HUNTIN⸺ ⸺IRPITZ

Royal Naval Operations against *Bismarck*'s Sister Ship

BRITANNIA NAVAL HISTORIES OF WORLD WAR II

University of Plymouth Press

This edition first published in the United Kingdom in 2012 by
University of Plymouth Press, Formation Zone, Roland Levinsky
Building, Drake Circus, Plymouth, Devon, PL4 8AA, United Kingdom.

Paperback   ISBN 978-1-84102-310-6
Hardback   ISBN 978-1-84102-309-0

The rights of this work have been asserted in accordance with the Crown
Copyright, Designs and Patents Act 1988.

A CIP catalogue record of this book is available from the British Library.

Publisher: Paul Honeywill
Commissioning Editor: Charlotte Carey
Publishing Assistant: Alex Hannon
Translation: Alrun Guenther
Series Editors: G. H. Bennett, J. E. Harrold and R. Porter

Content courtesy of Britannia Museum, Britannia Royal Naval College,
Dartmouth, TQ6 0HJ.

Cover image © Edward Stables 2012

Typeset by University of Plymouth Press in Janson 10/14pt.
Printed and bound by Short Run Press, Bittern Road, Sowton Industrial
Estate, Exeter, EX2 7LW.

The historical documents reproduced here appear as un-edited text, apart
from minor changes made to date formats and corrections to typing errors
found in the original.

MIX
Paper from
responsible sources
FSC® C014540

Britannia Royal Naval College

A majestic landmark, which towers above the harbour town of Dartmouth in Devon, Britannia Royal Naval College was designed by royal architect Sir Aston Webb to project an image of British sea power. A fine example of Edwardian architecture, the building has prepared future generations of officers for the challenges of service and leadership since 1905.

The Britannia Museum opened in 1999 to safeguard the College's rich collection of historic artefacts, art and archives and promote greater public understanding of Britain's naval and maritime heritage, as a key element in the development of British history and culture. It also aims to instil a sense of identity and ethos in the Officer Cadets that pass through the same walls as their forbears, from great admirals to national heroes to royalty.

Contents

Foreword

Admiral Sir Mark Stanhope

With this welcome new series of Second World War battle summaries, history once again speaks to posterity.

There is much in this nation's long and distinguished maritime and naval history upon which to reflect and celebrate. In so doing, we are reminded especially of our country's inextricable dependency on the sea for our prosperity and security.

We are also reminded that, within an ever-changing security environment, the characteristics of the sea and the attributes of maritime forces prevail. Enduring truths that the story of the hard-won pursuit of the *Tirpitz* illustrates so clearly. A story of determination, innovation and heroism. A story which demonstrates graphically *Tirpitz's* strategic significance because of her potential to prevent the flow of trade; always the lifeblood of ours and Russia's economies at a critical time. Consequently, the *Tirpitz* shaped the Admiralty's and British War Cabinet's thinking perhaps for longer than any other capability or platform during the War.

Dr Bennett's introduction helpfully sets the naval staff historians' accessible battle summaries in their wider context. Together, the Royal Navy's attempts to render the *Tirpitz* unusable – by deploying daring and imaginative raids, midget submarine attacks and Fleet Air Arm sorties – are as much inspirational as they are instructive. Indeed, I would commend readers, when absorbing these engaging pages, to reflect upon another enduring truth; the qualities of human endeavour: qualities of courage, leadership and professionalism – quietly, consistently and valiantly displayed for the nation and for freedom. Qualities that were tangible yesterday, are visible today and will be indispensable tomorrow.

I am most grateful to the Trustees of the Britannia Museum and the University of Plymouth Press for producing this immensely worthwhile series of battle summaries. The BRITANNIA NAVAL HISTORIES OF WORLD WAR II will be a valuable resource for anyone with either a professional, personal or even passing interest in British maritime and naval history.

Posterity should listen with attentiveness.

Mark Stanhope

Introduction

Dr G. H. Bennett

In 1941, the North Atlantic witnessed a desperate struggle as Germany's newest battleship *Bismarck* tried and failed to escape pursuing units of the Royal Navy. Making her sortie from the Baltic on 19 May 1941, *Bismarck* slipped into the North Atlantic via the Greenland–Iceland gap in search of the convoys running from North America to the United Kingdom. The Royal Navy countered by deploying most of its capital ships in the Atlantic and the Gibraltar based 'Force H' from the Western Mediterranean. On 24 May, the battlecruiser HMS *Hood*, the 'pride of the Royal Navy', and HMS *Prince of Wales*, Britain's newest battleship, engaged *Bismarck* and her escorting heavy cruiser *Prinz Eugen*. The battle was over in a matter of minutes as HMS *Hood* was destroyed with the loss of all but three of her crew of 1,418, and HMS *Prince of Wales*, fighting on alone for 13 minutes, retired to shadowing distance after sustaining damage. It was a stunning success for the German Navy, but other major units of the Royal Navy were already closing with the German task force. *Bismarck* had sustained apparently minor damage to her fuel bunkers in the encounter, but in the midst of an Atlantic dominated by the Royal Navy, it was enough to terminate the operation.

It was decided that *Bismarck* should head for St. Nazaire, which had the only dock on the Atlantic coast capable of accommodating the mighty battleship. It was a perilous voyage with an uncertain end, even if *Bismarck* succeeded in making port. In port, on the French coast, *Bismarck* would be in range of R.A.F. Bomber Command. *Prinz Eugen* was detached from *Bismarck* as both ships' companies prepared for a desperate race for safety. Aided by the vastness of the Atlantic, *Bismarck* succeeded in getting away momentarily from the shadowing British units. Reacquiring their target as *Bismarck* pushed steadily towards St. Nazaire, the Fleet Air Arm were able to deal a decisive blow: a torpedo strike from a Fairey Swordfish late in the evening of 26 May jammed *Bismarck*'s rudder and condemned her to steam in circles, miles short of her intended destination. The following morning, British vessels engaged the *Bismarck*. Within 45 minutes, *Bismarck*'s main armament had been silenced and British ships closed in to fire at her at point blank range. Almost two hours after the engagement had begun, at 1039, *Bismarck* slipped under the waves. The news was relayed to the Admiralty to be announced by the Prime Minister in the House of Commons.[1] After Churchill had made the announcement, the sense of relief within the Government and the House of Commons was palpable. Within the Royal

Navy there was satisfaction in accomplishing a job well done. Granted, HMS *Hood* had been lost, but equally Germany's newest and most powerful battleship had been sunk on her first war cruise.

The heavy units of the Royal Navy then set themselves to wait for the day that *Tirpitz*, *Bismarck*'s sister ship, would follow her departed sister ship into the Atlantic. In the meantime, the Naval Staff would examine a variety of innovative means to attack the German battleship. While Churchill worried about *Tirpitz* and the threat to the North Atlantic convoys on which Britain's war economy depended, the Royal Navy was impatient for battle. Churchill commented to US President Roosevelt on 28 May that *Bismarck* had been "a terrific ship, and a masterpiece of naval construction".[2] The First Sea Lord concurred with Churchill's concerns about what *Tirpitz* might do if she entered the Atlantic: "If the *Tirpitz* did manage to break out she could paralyse our North Atlantic trade."[3] The real danger to the North Atlantic trade lay not in the number of ships which *Tirpitz* might sink, but in the disruption to the flow and turn around of the convoys coming across the Atlantic. By 1941, the convoy system was highly organised and efficient as a result of careful organisation and planning. A German battleship in the Atlantic would throw out the careful organisation required to muster, convoy, unload and re-supply the merchant ships on which Britain's importing capacity depended. From the end of 1941, until early 1944, *Tirpitz* was to be the most important single maritime target confronting the Royal Navy. The threat would have to be contained, and if possible, neutralised.

Despite the public's impression, *Tirpitz* and *Bismarck* in wartime, backed by a number of post-war writers, were not a radical new design of super ship. They marked an evolutionary point along the line of German battleship design from World War I. With their eight, 15-in. gun, main guns grouped into four turrets, 31 knot maximum speed and operational displacement of over 50,000 tons, they were simply bigger, more heavily armed and better equipped than their predecessors. Part of Germany's Plan Z, developed in the 1930s as the blueprint for a navy able to compete against the British for control of the seas by 1944, *Bismarck* and *Tirpitz* were to be Nazi Germany's first true battleships. Added to the pocket battleships developed during the Weimar period and the intermediate design represented by *Scharnhorst* and *Gneisenau*, the *Bismarck* class would in turn be surpassed by battleships of even bigger design. According to Timothy P. Mulligan, *Tirpitz* and *Bismarck*, despite their later roles as commerce raiders, were always intended to serve as conventional battleships as part of a balanced fleet.[4] The outbreak of war in 1939 interrupted the development of this balanced fleet. War with the British was an unwelcome and surprising event, so far as the majority of the German naval staff were concerned. They would not be able to meet the Royal Navy on anything like equal terms.[5]

The keel of *Tirpitz* had been laid at Wilhelmshaven in late 1936 and she was launched on 1 April 1939.[6] *Tirpitz* was not yet operational when *Bismarck* embarked on her one-and-only war cruise. Finally ready for action at the end of 1941, a decision was taken to send *Tirpitz* to Norway. In part, this was a defensive move – the loss of *Bismarck* had made Hitler profoundly sensitive about the potential loss of other 'prestige units'.[7] Departing on 14 January 1942, it was envisaged that *Tirpitz* could play two roles: as a potential threat to any invasion force that attempted a landing in Norway; also as a commerce raider preying on the convoys running to and from the ports of North Russia.

In his 37th War Directive, issued on 10 October 1941, Hitler had stressed the vital need to "attack enemy supplies going by sea to Murmansk".[8] The convoys to Russia represented a rich potential target for *Tirpitz*. During the course of the war, 75 convoys totalling 775 merchant ships went to and from Russia. From the United Kingdom they carried "£308 million worth of military equipment" and a further "£120 million worth of other material".[9] Via this lifeline, the Soviet Union received 5,000 tanks and 7,000 aircraft from Britain. This was in addition to cargo delivered to the Soviet Union by the United States under the Lend-Lease scheme. The Russian convoys played a small but important role in the build-up of the Red Army and Air Force following disastrous losses in Operation 'Barbarossa', the German invasion of the Soviet Union, in 1941.[10]

Of much greater significance was the political importance of the continued running of the convoys. With Soviet forces suffering heavy losses, and vast areas of the western USSR in German hands, Stalin pressed his British and American counterparts to open a second front in Europe as quickly as possible. British and American planners eventually came to the conclusion that it would take a sustained build-up over many months before they could chance an invasion of Western Europe. In the meantime, Stalin would have to be content with a second front from the air, in the form of a bombing campaign against German cities by the British and American airforces, raids on the coast of Europe, and the delivery of significant quantities of military aid through convoys to Russia.

Tirpitz first went into action on 6 March 1942 as she attempted to intercept PQ12, a convoy heading to Murmansk. Traditional accounts suggest that bad weather played the key role in preventing the interception.[11] Only one straggler from the convoy fell victim to one of the destroyers escorting *Tirpitz*. During the course of her sortie, *Tirpitz* was sighted and attacked by British carrier-based aircraft. Twenty torpedoes launched resulted in no hits, as the battleship staged an impressive display with her anti-aircraft armament. The attacking aircraft pressed home their attack to such an extent that Admiral Ciliax was convinced that his flagship must have been hit by at least one torpedo which thankfully had not exploded.[12] It was almost with a sense of relief that *The Times*, 12 March 1942, carried the headline "First attack on *Tirpitz* – Torpedoes fired by Aircraft".[13] Battle had at last been joined between the Royal Navy and the Nazi leviathan. If the first attack had not been successful, it had certainly been a nasty surprise for Admiral Ciliax. Attacks by R.A.F. Bomber Command, and even by the Russian Air Force (five before the end of April 1942) would follow in 1942 and 1943.[14] The ineffectiveness of the attacks demonstrated the difficulties of attacking *Tirpitz* in the Norwegian fjords.

What the journalists of *The Times* did not appreciate, although the writers of many subsequent accounts did, was the failure of the attack on PQ12 and the launching of a strike against *Tirpitz* was not a coincidence. Allied code breakers had broken the German naval Enigma code in 1941; with varying degrees of success and speed they had been able to monitor the activities of every surface unit in the German Navy since the end of that year. Those code breakers had followed the final working-up exercises of *Tirpitz* in the Baltic in September 1941.[15] During her deployment to Norway, there was a considerable delay at Bletchley Park between receiving and breaking coded messages to and from *Tirpitz*. Only after she had sailed did decodes reveal German intentions. It was too late to mount an operation to intercept her.

To the work of the code breakers was added intelligence derived from photo reconnaissance, the Norwegian Resistance and the British Special Operations (SOE) Executive who reported separately on ship movements, the disposition of German units in Northern Norway and anything else that might yield clues about future operations.[16] The PQ12 episode in March 1942 came at a moment when Bletchley Park's code breakers were reading German naval traffic within two to three hours of its transmission.[17] Unfortunately, this time span was the exception rather than the rule, but from her first sortie onwards, British code breakers and the Norwegian resistance would feed the Royal Navy with valuable intelligence about the operational state and future movements of *Tirpitz*.

St. Nazaire Raid

The British Admiralty, in recognising the difficulties of destroying *Tirpitz*, was also alive to other options to limit her effectiveness. On 28 March 1942, British naval units and commandoes staged Operation 'Chariot': a daring raid on the port of St. Nazaire.[18] The primary purpose of the raid was to destroy the only dock on the Atlantic coast capable of receiving *Tirpitz*. It was the safety of the Normandie dock at St. Nazaire that a damaged *Bismarck* was seeking before she was sunk in 1941. Without a dock capable of receiving and repairing *Tirpitz* in France, the Royal Navy reasoned that the German Naval High Command would not risk her on a commerce raiding operation in the Atlantic.

In its primary objective, the St. Nazaire raid was entirely successful. Packed full of explosives, the old destroyer HMS *Campbeltown* was driven into the lock gates of the Normandie dock. The eventual explosion rendered the dock unusable for a considerable time afterwards. To those involved in the raid 'Chariot' appeared highly costly: (almost two-thirds of the raiding force of 612 men were killed or captured) even though the raid had placed significant limits on the options available to the German Naval High Command. One of the senior officers on the raid later commented that sadness at the scale of the losses was mitigated by the hope that in containing *Tirpitz* "many lives at sea on the convoys were saved".[19] However, such personal reflections should be viewed against the backdrop of the grand strategy of Allied operations. In the scheme of things, the losses on the raid were comparatively small when compared with the scale of the damage done to the facilities of St. Nazaire.

Keeping *Tirpitz* in Norwegian waters undoubtedly saved lives in the Atlantic, but the battleship cast a long shadow over the conduct of convoy operations. In July 1942, *Tirpitz* played a major role in the destruction of North Russian convoy PQ17.[20] The sailing of the convoy coincided with one of the periods when, following a change to the inner settings of the German enigma coding machine, the naval code breakers at Bletchley Park were struggling to break into the code again. On 4 July, the convoy scattered as a result of competing assessments over whether or not *Tirpitz* was about to attack the convoy. *Tirpitz* did not come over the horizon to attack the dispersed convoy, but the withdrawal of the convoy escorts had a devastating effect on the merchant ships of PQ17; easy pickings for German aircraft and submarines, only 11 of the convoy's ships reached port. The political repercussions between Britain and the Soviet Union were considerable, underlining the urgent need to put *Tirpitz* out of commission.

Attack by X-Craft

Reports following PQ17 that a Soviet submarine had torpedoed *Tirpitz* proved to be false.[21] The British Admiralty, therefore, began to consider its options concerning attacks against the German battleship. Mounting aerial attacks against *Tirpitz* was proving difficult and ineffective, since bombers were required to operate at the limit of their range. Conventional bombs stood little chance of damaging the battleship. Attacking a defended and camouflaged target, in the confines of a fjord, offered further challenges to both aircraft and the surface ships of the Royal Navy. The shallow depths of the fjord meant that a conventional attack by submarine would probably be detected long before the submarine was in torpedo range. At the end of October 1942, an attempt was made to attack *Tirpitz* using a pair of chariots: two-man human torpedoes.[22] The men would guide the chariot to the underwater target where they would place the explosive charge, making their escape before it exploded. The head of Operation 'Title' was Leif Larsen, a Norwegian who had escaped to Britain; the operation was dogged by bad luck. The trawler allocated to towing the chariots underwater, suffered mechanical problems. The chariots eventually broke free and sank within sight of *Tirpitz*. The trawler was scuttled and the personnel onboard walked to the safety of neutral Sweden.

The failure of 'Title' did not prevent the Royal Navy from attacking *Tirpitz* with submarines the following year – in September 1943. Six midget submarines were deployed against German naval targets in Norwegian waters.[23] Three submarines – X5, X6 and X7 – were to target *Tirpitz* in Kaa fjord, while X9 and X10 targeted *Scharnhorst* in Kaa fjord and X8 attacked *Lützow* in Langefjord. While it appears that X5 came to the surface and was destroyed by gunfire, X6 and X7 succeeded in placing their side charges underneath *Tirpitz*. Aware of the danger, the crew were in the process of moving the battleship when the charges exploded. Eight hundred cubic meters of water had entered the ship within two and a half hours of the attack and severe damage was reported to electrical and propulsion systems.[24] *Tirpitz* would be non-operational for months, and even after some time, questions would remain over whether she was truly fit to go to sea. The Admiralty released details of Operation 'Source' on 11 October 1943, which *The Times* published the following day with the headline "*Tirpitz* hit in Fjord Raid – Gallant Midget Submarines".[25] The tone of the report was subdued, with substantial damage to the ship only hinted at through reference to an oil slick and vessels, "possibly repair ships", clustered around *Tirpitz*. The Admiralty knew that, if they had not killed the beast, then they had gravely wounded it.

Attack by the Fleet Air Arm

The war at sea had turned decisively against the German Navy by the end of 1943, with the loss of *Scharnhorst* that December, *Tirpitz* constituted the last remaining major surface vessel in Hitler's fleet. Badly damaged as a result of Operation 'Source', and with dwindling confidence in her capabilities in Berlin, *Tirpitz* increasingly constituted "less of a threat than a target" particularly for aerial attack.[26] Her every move was monitored by R.A.F. photo reconnaissance and by the code breakers at Bletchley Park. To make matters worse, the German Navy and Air Force were increasingly short of fuel. Lack of fuel and the danger of further attacks imposed severe restrictions on the ability of *Tirpitz's* crew to 'work-up' the battleship in preparation for the completion of repairs and before undertaking an operation.[27] Shortages of fuel oil restricted the options to regularly move the ship in order to make attacks on her more difficult. The same problem similarly affected the Luftwaffe units tasked with defending the battleship from the air.

Launched on 3 April 1944, Operation 'Tungsten' was a pivotal moment in the history of *Tirpitz* and the development of the Royal Navy during World War II. The Royal Navy's Fleet Air Arm had been engaged in a major programme of expansion since 1941. A large part of that expansion was due to American generosity. In May 1941, several months before America joined World War II, the US Navy agreed to help the Royal Navy train the thousands of pilots which it urgently required.[28]

By 1944, the Towers scheme was providing 44 per cent of the pilots required by the Fleet Air Arm.[29] During this period, under the Lend-Lease scheme, American industry was providing many of the aircraft types (Corsair, Hellcat and Wildcat) and escort carriers operated by the Royal Navy, and the Royal Navy in the Atlantic was capable of staging mass air attacks from its Fleet and Escort Carriers. *Tirpitz* was an obvious and significant target on which to test the rapidly developing capabilities of the Fleet Air Arm.

The idea of attacking *Tirpitz* with carrier aircraft had first been raised in late 1943, as the Royal Navy considered how best to capitalise on the damage done to the battleship in Operation 'Source'. With urgent repairs underway on *Tirpitz* in the winter of 1943–1944, it was clearly imperative that fresh attacks were mounted against her at the earliest opportunity; the darkness of the Norwegian winter would limit the possibility of attacks until the Spring. (By that time, both the Germans and the British were considering *Tirpitz* as a potential factor in the opening of a second front. Hitler was convinced that Norway constituted a prime location for an Allied landing and was convinced of the value of *Tirpitz* as a deterrent, or counter, to such a move.)

In January 1944, the Commander-in-Chief Home Fleet had received a signal from the Admiralty instructing him to prepare to attack *Tirpitz* in mid-March.[30] The operation was postponed to April but in the meantime, pilots and aircrew rehearsed the attack at Loch Eriboll, which was transformed into a mock-up (complete with a model of *Tirpitz* and simulated anti-aircraft defences) of Kaa fjord, where *Tirpitz* lay at anchor. The slight delay meant that two extra squadrons of Corsair aircraft, 1834 and 1836, would be ready for the attack. They had only joined HMS *Victorious* in February and early March. Also available for the attack would be the new 1,600 lb bomb which was just entering fleet service.

On 30 March, Force I (consisting of battleships *Duke of York* and *Anson*, aircraft carrier *Victorious* and cruiser *Belfast* together with destroyer escorts) sailed as cover for convoy JW-58. Later that day, Force II sailed. It consisted of the cruisers *Royalist*, *Sheffield*, and *Jamaica*, the escort carriers *Searcher*, *Emperor*, *Fencer*, and *Pursuer* and the fleet carrier *Furious* together with escorting destroyers and two fleet oilers. Force I and Force II made rendezvous on 2 April and were in a position to launch a strike the following morning.

The launch and approach to target of the first wave of aircraft was later described by Commander Anthony Kimmins:

"At first light, at exactly the prearranged minute, Commander Flying shouted the welcome order 'start up!' The words were hardly out of his mouth before there was a roar of engines. By now the carriers and the escorting ships were all heeling over and swinging into wind. A final nod from the Captain, a signal from Commander Flying, the Flight Deck officer raised his green flag, the engines started to rev up, the flag dropped and the first aircraft was roaring away over the bow. One after the other they followed in rapid succession, and nearby you could see the same thing going on. More Barracudas, Seafires, Corsairs, Wildcats and Hellcats. In a few minutes the sky was full of them, and as the sun started to rise and the clouds turned pink at the edges, they formed up in their squadrons.

It wasn't long before the mountains in the coastline showed up ahead. As they gained height and crossed the coast the sun was rising to their left, shining across the snow-covered mountains, throwing shadows in the gorges and against the snow-covered trees in the valleys, and lighting up the deep blue of the calm fjord. Down to the left were two or three enemy ships, but these took no visible interest in the proceedings. Everything seemed calm and peaceful, but I'll bet that down below the wires were humming and that up at the far end of the fjord alarm bells were ringing, fat-headed Huns were falling out of bed, rubbing their eyes and cursing the British as they threw on some clothes and stumbled out to their cold action stations. By now the strike was passing its next landmark, a huge glacier on the top of a mountain. Soon they were crossing the final ridge and sighted a flak ship on the far side of the fjord. She immediately opened up, but raggedly, and without great effect. And then, as they crossed over the final ridge, they had a thrill which none of those aircrews will ever forget. There, nestling under the sheer mountains in a fjord not much wider than the Thames at London, lay one of the largest battleships in the world – the *Tirpitz*."[31]

Forty Fairey Barracuda (827, 829, 830 and 831 Squadrons) and 81 fighters (mostly Corsairs from 1834 and 1836 Squadrons) together with Hellcats from 800 and 804 Squadrons delivered the attacks. Meanwhile Wildcats from 882 and 898 Squadrons flew in support. Combat air patrols over the British fleet and an anti-submarine patrol were maintained by Wildcats, Seafires (801 and 880 Squadrons) and Swordfish aircraft (842 Squadron).

In the excitement of the run into the target, many of the aircraft assigned to make bomb runs against *Tirpitz* flew lower than the mission altitude of 3,000 ft. (See Part III, pages 135–176). This was considered the optimum height to allow a bomb to punch through the armoured deck before exploding. Critically, for many of the Fleet Air Arm aircrew the site of the battleship exercised a magnetic effect drawing them lower than 3,000 ft. One telegraphist air gunner was later questioned about his impressions of the bomb run:

> "'What was your overwhelming impression of that raid?' He replied, 'The sheer size of the battleship.' He said, 'We came down sharply, as you can imagine, and flew the length of the ship. As I was the telegraphist air gunner I was facing rearwards, and I could see the length of the ship unrolling as we flew along. It went on and on.' I asked him a rather obvious question: 'Do you think you hit it?' He allowed himself the ghost of a smile. 'Couldn't really miss from that height,' he said." [32]

Overall, the operation went according to plan, with the fighters carrying out ground strafing attacks, as a distraction for the bombers, while providing top cover against enemy fighters. But the outcomes of the attack were somewhat unexpected. Only four Fleet Air Arm aircraft had been lost – with eight men killed.[33] Fourteen confirmed hits on *Tirpitz* had been scored. The ship had been damaged and further crippled.

A hero's welcome greeted the ships that had carried out Operation 'Tungsten'. A Reuters correspondent described the scene:

> "The flagship and other ships of the Home Fleet cleared the lower decks, and gave three rousing cheers as the fleet carrier force that smashed the *Tirpitz* steamed line ahead into port. The carriers were welcomed home with full honours. As we passed each ship, the officers and ratings lining the quarterdecks, took off their caps and cheered, the sound reverberating across the blue waters. It was an inspiring sight, and, standing on the Admiral's bridge of the carrier, I felt very proud of being in such a ship. The sleek, green Barracudas that had done the job were lined up astern on the flight deck and up forward, and the blue-uniformed pilots, observers and gunners stood in line. The Fleet Air Arm boys are happy tonight and they deserve to be." [34]

Ongoing photo-reconnaissance gradually revealed the scale of the damage done to *Tirpitz*. Throughout early April, the British press became steadily more excited at the wounds inflicted on the battleship. On 3 April, the Admiralty revealed that Fleet Air Arm aircraft had attacked *Tirpitz*. *The Times* cautiously announced the following day: "*Tirpitz* bombed by Navy – Several Hits Scored".[35]

The following day *The Times* attacked a report from the German Overseas News Service, the British newspaper stated that the aerial attacks on *Tirpitz* had been made in a convoy action which had resulted in the loss of a number of British destroyers.[36] The first full report on the action was given by the Admiralty on 5 June. *The Times* headline the following day declared: "*Tirpitz* left on Fire: Many Bomb Hits".[37] Two days later the newspaper quoted a Reuters correspondent who had sailed with the carrier force and was able to quantify the damage done: "16 Direct Hits on the *Tirpitz*". *The Times* was happy to conclude that *Tirpitz* had been put out of action for several months. Despite its growing excitement at the success of Operation 'Tungsten', the newspaper carried no first-hand accounts of the attacks.

The aerial attack on *Tirpitz* was discussed at the Führer Naval Conference at the Berghof on 12 April.[38] The minutes of Hitler's meeting with Grand Admiral Dönitz are extremely revealing in terms of attitudes towards *Tirpitz*. Hitler had become increasingly sceptical about the value of Germany's heavy ships. In January 1943, following a row that had seen the retirement of Dönitz's predecessor as head of the German Navy, Hitler had scheduled the decommissioning of the remaining large units of the German Navy. Dönitz had been able to persuade Hitler to change his mind but, if carried through, *Scharnhorst* would have been decommissioned in July 1943 and *Tirpitz* in October.[39]

Hitler's prejudices and Dönitz's skilful politicking could be seen again in the meeting at the Berghof, following Operation 'Tungsten'. While it was recognised that her continued existence tied down enemy forces it was considered that she was of limited value in a practical military sense, either as a battleship or as a floating military battery of potential use against an invasion force off the Norwegian coast. A return to Germany was considered out of the question because the long journey would make her vulnerable to attack, and also because it was recognised that whichever north German port she sought sanctuary in would be immediately devastated by the heavy bombers of the Royal Air Force. The crew of *Tirpitz* were effectively exiles: they were awaiting either the end of the war, or of their ship.

Following Operation 'Tungsten', the Royal Navy launched a series of repeat air strikes against the battleship, although they were less successful than the April attack had been. For example, Operations 'Goodwood I' and 'Goodwood II' were launched on 22 August 1944,[40] when three aircraft were shot down. The Admiralty, probably aware from ULTRA that *Tirpitz* was undamaged in the attack, were reluctant to ascribe particular damage to the ship, but commented more generally that a total of 19 German vessels had been damaged or sunk.[41] 'Goodwood III' and 'Goodwood IV' followed later that month. The strikes further underlined the difficulties of attacking surface ships in the Norwegian fjords, except under ideal weather conditions.

The R.A.F. attacked *Tirpitz* on 15 September, using Lancaster four-engined bombers carrying 12,000 lb Tallboy bombs. The attack force, with bombs onboard, had arrived at a Russian airbase near Archangel on 11 September.[42] Poor weather had kept the Lancasters on the ground until 15 September. The Air Ministry announced that one of the bombs had scored a direct hit on *Tirpitz*. If Operation 'Source' had ended *Tirpitz*'s days as a naval unit able to sortie into the Atlantic or Arctic Oceans, the bomb attack on 15 September effectively ended her days as a warship. Dönitz ordered that henceforth *Tirpitz* would constitute only a floating gun battery for the defence of Norway.[43] The mighty ship was taken to a new shallow water anchorage near Tromsø, in the hope that she would not capsize here if she suffered further heavy damage. Sand and dredged material was dumped around the ship, to decrease the depth of the fjord still further, and this was continuing when the crippled battleship was attacked again, on 29 October, by Lancasters armed with 12,000 lb bombs. The Air Ministry revealed that the bombers had flown a round trip of 2,400 miles from British bases and had scored "at least one direct hit".[44]

The bombers returned on 12 November 1944. Lancaster four-engined bombers from 617 and 9 Squadrons attacked *Tirpitz* with 12,000 lb Tallboy bombs. The approach to the target was marked by excellent visibility as Wing Commander J. B. Tait, who commanded the attack, later recalled:

"The water of the fjord was like crystal, and against its background the battleship looked like a big, squat island. This was the clear sort of run for which they had been waiting. When the Lancasters were still about 10 miles away the *Tirpitz* opened fire with her big guns, and as they closed in flak got intense, although it was not as accurate or as bad as at Brest for instance. Soon after the first bombs had gone down the whole ship was enveloped in greyish-brown smoke." [45]

The task of the bombers was made easier by the complete absence of Luftwaffe fighter aircraft. In fact, the approach of the bombers had been detected and German aircraft had been scrambled. Unfortunately, there appears to have been a breakdown in communications and the fighters were sent to *Tirpitz's* former anchorage at Kaa fjord. Kapitaen Bernard Schmitz, a *Tirpitz* officer, later recalled:

"We knew well in advance we were to be attacked and we requested the presence of the fighters. The request was granted and the takeoff was reported to us. When 28 Lancasters came into sight from the south we enquired as to the whereabouts of our fighters only to discover that they had flown to our old berth".[46]

Leading 617 Squadron, the November attack was J. B. Tait's third attack on *Tirpitz*. It was to be his last.[47] A film unit was onboard the aircraft, flown by an Australian pilot, Flight Lieutenant B. A. Buckham:

"The first bombs fell just beyond the ship. Agonizing moments! Then came three direct hits in quick succession, the first amidships, the next in the bows, and the third towards the stern. Her guns had been firing like blazes when we first arrived, but after the first bomb had hit her the guns stopped firing. Not a shot came up after that. Smoke began to pour up. It spiralled at first in a column. Then it spread over the doomed ship in the shape of a mushroom. Afterwards there were several explosions. One of them was very big and one of my crew shouted out: 'she's on fire skipper; she's on fire'. The fire did not seem to last long. Finally she capsized." [48]

While most of the bombers started the return leg of their journey, Buckham's aircraft remained on-station to observe the damage to *Tirpitz*. His rear-gunner used the intercom to tell the pilot that *Tirpitz* was listing, just as Buckham was about to set off for home. Making one last circuit, he was able to observe *Tirpitz* lying on her side and half-submerged before Buckham finally left the target area. On 13 November, the Air Ministry announced the details of the sinking of *Tirpitz*.[49] It was the lead story on the first page of the *Daily Telegraph* complete with photographs of the attack.[50]

In a career that was less than glorious, *Tirpitz* had not been a happy ship.[51] The bombardment of the Allied base on Spitzbergen, in September 1943, was the ship's only wholly successful operation of the war. If she had not been as successful as the other vessels in the German surface fleet, then strategically she had still been important. For three years she had exerted a powerful effect on the 'thinking' within the British War Cabinet. The Royal Navy had approached the problem of *Tirpitz* with intelligence and inventiveness. Desperately hoping that *Tirpitz* would meet the same fate as *Bismarck*, the Naval Staff had come up with clever and surprising means to limit her radius of action, utilise new weapons to attack her, and to reduce the threat in a proportionate and cost effective manner. The R.A.F.'s bomb attacks on *Tirpitz*, in late 1944, completed a job that had been 80 per cent completed by the Royal Navy. The critical damage done to *Tirpitz* in Operations 'Source' and 'Tungsten', in 1943 and 1944, had effectively ended her threat to the convoy routes. The Kriegsmarine High Command knew it and it would be left to the bombs of the Royal Air Force to complete the process of turning *Tirpitz* into scrap steel.

During the late 1940s, the wreck of the *Tirpitz* was broken up. In 1950, a section of engine room bulkhead featuring an image of *Tirpitz*, and carrying the slogan *"Gegen Engeland"*, was presented to the R.A.F. by Norwegian salvors. Later, in 1973, a Halifax bomber that had crashed into a Norwegian lake in April 1942 on an operation against the German vessel was recovered from the depths, largely intact.[52] Both now reside in the R.A.F. Museum at Hendon. In the fjord which became the lonely grave of *Tirpitz* in 1944 there is still just enough of the ship on the sea bed to glimpse her ghostly outline from the air. It may have been the R.A.F., in late 1944, that finished off *Tirpitz*, but the Royal Navy had already done enough, by the end of 1943, to ensure that she would never leave Norwegian waters.

The Battle Summaries on the following pages chart some of the Royal Navy's operations to deal with the threat of *Tirpitz*. Damage summaries further illustrate the effectiveness of the operations against the ship, and a report of first-hand accounts of the sinking of *Tirpitz*, by Klaus Rohwedder, provides a powerful reminder of the human stories involved in the life and death of the 'lone queen of the North'.

Operation 'Chariot', Operation 'Source' and Operation 'Tungsten' represented innovative attempts by a nation at war to neutralise a major enemy unit. From the men who staged the raid on St. Nazaire, to the submariners in their X-Craft and the Fleet Air Arm crews flying in the confines of the fjords of Norway, an aggressive and determined spirit was in evidence. The operations against *Tirpitz* also underlined the Royal Navy's efficiency when it came to planning, logistics and training. *Tirpitz* spent almost the entire war on the defensive, hiding from her pursuers while trying to make a contribution to the war effort. While the writers of the Summaries had privileged access to intelligence reports and key participants on the British side, there was still much that they could not know and even more that they could not reveal. The Summaries were pulled together quickly as the officers of the Royal Navy tried to learn lessons for the future from recently concluded operations.

The German perspective on these operations would not emerge until after 1945, and the ULTRA secret which allowed British code breakers a remarkable insight into the life of Nazi Germany's biggest battleship would remain out of the public domain until the 1970s. References to "special intelligence" in post-war official histories were the only permitted hint to the significance of the ULTRA secret. The writers of the Battle Summaries who were aware of the ULTRA secret had to be careful not to expose what they knew in their writing. Seventy years on from the events they analyse, the Battle Summaries make interesting reading. They constitute an important part of the process by which the Royal Navy began to produce a first draft of the history of the war at sea.

Endnotes

1. Churchill, W. S. (27 May 1941), *Debate on the War Situation, House of Commons Debates* vol. 371, col.1718.

2. Churchill to Roosevelt. (28 May 1941) reproduced in Churchill, W. S. (1952), *The Second World War*, vol. 3, The Reprint Society, London, p.259.

3. First Sea Lord to Prime Minister, (28 August 1941), reproduced in Churchill W. S. (1952), *The Second World War*, vol. 3, The Reprint Society, London, p.669.

4. Mulligan, T. P. (October 2005), *'Ship-of-the-Line or Atlantic Raider?' Battleship Bismarck Between Design Limitations and Naval Strategy*, The Journal of Military History, vol. 69, pp.1013–1044.

5. The order for the construction of *Graf Zeppelin* was given on 16 November 1935 with her keel being laid down by Deutsche Werke at Kiel on 28 December 1936. *Graf Zeppelin* was launched on 8 December 1938. However, the ship was never completed. Scuttled in shallow water near Stettin in 1945, the wreck was captured by the Russians. Refloated and repaired, the Russians floated *Graf Zeppelin* for bombing practice on 18 August 1947. The wreck was found in 2006 by a vessel carrying out underwater survey work.

6. 'Germany's Second Big Battleship – Launch of the *Tirpitz*', *The Times*, 3 April 1939, p.13.

7. Testimony by Grand Admiral Raeder, 18 May 1946, Trial of the Major War Criminals Before the International Military Tribunal, International Military Tribunal, Nuremberg, 1948, p.127.

8. Directive No. 37, 10 October 1941, reproduced in Trevor-Roper, H. R. (1964), *Hitler's War Directives 1939–1945*, Pan, London, pp.159–163.

9. Statement by the Parliamentary and Financial Secretary to the Admiralty Mr John Dugdale, House of Commons Debates, 17 December 1946, vol. 431, col. 1777.

10. For further discussion see Llewellyn-Jones, M. (2006), *The Royal Navy and the Arctic Convoys*, Routlege, London.

11. Bekker, C. D. (1953), *Swastika at Sea*, William Kimber, London, pp.151–152. See also Llewellyn-Jones, M. (2006), *The Royal Navy and the Arctic Convoys*, Routlege, London, 2006.

12. Von der Porten E. (1970), *The German Navy in World War Two*, Pan, London, pp.219–220.

13. 'First attack on *Tirpitz* – Torpedoes fired by Aircraft', *The Times*, 12 March 1942, p.4.

14. Tarrant V. E. (1994), *Last Year of the Kriegsmarine: May 1944–May 1945*, Arms and Armour, London, p.127.

15. See for example details of refuelling at sea exercises, 9 September 1941, British National Archives (hereinafter TNA:PRO) HW1/64 and torpedo firing exercises, 17 September 1941, TNA:PRO HW1/73. For the PQ12 episode see TNA:PRO HW1/394.

16. See Special Operations Executive file on Operation Frodesley 1941–1942, TNA:PRO HS8/785.

17. Sebag-Montefiore H. (2001), *Enigma: The Battle for the Code*, Phoenix, London, p.230. Some of the key PQ12 decrypts are reproduced in Kennedy, L. (1979), *Menace: The Life and Death of the* Tirpitz, Sidgwick and Jackson, London, pp.46–53.

18. 'The Attack on St. Nazaire, 1942', Supplement to the *London Gazette*, 2 October 1947.

19. Lieutenant Colonel Charles Newman, VC, OBE in David Mason, *Raid on St. Nazaire*, Macdonald & Co, London, 1970, p.7.

20. For the role of *Tirpitz* in PQ17 see Bekker, C. (1974), *Verdammte See*, Verlag Ullstein, Berlin, pp.261–268. 'Convoys to North Russia 1942, Admiralty Report, Supplement to the *London Gazette*, 13 October 195, pp.5139–5154. See also Hinsley F. H. & Eastaway T. E. (1990), *British intelligence in the Second World War: its influence on strategy and operations*, Volume II, HM Stationery Office, London, pp.213–214.

21. 'Attack on *Tirpitz* – Soviet Commander's Report', *The Times*, 10 July 1942, p.4.

22. For Operation 'Title' see TNA:PRO HS2/202 and HS2/203.

23. Among the many accounts, see Gallager, T. (1971), *The X-Craft Raid: A True Story of a Secret World War II Mission Unparalleled in the Annals of the Sea*, Harcourt Brace, New York.

24. The Attack on the *Tirpitz* by Midget Submarines on 22 September 1943, despatch submitted to the Admiralty, 8 November 1943, by Rear-Admiral C.B. Barry published Supplement to the *London Gazette*, 11 February 1948, pp.993–1008. See also ULTRA decrypts relating to Operation Source in TNA:PRO HW1/2036, 2039 and 2041.

25. '*Tirpitz* hit in Fjord Raid – Gallant Midget Submarines', *The Times*, 12 October 1943, p.4.

26. Willmott, H.P. (2002), *Battleship*, Cassell, London, p.165.

27. Essay on the war at sea 1939–1945 completed by General Admiral Otto Schniewind and Admiral Schuster, 10 November 1946, TNA:PRO ADM223/696.

28. Air Commodore Pirie to Admiral Towers, May 1941 and British Air Military Mission, Washington DC, to Air Ministry 18 June 1941, TNA:PRO AIR42/2.

29. Survey of Royal Navy Training in the United States, May 1945; see also Towers Training Scheme File OP-05D4, Office of US Naval History, Washington DC,TNA:PR0 ADM117/17286. See also Guinn, G. S. & Bennett, G. H. (2007), *British Naval Aviation in World War II: The US Navy and Anglo-American Relations*, London, I. B. Tauris.

30. Sweetman J. (2000), *Tirpitz: Hunting the Beast: Air Attacks on the German Battleship 1940–44*, Stroud, Sutton, p.57.

31. 'I Was There! – We Struck at and Crippled the Mighty *Tirpitz*', *The War Illustrated*, vol. 7, No. 180, 12 May 1944, pp.794–795.

32. Dr. Lewis in adjournment debate, House of Commons Debates, 9 June 2004, vol. 422, col. 317.

33. The following British Fleet Air Arm casualties from Operation 'Tungsten' are buried in the Commonwealth War Graves Cemetery at Tromsø: Sub-Lieutenant (A) THOMAS CHARLES BELL (F.A.A. 830 Sqdn. HMS *Furious*., Royal Naval Volunteer Reserve) age 21; Leading Airman GEORGE JOSEPH BURNS (F.A.A. 830 Sqdn. HMS *Furious*., Royal Navy) age 20; Sub-Lieutenant (A) ANDREW GEORGE CANNON (F.A.A. 829 Sqdn. HMS *Victorious*, Royal Naval Volunteer Reserve) age 21; Sub-Lieutenant (A) ROBERT NORMAN DRENNAN (F.A.A. 830 Sqdn. HMS *Furious*, Royal Naval Volunteer Reserve) age 23; Sub-Lieutenant (A) HUBERT HORACE RICHARDSON (F.A.A. 829 Sqdn. HMS *Victorious*., Royal Naval Volunteer Reserve) age 22. Leading

Aircraftsman E. CARROLL flying in a Baracuda II with RICHARDSON and CANNON managed to bail out. He spent the rest of the war as a prisoner. The crew of the 827 Squadron Barracuda flying from HMS *Victorious* which crashed into the sea were COLWILL, Colin Leading Airman; WHITTAKER, John P., Ty/Lieutenant (A), RNVR; BOWLES, Francis Ty/Sub Lieutenant (A), RNVR. They were all killed in the accident.

34. Lt-Cmdr M. Apps, (1971), *Send her Victorious*, Purnell, London, pp.139–40.

35. '*Tirpitz* Bombed by Navy: Several Hits Scored', *The Times*, 4 April 1944, p.4.

36. 'Enemy Story of the *Tirpitz* – Convoy Operation', *The Times*, 5 April 1944, p.4.

37. '*Tirpitz* left on Fire: Many Bomb Hits', *The Times*, 6 April 1944, p.4.

38. Minutes of the Führer Naval Conference, the Berghof, 12 and 13 April 1944, *Führer Conferences on Naval Affairs, 1939–1945*, Greenhill Books, London, 1990, pp.388–389.

39. Breyer S. & Koop G. (1989), *The German Navy at War 1935-1945*, vol.1, Schiffer, West Chester [PA], p.165.

40. 'Daring attacks on the *Tirpitz* – Day by Day Diary of Operations', *The Times*, 6 September 1944, p.3.

41. '*Tirpitz* bombed in Fjord – 19 Ships Destroyed or Damaged', *The Times*, 6 September 1944, p.4. For the ULTRA decrypts see relating to the attack on 22 August see TNA:PRO HW1/3186.

42. '12,000 lb bomb Bomb Hit on the *Tirpitz* – R.A.F. Attack Launched from Russia', *The Times*, 5 October 1944, p.4.

43. Essay on the war at sea, 1939–1945 by Grand Admiral Dönitz, 24 September 1945, TNA: PRO ADM223/688. *Admiral Dönitz, Memoirs: Ten Years and Twenty Days*, Weidenfeld and Nicolson, London, 1958, p.386. More generally see Bennett, G. H. & Bennett, R. (2004), *Hitler's Admirals*, US Naval Institute Press, Annapolis (MD.), pp.187–189.

44. '*Tirpitz* hit again – Dawn Attack by R.A.F.', *The Times*, 30 October 1944, p.4.

45. 'How *Tirpitz* was Sunk – R.A.F. Crews' Own Stories', *The Times*, 15 November 1944, p.4.

46. Reproduced in Cooper A. (1991), *Beyond the Dams to the Tirpitz: The Later Operations of 617 Squadron*, Goodall Publications Ltd, London, p.111.

47. Supplement to *The London Gazette*, No. 36883, 5 January 1945, p.273.

48. 'R.A.F. Lancasters sink the *Tirpitz* – Capsized in Fjord after hits by 12,000 lb Bombs', *The Times*, 14 November 1944, p.4.

49. 'R.A.F. Lancasters sink the *Tirpitz* – Capsized in Fjord after hits by 12,000 lb Bombs', *The Times*, 14 November 1944, p.4. Further confirmation came via the ULTRA decrypts TNA: PRO HW1/3321.

50. '*Tirpitz* sunk by 29 Lancasters', the *Daily Telegraph*, 14 November 1944, p.1.

51. Woodward D. *Tirpitz*, New English Library, London, 1974, p.113.

52. 'Souvenir of *Tirpitz* Sinking', *The Times*, 15 February 1950, p.8. 'Norwegian Lake Yields up *Tirpitz* bomber', *The Times*, 5 July 1973, p.5.

PART I

B.R. 1736 (34) (48)

BATTLE SUMMARY No. 12

THE ATTACK ON ST. NAZAIRE
28 March, 1942

T.S.D 35/48
TACTICAL, TORPEDO AND STAFF DUTIES DIVISION
(HISTORICAL SECTION),
NAVAL STAFF, ADMIRALTY, S.W.1.

The following Battle Summary was originally completed in July 1942. At that time, though the main facts of the operation were fairly well established, many of the details were in doubt, owing to the heavy casualties sustained by the motor launches and the capture by the enemy of almost all the commandos who got on shore.

Since the surrender of Germany in 1945, a considerable amount of additional information has been obtained from returned prisoners of war and the examination of captured German documents dealing with the raid. This information has been embodied in the following version.

A fuller account of this unique exploit may be read in the book by Commander Ryder, V.C., published by Messrs. John Murray in 1947.

This edition cancels the previous edition of Battle Summary No. 12. B.R.1736 (7), 1943, all copies of which should be destroyed.

CONTENTS

Abbreviations

A.A.	Anti-aircraft.
A/S	Anti-submarine.
C.O.	Commanding Officer.
D/F	Direction finding.
M.G.B.	Motor gunboat.
M.L.	Motor launch.
M.T.B.	Motor torpedo boat.
O.C.	Officer Commanding.
R.D/F.	Radio direction finding.
S.N.O.	Senior Naval Officer.
T.B.	Torpedo boat.
W/T	Wireless telegraphy.

Introduction

St. Nazaire is situated on the north bank of the River Loire, about 120 miles south-east of Brest. Ideally placed for operations against commerce in the Atlantic, the port had been developed by the Germans as a submarine base and could also boast of the only dry dock on the west coast of France capable of accommodating German capital ships.

The enemy had not neglected the defences of this important base, and the raid on 28 March, 1942, was in fact a frontal attack on a heavily defended port by a force of small unarmoured vessels. In surprise, therefore, lay the principal promise of success much as it did at Zeebrugge in 1918. But there the task was not so difficult. Four hundred miles was the distance to St. Nazaire compared with eighty to Zeebrugge, and the passage had to be accomplished by a large number of weakly armed vessels, without detection by aircraft or R.D/F. Zeebrugge, too, had an entrance open to the sea, while St. Nazaire lies 5 miles up a river. Finally, the great development during the last 25 years of close range quick-firing weapons constituted a formidable threat to the wooden petrol-driven craft assigned to the operations.[1] These handicaps had to be faced in drawing up the naval and military plan of attack.

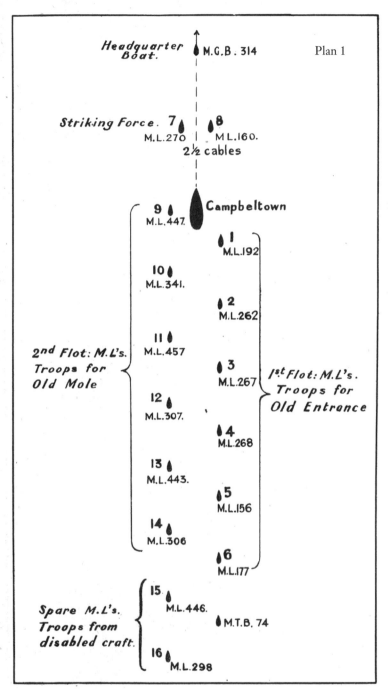

Cruising order for approach

Distance between columns and ships in column - 1 cable

Object of Operation and Forces

The port of St. Nazaire consists of an avant port, and two basins entered by locks. (Plan 2.)

The St. Nazaire basin, on the western side of which are the submarine shelters, is situated north of the avant port and is about 650 yards long. The main entrance is from the avant port by the south lock, which is crossed by two swing bridges, but small craft can enter from the river by the east lock in the Old Entrance.

Connected with the St. Nazaire Basin on the north is the Penhouet Basin, at the north-eastern corner of which are three graving docks. Since 1932 the south-east corner of this basin has had direct access to the River by a large lock, which could itself be used as a dock, known as the "Normandie" Dock after the 83,400 ton liner for whose accommodation it had been specially constructed. At each end of this dock was a massive caisson, operated by hydraulic machinery.[2]

The immobilisation of the Normandie dock – the only one large enough to take the *Tirpitz* – was the principal object of the raid, subsidiary objects being to open the St. Nazaire basin to the tide and to do as much damage as possible to the dock entrances, lock machinery, etc.

The scheme was briefly as follows. The destroyer *Campbeltown* was to ram the lock gate at the southern end of the Normandie dock and be scuttled there, having onboard 3 tons of high explosive timed to blow up some 2½ hours later.

Commando troops were to land on the lock gates from the *Campbeltown*, and from motor launches at the Old Mole and the Old Entrance, to carry out demolitions in the dockyard, and to hold the area east of the St. Nazaire basin and locks – which consisted of two small islands, known as I. de Penhouet to the north of the Old Entrance and I. de St. Nazaire to the south – until re-embarkation in the motor launches was ordered. It was hoped to get well in undetected and then to "bluff" the enemy for just sufficient time for the *Campbeltown* to reach the lock gate, but it was realised that to get out again would be another matter; for this purpose cover by smoke had to be relied on.

The naval side of the operations was entrusted to Commander R. E. D. Ryder, R.N., and the forces employed consisted of M.G.B.314, as headquarter boat, carrying the S.N.O. and Lieut.-Colonel A. C. Newman, the Military Commander, 16 M.Ls. organised in two flotillas, the destroyer *Campbeltown* and M.T.B.74.[3] Embarked in the motor launches and *Campbeltown* were the Commando troops.

The destroyers *Atherstone* and *Tynedale* accompanied the force as escorts, but did not enter the River Loire.

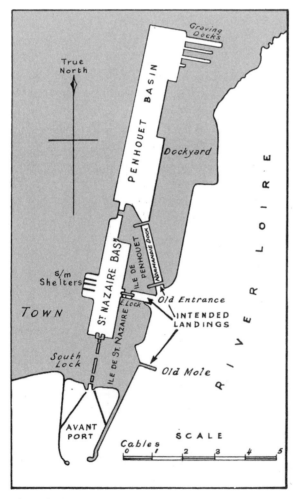

Plan 2 St. Nazaire

Preparations and Plan

The force detailed for the operation, which was known as 'Chariot', assembled at Falmouth, where training was carried out between 12 and 25 March.[4] In order to ensure secrecy, all vessels taking part were referred to collectively as the 10th A/S Striking Force, and all training programmes were worded accordingly. The essence of the various security measures adopted, such as the issue of tropical clothing to the M.Ls. crews, was to discourage any implication of "super" secrecy. When troops were embarked for training, it was announced that this was in connection with exercise "Vivid" to test the defences of Plymouth – an exercise actually carried out – somewhat to the annoyance of the "10th A/S Striking Force", with whose "programme" it interfered. After returning to Falmouth on its conclusion on 23 March, the force was kept at short notice; contact with the shore virtually ceased, and the details of the operation were explained to the officers and key ratings, though the name of the actual locality was withheld.

It had been agreed by the naval and military Force Commanders that the *Campbeltown*, being the main unit, should receive prime consideration in every respect. Light craft were to lead her in and give her full supporting fire.[5]

Detailed operation orders dealing with the organisation and assembly of forces, the passage, final approach, attack, and withdrawal were issued by Commander Ryder to the Naval Forces. The organisation, together with the names of the Commanding Officers, will be found in Appendix A; for the sake of clarity, the motor launches will be designated by their flotilla numbers (see Plan 1) as well as their List of Navy numbers throughout this narrative.

For the final approach[6] and attack the special cruising order shown in Plan 1 was laid down.

Commander Ryder, in M.G.B.314, with an M.L. from the 1st Flotilla on either quarter (Nos. 7 and 8), led the force. These two motor launches had no troops onboard, but carried torpedoes, and formed a striking force under his immediate orders, to deal with any surface craft that might offer resistance. It was stressed that the policy was to pass through unseen or by "bluff," but any vessel showing definite opposition was to be sunk at once by torpedoes. About 2½ cables astern of M.G.B.314 followed the *Campbeltown*, acting as guide, with the 2nd Flotilla of M.Ls. carrying the Commando troops destined for the Old Mole on her port quarter, and the remainder of the 1st Flotilla with the troops for the Old Entrance on her starboard quarter. The two last boats in the port column carried no troops; their primary duty was to land the troops from any ships which might be disabled, and they were also to deal with enemy craft interfering with the rear. M.T.B.74 was in the rear of the starboard column; she was to act as the S.N.O. might direct, as the assault developed.

The *Campbeltown* was given liberty to increase speed should the force be fired on, in order to reach her objective as quickly as possible; and emphasis was laid on the importance of careful fire control by all British ships, to avoid endangering friendly craft.

As soon as their tasks on shore were completed, the crew of the *Campbeltown* and the troops were to re-embark, the M.Ls. leaving independently as they filled, in order to avoid congestion. Smoke was to be used freely to cover the withdrawal. All were to rendezvous with the destroyers at 0600/28 in position Y, some 25 miles south-west of St. Nazaire. It was emphasised that the best defence against the air attacks which were expected was for all ships to remain concentrated, and that "we must all stand by our lame ducks regardless of the speed or condition of our own craft."

The night of 27/28 March was provisionally selected for the attempt.[7] On 24 March, the destroyers *Tynedale* and *Atherstone* arrived at Falmouth, and Commander Ryder and his staff embarked in the latter. During the nights of 24/25 March, all military stores and equipment were transferred from the Special Service Ship *Princess Josephine Charlotte*, in which the troops were accommodated, to the *Campbeltown* and motor launches; the troops followed on receipt of the order "Preparative Chariot" from the C.-in-C., Plymouth, at 0930/26, care being taken to keep them out of sight after embarkation. At 1230/26 came the executive order "Carry out Chariot" and Colonel Newman, with the remainder of the Headquarters Staff, embarked in the *Atherstone*.

Outward Passage
(Plan 3)

At 1400, 26 March, the 10th A/S Striking Force sailed from Falmouth. During daylight the motor launches were spread 2 cables apart ahead of the three destroyers, thereby simulating a routine A/S sweep, in case of observation by enemy aircraft. M.G.B.314 was towed by the *Atherstone* and M.T.B.74 by the *Campbeltown*.

Commander Ryder, in the *Atherstone*, gave the *Lizard* a wide berth, and shaped course at 13 knots to follow a route carefully chosen so as to keep the force out of the track of enemy reconnaissance flights.[8]

The weather was favourable during the afternoon of 26 March, the wind E.N.E., force 4, with considerable haze. At about 0230/27, the haze cleared, and when dawn broke visibility was extreme. At 0700/27, the force was in position C (about 160 miles to the westward of St. Nazaire), and course was altered to 112°. As there was time in hand, speed was reduced to 8 knots, in order to minimise the chances of being spotted from the air.

Twenty minutes later, in lat. 46° 34' N., long. 5° 41' W., the *Tynedale* reported an object[9] bearing 002°, which proved to be a submarine. The *Tynedale* closed at high speed; when some 5 miles distant the submarine fired a recognition signal, which was replied to with five long flashes. This appeared to satisfy her, and she continued on the surface until at 0745 the *Tynedale* broke the white[10] ensign and opened fire at a range of about 5,000 yards.[11] The submarine crash dived, but a depth charge attack carried out at 0758 forced her to break surface when she was engaged by every gun which would bear, and was seen to be hit; she disappeared with a heavy list to port after a few seconds.

The *Atherstone* then joined in, and the submarine was hunted by the two destroyers until 0920 when they shaped course to the south-westward and rejoined the remainder of the force by an indirect route.

It seemed probable that the submarine had been sunk, but, if not, it was possible that she might later surface and make an enemy report. Commander Ryder considered, however, that as she had not sighted the motor launches, she would merely report two destroyers steering south-west.

Actually, the submarine (U.593, which chanced to be returning from a patrol) had sighted some of the motor launches before she was attacked. Nor had she been sunk. After the attack, she remained submerged till 1347, when she surfaced in position lat. 46° 50' N., long. 5° W. and made the following report: "0620[12]: 3 destroyers, 10 M.T.Bs. 46° 52' N. 5° 48' W. course West." This report was picked up by the German Group Command, West, at 1420. Fortunately, the westerly course mentioned in the signal led the Germans to appreciate that either the British force was withdrawing after a minelaying operation, or that the M.T.Bs. were being transferred to Gibraltar. The possibility of an attack from the sea on a port on the French coast was not considered.

After this episode the sky became covered with low cloud, which greatly reduced the chances of detection from the air. Shortly before noon a couple of trawlers were met, which were sunk by the *Tynedale* and *Atherstone*, the crews first being taken off. They were French, and appeared well disposed. From what they said it seemed clear that none of the fishing craft carried wireless, and consequently the large number of trawlers sighted in the course of the afternoon were not interfered with.

At 1240/27, a signal was received from the C.-in-C. Plymouth, stating that five German torpedo boats previously reported at St. Nazaire had been located at Nantes on 25 March, but at 1718/27, a further signal reported that they had reappeared in the neighbourhood of St. Nazaire. These torpedo boats constituted a superior force, but as the U-boat had apparently sent no report, and as the British force had not been sighted from the air,[13] it appeared probable that its presence was unknown to the enemy, and there seemed to be no reason for any change of plan. In point of fact, as previously mentioned, the German Group Command had then been in possession of U.593's report for some three hours, but paradoxically this worked out to the advantage of the British, since the enemy, adopting the supposition that the British Force was returning home after minelaying, ordered the torpedo boats to carry out a sweep in the sea area off St. Nazaire during the night. They were consequently already at sea by the time Commander Ryder's Force entered the Loire and well out of the way during the critical period of the raid.

Half an hour after sunset, Commander Ryder and Colonel Newman transferred from the *Atherstone* to M.G.B.314, and the special cruising order designed for the attack was taken up.[14] (see pages 35-36). Course was set to the north-eastward for position Z – some 40 miles from St. Nazaire – where it had been arranged that the submarine *Sturgeon* (Lieutenant P. H. B. Brunner, R.N.) should show a light as a beacon. To assist in picking her up, the *Tynedale* and *Atherstone* were spread on either beam during this stage of the approach.

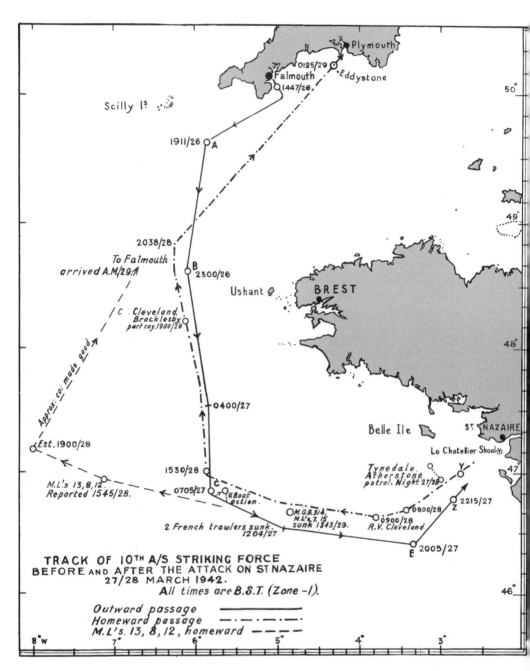

Plymouth
0125/29
Eddystone
Falmouth
1447/26
50°
Scilly Is.
1911/26   A
49°
2038/28
To Falmouth
arrived A.M./29/1
B
2300/26
Ushant
BREST
48°
C. Cleveland
Brocklesby
part coy.1900/28
Approx. co: made good
0400/27
Belle Ile
St NAZAIRE
Est.1900/28
Le Chatellier Shoal
47°
1530/28
Tynedale
Atherstone
patrol. Night 27/28
Y
M.L's 13,8,12.
Reported 1545/28.
0705/27   C
U.Boat
action
2215/27
Z
M.G.B.314.
M.L's 7, 15
sunk 1343/29.
0800/28
0900/28
R.V. Cleveland
2 French trawlers sunk.
1204/27
E   2005/27
46°

TRACK OF 10TH A/S STRIKING FORCE
BEFORE AND AFTER THE ATTACK ON St NAZAIRE
27/28 MARCH 1942.
All times are B.S.T. (Zone −1).

Outward passage ——————
Homeward passage —·—·—·—
M.L's. 13, 8, 12, homeward — — — —

8°W   7°   6°   5°   4°   3°

Plan 3

The Approach
(Plans 3 and 4)

The *Sturgeon's* light was sighted right ahead at 2200 and the flotilla passed within hailing distance at 2215/27, the *Atherstone* and *Tynedale* parting company to patrol to the north-westward.

After the *Sturgeon* had been passed, mist came down and visibility decreased to about 2 miles.

From about midnight, gun flashes were seen to the north-eastward, and half an hour later the wide arc over which they extended, together with considerable flak, indicated some sort of air activity.[15]

No land was sighted until 0045/28, when the northern shore could be dimly discerned from the vicinity of Le Chatelier Shoal (7 ½ miles from St. Nazaire). The *Campbeltown*, as guide, was given a course to steer, thereby leaving M.G.B.314 free to manoeuvre as required to take soundings or obtain R.D/F ranges from the shore.[16]

At 0125 Les Morees Tower was passed. So far all had gone well; no searchlights had been switched on and the flotilla had obviously not been detected;[17] it was only a mile and three-quarters to the lock gate. Just then, however, one searchlight from No. 3 heavy coastal battery was switched on down the Charpentier Channel, followed by all the searchlights on both banks of the river, and from that moment the entire force was flood lit. Commander Ryder at once made a bogus identity signal to the shore signal station at No. 3 battery, and signalled in German that they were "proceeding up harbour in accordance with instructions." On receipt of this signal some of the searchlights were switched off, but he was then called up from the South Entrance, to which he replied with a similar message. While this was in progress the force was fired on by light flak from one position, so the signal for "a vessel considering herself to be fired on by friendly forces" was made, and the firing ceased.

Four priceless minutes – one mile – had been gained by stratagem, but a few seconds later the force must have been recognised as hostile, for, suddenly, a heavy fire was opened on it, and the action became general. To quote Commander Ryder, "It is difficult to describe the full fury of the attack that was let loose on both sides, the air became one mass of red and green tracer, most of it going over." From the head of the line it did not appear that any of the shore surface batteries opened fire, though it is possible that they fired on the rear.

As the action started a flak ship was seen right ahead, which opened fire with some small automatic weapon; she was speedily silenced by M.G.B.314's pom-pom, but had to be passed unpleasantly close.

ATTACK ON St NAZAIRE
27/28 MARCH 1942
THE APPROACH.
SHEWING
POSITION OF FORCE WHEN FIRST FIRED ON.
APPROXIMATE POSITIONS OF ENEMY DEFENCES.
Reduction from Chart 2989
KEY
⊕.......*Heavy A/A Batteries (3/4 guns).*
⚔.......*Light Flak Positions.*
⊟.......*Coastal Battery. (Low Angle). (3/4 guns).*
⊙⟨......*Searchlights.*

Scale
0 1 2 3 4 5 6 7 8 9 10 *Cables.*

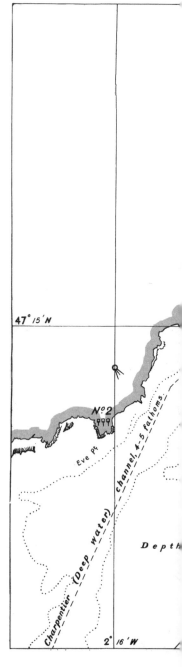

Plan 4

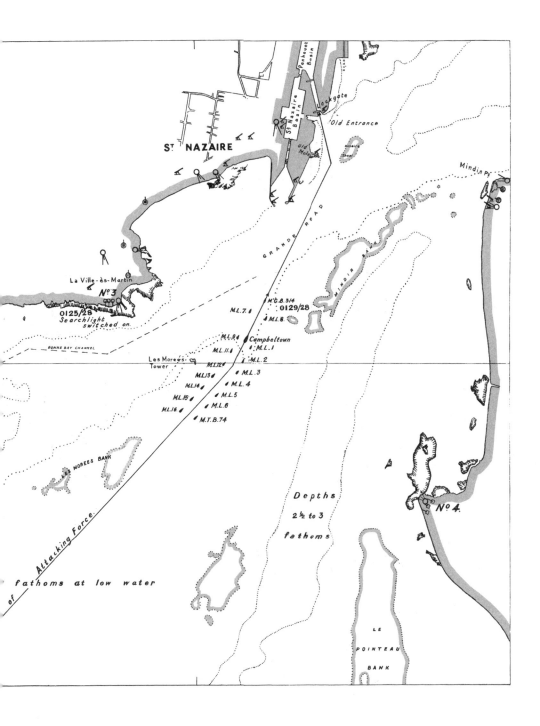

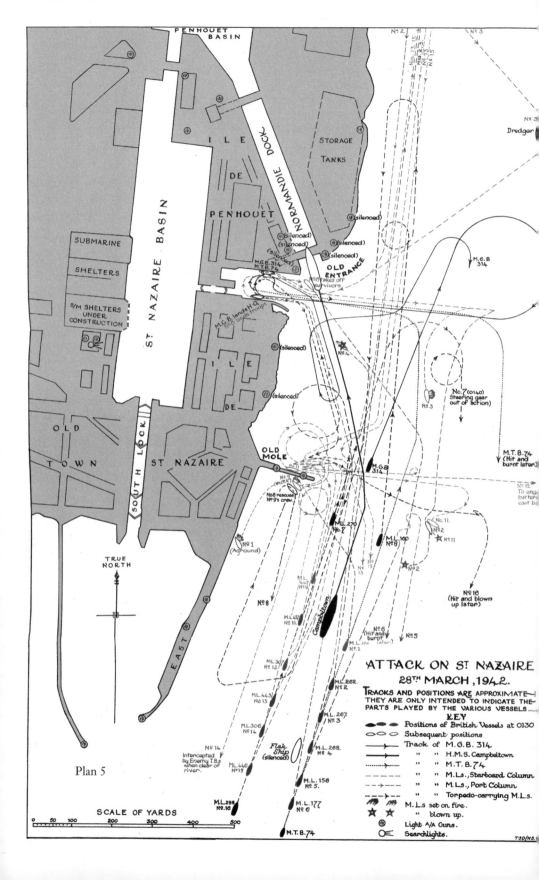

PENHOUET BASIN

ILE DE PENHOUET

NORMANDIE DOCK

STORAGE TANKS

SUBMARINE SHELTERS

S/M SHELTERS UNDER CONSTRUCTION

ST NAZAIRE BASIN

No. 2
No. 3
No. 3
Dredger

(silenced)
(silenced)
(silenced)
(silenced)
(silenced)
(silenced)
M.G.B. 314
M.T.B. 74

OLD ENTRANCE
M.G.B. takes off survivors

M.G.B. 314

ILE DE ST NAZAIRE

M.G.B. lands H.Q.
M.G.B lands troops

(silenced)

(silenced)

No. 4

No. 7 (0140)
Steering gear out of action

No. 3

OLD TOWN

SOUTH LOCK

OLD MOLE

No. 7 (sunk)
No. 8 rescued No. 9's crew.

M.G.B. 314

M.T.B. 74
(Hit and burnt later)

No. 12
To eng. battery cast ba...

EAST

No. 11

M.L. 270
No. 7

M.L. 160
No. 8

No. 2

No. 11

No. 1
(Aground)

No. 15
No. 13

No. 2

TRUE NORTH

M.L. 447
No. 9

No. 16
(Hit and blown up later)

No. 8

M.L. 457
No. 11

Campbeltown

No. 6
(Hit and burnt later)

No. 5

M.L. 307
No. 12

M.L. 156
No. 1

M.L. 262
No. 2

M.L. 443
No. 13

M.L. 267
No. 3

M.L. 306
No. 14

Flak Ship
(silenced)

M.L. 268
No. 4

No. 14
Intercepted by Enemy T.Bs when clear of river.

M.L. 446
No. 15

M.L. 156
No. 5

Plan 5

M.L. 298
No. 16

M.L. 177
No. 6

M.T.B. 74

ATTACK ON Sᵗ NAZAIRE
28ᵀᴴ MARCH, 1942.

TRACKS AND POSITIONS ARE APPROXIMATE—
THEY ARE ONLY INTENDED TO INDICATE THE
PARTS PLAYED BY THE VARIOUS VESSELS.....

KEY

● ● ●	Positions of British Vessels at 0130
○ ○ ○	Subsequent positions
——→	Track of M.G.B. 314
——→	" " H.M.S. Campbeltown
·····→	" " M.T.B. 74
– – –	" " M.Ls., Starboard Column
– ·→	" " M.Ls., Port Column
— —	" " Torpedo-carrying M.Ls.
🔥	M.Ls set on fire.
★ ★	" blown up.
Ⓑ	Light A/A Guns.
⋐	Searchlights.

TSD/H3...

SCALE OF YARDS

0   50   100   200   300   400   500

The Attack
(Plan 5)

The Old Mole was passed by M.G.B.314 at a distance of 1½ cables and she then sheered off to starboard to clear the course for the blockship.

With but 500 yards to go, Lieut.-Commander Beattie[18] drove the *Campbeltown* at his objective. Though repeatedly hit throughout her length by shells and bullets of about 4in. calibre and downwards, no essential parts of the ship were damaged. The Coxswain was wounded, as was the rating who relieved him; Lieutenant Tibbits then took the wheel, and at 0134 – only 4 minutes after the scheduled time – she struck deep into the lock gate, her forecastle ablaze and her Oerlikons firing fiercely.[19] Some relief was afforded to her by M.L.160 (No. 8) – the torpedo carrying M.L. at the head of the starboard column – which opened an accurate fire with her 3-pdr. on the light A.A. positions to starboard of the *Campbeltown* and silenced them.

With the *Campbeltown* firmly wedged in the lock and her scuttling charges momentarily expected to go off, the main objective of the expedition had been attained. Every precaution that ingenuity and experiment could suggest had been taken to ensure the detonation of the explosive charges she carried in due course, and unless some unforeseeable circumstance intervened, the doom of the lock gate seemed inevitable. No more could be done, and the interest accordingly shifted to the subsidiary objects. In these, too, a remarkable measure of success was quickly achieved especially in view of the fact that only about 40% of the troops got ashore, owing to the severe opposition encountered by the motor launches.

Turning then to the motor launches,[20] it will be convenient to consider the attempts at the Old Entrance and the Old Mole separately, though it must be borne in mind that both were actually taking place simultaneously. It will be remembered that the starboard column was carrying the commandos destined for the Old Entrance (see Plan 1). Covering fire for these attempts was provided by M.L.270 (No. 7) for the first five minutes after the *Campbeltown* struck, but she was then badly damaged by shellfire, and obliged to withdraw. Most unfortunately, the leading troop carrying M.L. of this column – M.L.192 (No. 1), in which were embarked the Senior

Naval Officer, M.Ls., and the Commando assault unit – was the first to be hit; she burst into flames and, shooting across the bows of the port column, beached herself south of the Old Mole, ablaze from end to end. The next two in the line – M.Ls.262 (No. 2) and 267 (No. 3) – were dazzled by the glare and missed the landing place. They ran on some way up river before ascertaining their position; then, returning, succeeded in landing their troops in the Old Entrance later on, but these were repulsed and had to be re-embarked. Both motor launches were destroyed by gunfire shortly afterwards. No. 4 (M.L.268) turned in towards the landing place correctly, but was hit while approaching and enveloped in flames; No. 5 (M.L.156) had been hit early in the action, and with steering gear broken down and most of her personnel casualties, was forced to withdraw on one engine. The last boat in the line, No. 6 (M.L.177), alone reached the Old Entrance and landed her troops on the south side as planned. In the glare and confusion prevailing at the time, these events were of course unknown to Commander Ryder, who subsequently reported that at this stage it appeared to him that the situation was being got under control; firing had decreased and was mostly confined to positions on the housetops.[21]

While all this was going on at the Old Entrance, the Port Column was meeting equally fierce resistance at the Old Mole. There the landing place was protected by two massive pill boxes, and the defenders had no such distraction as the sudden arrival of the *Campbeltown* with her commandos in their midst to occupy their attention. The leading boat, M.L.447 (No. 9), grounded while still 10 ft. off the jetty; she encountered a withering fire and was set ablaze almost at once. Backing out, she sank, the troops and crew being rescued most gallantly by M.L.160 (No. 8 – one of the van torpedo carrying craft), which subsequently made good her escape at 0220. The next boat in the line, M.L.457 (No. 11),[22] succeeded in landing her troops – the only craft in the column to do so – but was hit later, and after drifting off the Old Mole for some time, again came under fire and blew up. No. 12 (M.L.307) ran aground close in to the Mole, and could not get alongside; after suffering many casualties and inflicting some, she backed out and engaged batteries and searchlights on the eastern bank of the river till 0230, when she withdrew, shooting up a merchant ship on the way out. M.Ls. 443 (No. 13) and 446 (No. 15) missed the Old Mole in the glare of the searchlights; returning later, each found it impossible to get alongside and withdrew, the latter suffering heavy casualties. M.L.306 (No. 14), too, failed to get alongside, as by the time she arrived off the Mole she found both sides obstructed by burning motor launches;[23] after several attempts, under heavy gunfire, she was forced to withdraw. The last craft in the port column – M.L.298 (No. 16), which carried no troops – passed close to the Old Mole and, after engaging batteries north of the Normandie Dock and later the Old Mole defences, she caught fire passing through some burning petrol and was subsequently blown up by enemy gunfire on her way out.

Meanwhile, Commander Ryder, having seen the *Campbeltown* strike the lock, had taken M.G.B.314 to the south side of the Old Entrance and landed Colonel Newman, who hastened off with his Staff to join his men. M.L.177 (No. 6) had then just landed her troops and as she cast off, Commander Ryder ordered her to go alongside the *Campbeltown*'s stern. This she did, and was seen to shove off with a considerable number of the destroyer's crew onboard, but she failed to appear at the rendezvous next morning and it was long before her fate was known.[24] M.G.B.314 then turned round and secured by the north side of the entrance, where she received onboard between 20 and 30 of the *Campbeltown*'s crew, while M.T.B.74 reported for instructions. Commander Ryder had it in mind that she might be required to torpedo the *Campbeltown*, in event of the scuttling charges failing. He therefore landed and examined the *Campbeltown* – by then apparently deserted – from the dockside. After seeing four of the scuttling charges go off he decided that all was well, and ordered M.T.B.74 to torpedo the lock gate in the Old Entrance and then withdraw at high speed independently.

During this time, Commander Ryder stated, they could hear the military demolition parties "doing good work and with surprising rapidity." Nearby, the building which housed the lockworking machinery was blown up, wounding two men onboard M.G.B.314. This was followed by the pumping house, and another shed was set on fire, the flames casting a lurid glow which silhouetted the craft in the river to the batteries on the opposite bank. [25]

Commander Ryder, having seen M.T.B.74 hit the Old Entrance lock gate with her two torpedoes[26] and start off down river,[27] took M.G.B.314 round to see how the assault on the Old Mole was progressing. It was at once apparent that matters had fared badly there. The approaches were flood-lit by searchlights and a deadly fire was being poured on the motor launches still bravely attempting to get alongside. M.G.B.314 at once gave what support she could, but she herself was frequently hit and soon only the pom-pom remained in action. The pom-pom gunlayer, Able Seaman W. A. Savage, whose skill and gallantry was outstanding throughout the operation until he was eventually killed at his post, engaged various A.A. positions[28] and twice silenced the pillbox on the Mole, but on each occasion it re-commenced firing after an interval.[29] At one time the fire slackened and Commander Ryder was of the opinion that if a force reserve could have been rushed in at that moment, these positions so vital for the retirement might well have been carried. There was, however, no such reserve, and it had to be recognised that at both landing places the enemy was getting the upper hand.

The story of the end of the assault is best told in the words of Commander Ryder's report. "All this time," he wrote, "we were lying stopped about 100 yards off the Old Mole, and although fired on fairly continually by flak positions and hit many times we were, by the grace of God, not set ablaze. On looking round the harbour, however, we could count about seven or eight blazing M.Ls., and were forced to realize that we were the only craft left in sight. In consequence of this a more concentrated fire was directed upon us, so we dropped a naval smoke float while I called a council of war. No withdrawal signal[30] had been sent, and no contact made with the shore by wireless. There was still at least another half hour before one could expect the landing party to reach the point of evacuation. We would have returned to the Old Entrance, but we could see a heavy cross fire across this inlet, and it appeared that enemy forces on both banks were shooting at each other. It was clearly impossible for us to return. With some thirty to forty men onboard and our decks piled with seriously wounded, I decided at 0250 that we were in no position to take off the soldiers we had landed. It was unlikely that we would survive another five minutes with the fire that was then being concentrated in our direction, and so we left at high speed."[31]

Almost at the same moment that Commander Ryder was making his difficult decision to withdraw, Colonel Newman, having reached a similar conclusion as to the impossibility of evacuation by water, was organising his troops for an attempt to escape inland. Some account of their activities on shore and their desperate bid for freedom will be found in the following section.

The Commando Operations

Before following the fortunes of the Commandos on shore, it is necessary to consider briefly the main features of the military plan.

The essence of this plan was the rapid seizure of the islands of St. Nazaire and Penhouet. These two islands were then to be isolated by the destruction of the bridges and locks connecting them to the mainland,[32] and held long enough for the demolition parties to do their work, which was specified in great detail, after which the withdrawal was to be carried out.

The Old Mole was chosen as the point of re-embarkation, the troops from Penhouet Island passing over by the bridge across the Old Entrance, which was then – together with the two small lock gates – to be blown up. While this was being done, a final bridgehead was to be formed round the base of the Old Mole, through which it was hoped an orderly withdrawal to the motor launches could be effected.

In order to give effect to this plan, Colonel Newman organised his force in three main groups. Each group contained two assault parties, which were to clear the area in the first instance, and a number of demolition parties to follow up. The latter each included a small protection party of fighting troops to prevent interference from snipers or enemy who might infiltrate into the occupied areas.

Group I, landing at the Old Mole, was responsible for St. Nazaire Island to the southward of the northern lock of the South Entrance.

Group II, landing at the Old Entrance, was responsible for the north and west of Penhouet Island. At the last moment, a special party was added to this group to strike south into St. Nazaire Island, and deal with two gun positions which air photographs revealed on the water front between the two landing places.

Group III, under Major Copeland – Colonel Newman's Second-in-Command – was to land from HMS *Campbeltown* on to the caisson and deal with the adjacent areas on each side of the Normandie Dock. These areas contained the most important demolition objectives – the dock pumping machinery and hydraulic lock machinery to the west and the oil fuel storage tanks to the east.

Colonel Newman himself intended to set up his Headquarters on St. Nazaire Island, close south of the Old Entrance lock, where he would be centrally placed, and in a good position to control the evacuation of Penhouet Island and subsequent re-embarkation at the Old Mole.

The following summary shows the composition of the Groups, together with the individual tasks of each party; for convenience, a brief reference has been included, indicating which parties actually succeeded in getting ashore.

A. Landing at Old Mole.
Group I, commanded by Captain E. S. Hodgson.[33]

Party and Task	Embarked In	Remarks
Captain D. Birney: 14 All Ranks. Assault 2 pill boxes on Old Mole (A). Form bridgehead at landward end of Old Mole and protect M.Ls. berthing there for withdrawal	M.L.447 (No. 9)	Failed to get alongside
Captain E. S. Hodgson: 15 All Ranks. Assault 2 flak positions on East Jetty (B). Form protection post at landward end of East Jetty: picket and patrol built-up area opposite Old Mole	M.L.341 (No. 10) Transferred to M.L.446. (No. 15). 1830/27.	Failed to get alongside
Lieut. P. Walton: 10 All Ranks. Destroy northern lock gate and operating mechanism and lifting bridge across South Entrance (C)	M.L.457 (No. 11)	Landed successfully
Captain W. H. Pritchard, Lieut. W. H. Watson: 7 All Ranks. Demolition control party	M.L.457 (No. 11)	Landed successfully
Capt. E. W. Bradley: 7 All Ranks: 2 Medical Orderlies. Destroy centre lock gate, South Entrance (D). Covering party for demolition work in Power Station (E)	M.L.307 (No. 12)	Failed to get alongside
Lieut. J. A. Bonvin: 15 All Ranks. Destroy Power Station and Boilerhouse near South Entrance (E)	M.L.443 (No. 13)	Failed to get alongside
Lieut. R. O. C. Swayne: 14 All Ranks. Destroy swing bridge and 2 lock gates across south end of South Entrance	M.L.306 (No. 14)	Failed to get alongside

B. Landing at Old Entrance.
Group II, commanded by Captain M. Burn.

Party and Task	Embarked In	Remarks
Captain M. Burn: 14 All Ranks. Destroy 2 flak towers at north end of Penhouet Island and flak position on building across adjacent swing bridge (G). Form defensive block at north end of Normandie Dock and cover approach along east side of Penhouet Basin	M.L. 192 (No. 1)	Ran ashore near East Jetty
Lieut. M. Woodcock: 14 All Ranks. Destroy 2 lock gates and operating mechanism and swing bridge across Old Entrance (H)	M.L. 262 (No. 2)	Troops landed but forced to re-embark
R.S.M. A. Moss: 14 All Ranks. Reserve: engage enemy vessels in St. Nazaire Basin	M.L. 267 (No. 3)	Troops landed but forced to re-embark
Lieut. M. Jenkins, Lieut. H. Pennington: 15 All Ranks. Destroy swing bridge at north end of St. Nazaire Basin (J)	M.L. 268 (No. 4)	Failed to get alongside
Captain R. H. Hooper: 15 All Ranks. Assault guns on waterfront between Old Mole and Old Entrance (K). Fire on any vessel in dock. Come in to reserve	M.L. 156 (No. 5)	Failed to get alongside
T.S.M. G. Haines: 14 All Ranks. Assist Captain Hooper's party	M.L. 177 (No. 6)	Landed successfully

C. Landing at South Lock, Normandie Dock,
From HMS *Campbeltown*.
Group III, commanded by Major W. O. Copeland

Party and Task	Remarks
Captain D. Roy: 14 All Ranks. Assault flak positions at S.W. Corner of Normandie Dock and on roof of pumping-house. Form bridgehead to cover withdrawal of all parties across Old Entrance, and resist possible attack from escort vessels in St. Nazaire basin	
Lieut. J. Roderick: 14 All Ranks Assault flak positions at S.E. Corner of Normandie Dock and in vicinity of fuel storage to eastward of dock. Destroy fuel storage units (L). Prevent enemy from approaching from area to the north-east of dock	All landed according to plan
Lieut. S. W. Chant: 22 All Ranks Destroy main pumping-house and caisson-operating machinery in winding hut at south end of Normandie Dock (M)	
Lieut. W. W. Etches: 17 All Ranks. Destroy caisson at north end of Normandie Dock, and operating machinery in winding hut (N)	
Major W. O. Copeland: 8 All Ranks. Military Second-in-Command: responsible for organisation of re-embarkation	

This, then was the military plan. In the event it achieved a remarkable degree of success as far as the demolitions were concerned, but the heavy casualties suffered from the outset by the motor launches foredoomed the withdrawal to failure.

Taking the landings in turn, at the Old Mole, as already mentioned, out of the six motor launches carrying Group I, one only succeeded in landing her troops. This party, which included Captain Pritchard, the principal demolition Officer, had as its task the destruction of the lifting gate across the South Entrance and the adjacent lock gate. How this party fared is not known; later, Colonel Newman noticed two small vessels sunk across the north end of the South Entrance lock, which he presumed to be the work of some of them.[34] Since no other troops of Group I got ashore, their part in the plan was perforce omitted; neither the power station nor the South Entrance locks were destroyed and for some time the only fighting troops in this area were five men under Lieutenant Watson, who had landed from M.L.457 as protection for her demolition party. They remained in the vicinity of the Old Mole, fighting fiercely – a diversion subsequently of great value to the troops withdrawing from Penhouet Island, with whom they eventually linked up.

At the Old Entrance, Group II had little better fortune. Here again one motor launch only – M.L.177 (No. 6) – managed to land her party.[35] This was one of the assault parties detailed to deal with the water front guns to the southward; it subsequently joined up with Colonel Newman, who had landed just afterwards from M.G.B.314. Group II's objectives on Penhouet Island were thus left unmolested – with one exception. The two flak towers at the northern end of the island had been the objective of a party under Captain Burn, embarked in M.L.192, the leading craft of the Starboard Column. This motor launch, it will be remembered, had been set on fire and forced ashore while still south of the Old Mole. She fetched up somewhere near the East Jetty. From this position, Captain Burn managed to struggle ashore and, finding his way all alone right across the two islands, set fire to the flak towers, which, as it chanced, were unoccupied. Meanwhile, Colonel Newman, on arrival at the house earmarked for his headquarters, had found it already occupied by a German headquarters. At the same time, his party came under point blank fire from one or two vessels in the St. Nazaire basin and heavy plunging fire from the roofs of a nearby house and the submarine shelters. Most of the H.Q. Staff had been lost in M.L.267, and the arrival of the party under T. S. M. Haines from M.L.177 shortly afterwards was very welcome. The enemy guns and craft were engaged with a 2-in. mortar with good effect and the German headquarters personnel were dealt with by hand grenades. By this time explosions were taking place in the Normandie Dock area and Colonel Newman took up a position to check up the returning demolition parties and direct them to the Old Mole. In small groups they came over the Old Entrance bridge, each one reporting success.

Indeed, in that area, everything had gone almost exactly as planned. Led by their assault parties, the troops had scrambled down from the *Campbeltown's* forecastle as soon as she struck the caisson. The flak positions east and west of the entrance were speedily silenced by the assault parties led respectively by Lieutenant Roderick and Captain Roy. The former then advanced over the top of the oil fuel storage for about 100 yards; running into heavy opposition, they held a perimeter on this line. Captain Roy's party, after silencing two guns on the roof of the pumping–house, which they reached by scaling ladders, formed the bridgehead north of the Old Entrance, for the first stage of the withdrawal.

Meanwhile, on Penhouet Island, Lieutenant Chant's demolition party destroyed the machinery in the southern winding hut and the nearby pumpinghouse, while further north, Lieutenant Etches with his party wrecked the northern caisson, destroyed the winding hut machinery and finally set fire to the hut itself. All this work was completed in about an hour (by approximately 0230).

Group III had thus completed all its tasks, an achievement the more remarkable in view of the fact that many of the troops had been severely wounded in the *Campbeltown* before ever they got ashore. The only disappointment lay in the failure (for some unexplained reason) of the incendiary bombs dropped down the ventilators of the fuel installation to set it on fire.

All this was very cheering, as was the report on the *Campbeltown* and the evacuation of the wounded from her made by Major Copeland, who arrived with his small headquarters party a few minutes later. Major Copeland had fallen in with Captain Burn, and so knew that he alone of his party had reached Penhouet Island; this left only Lieutenant Pennington's party unaccounted for there[36] and Colonel Newman decided that the time had come to withdraw to the Old Mole area.

The first step was to call in Captain Roy's bridgehead party from Penhouet Island. Since the withdrawal rockets had been lost, this had to be done by runner – a duty gallantly performed by Corporal Harrington, who succeeded in crossing the bridge over the Old Entrance under heavy fire, and returned, followed in due course by the party.

By this time – about 0245 – Colonel Newman had moved to a position just west of the Old Mole. It was not until his arrival there that he realised that the St. Nazaire Island demolition parties had not got ashore and that consequently the South Entrance locks, etc., were probably still intact. A few moments' reflection convinced him of the impossibility of carrying out these demolitions with the troops at his disposal, since all the explosive charges had either been used, or sunk in the motor launches.

There was a "good sized battle going on in the old Mole area".[37] Colonel

Newman first busied himself trying to get an idea of what was happening, while Major Copeland organised a very effective protective screen round the base of the Mole. The Mole itself was still in enemy hands, no motor launches were alongside and the general view of the river presented a picture of burning and sinking craft. Clearly there could be no withdrawal by water. On the other hand it was essential to escape from the dock side as quickly as possible. "It was the focal point for all German reinforcements to make for; there was no room to manoeuvre, and six tons of unexploded explosive was just behind us,"[38] (in the *Campbeltown*).

The scene at the bridgehead at this time was well nigh indescribable. "Fires and smoke were everywhere and small arms fire was coming from most of the buildings around us... Everyone was behaving magnificently and coolly returning the fire with ever decreasing ammunition."[39] Several nearby railway trucks afforded good cover for the 80 or 90 commandos congregated in the area; near one of these trucks Colonel Newman reviewed the situation with Major Copeland and the Adjutant, Captain Day. A stick grenade fell at their ft. and burst; miraculously, not one of them suffered a scratch. In this desperate pass Colonel Newman decided to break inland, in the hope of eventually reaching Spain.

To carry out this attempt, the troops were rapidly organised into parties of about twenty and the leaders were instructed to fight their way inland separately, using "fire and movement" as they advanced. The inner bridge over the South Lock offered the best prospects of escape, but enemy fire rendered a direct approach from the Mole impossible, and most of the parties moved off to try to work their way round and carry the bridge from its northern flank. Good progress was made, despite the fact that more than half the survivors were wounded by this time.

Colonel Newman's group paused for a while in a bomb hole made by the R.A.F. where a railway shed had once been, and then made for the Inner basin. Finely led by Captain Roy, they fought their way to the bridge, which they rushed under heavy fire, the bullets ricochetting off the girders over their heads,[40] and burst into the town – a smaller party, but still able to move. "The sequence of events during the next half hour," wrote Colonel Newman, "I cannot adequately describe. We seemed to be one moment jumping over a wall into someone's back garden, bursting through houses into the road... I remember going head first through a window into somebody's kitchen – there to see the breakfast or supper laid out on a check table cloth and thinking how odd it all was. The next moment we were dashing along a road when an armoured car appeared with the turret spitting fire on all and sundry – including Germans – we were lucky to find a small alley to dodge into as she passed. Someone scored a good hit as a motor cycle and sidecar, full of Germans, came dashing across a square. The troops pitched out and the bike crashed into a wall."

This hectic rush could not go on indefinitely, however. Major Copeland found a lorry, which seemed to offer a chance of getting to the open country, but no effort could persuade it to start. By this time dawn was breaking, ammunition was running very short, and the wounded, some of whom, like Lieut. Etches, had been badly hit before landing, but yet had completed their tasks in the docks and kept up in the wild rush through the town, were in sore need of rest and treatment. Every cross road seemed picquetted with an enemy machine gun and movement was very difficult so shelter was sought in a convenient cellar, where wounds were dressed and plans laid to continue the following evening.

In the course of the day, however, they were discovered by a German search party, and being in a hopeless position to fight down there, there was nothing left for it but surrender.[41]

The other parties which had split up met with varying success, but most suffered a similar fate to that of Colonel Newman's, being rounded up within the next twenty-four hours. Not all of this determined force, however, fell into the hands of the enemy; five of them – Corporal Wheeler, Lance-Corporals Douglas, Howarth and Sims, and Private Harding eluded capture, and after remarkable adventures reached England in due course.

The Withdrawal

To return to the Naval force. Having decided that no more could be done at St. Nazaire, Commander Ryder headed to the southward at 24 knots at 0250/28. During her withdrawal, M.G.B.314 was flood-lit by searchlights and subjected to intense fire from both banks of the river. When abreast of the south Mole she passed a surviving motor launch for which she laid smoke, at the same time ordering her to follow. As they passed Les Morees Tower the coastal artillery opened fire and straddled them continuously until they reached the neighbourhood of Le Chatelier Shoal – about 4 miles from the land-shell splinters causing further casualties onboard M.G.B.314.

When at last they were getting out of the searchlight beams, they encountered an armed trawler, which opened an unpleasantly heavy fire, but fortunately did no serious damage. Soon afterwards, M.L.270 (No. 7) was met, damaged and steering from aft; she was capable, however, of 15 knots and joined the motor-gunboat. Ten minutes later a short action was seen taking place to the north-westward and course was altered to the southward to keep clear. Another action to the south-westward was observed at 0330, and a very heavy explosion in the direction of St. Nazaire at 0400 signified – it was hoped – the end of the *Campbeltown* and the lock gate.[42]

The rendezvous – position Y – was reached at 0430, but in view of possible interference by the five enemy torpedo boats reported the previous evening, Commander Ryder continued to the westward at 12 knots.

The reality of this danger was proved by the fate which overtook M.L.306 an hour later. This motor launch, after vain attempts to get alongside the Old Mole, had left St. Nazaire about 0200, and under cover of smoke succeeded in making the passage down river. At 0530, when 45 miles out, she sighted several large vessels approaching her fine on the port bow. These were the torpedo boats returning from their sweep.

Uncertain as to whether they were friend or foe, the Commanding Officer (Lieutenant Henderson), stopped engines, hoping to escape notice in the dark, and the enemy passed within 100 yards of her. On re-starting her engines, however, she was sighted by the rear ship and illuminated by

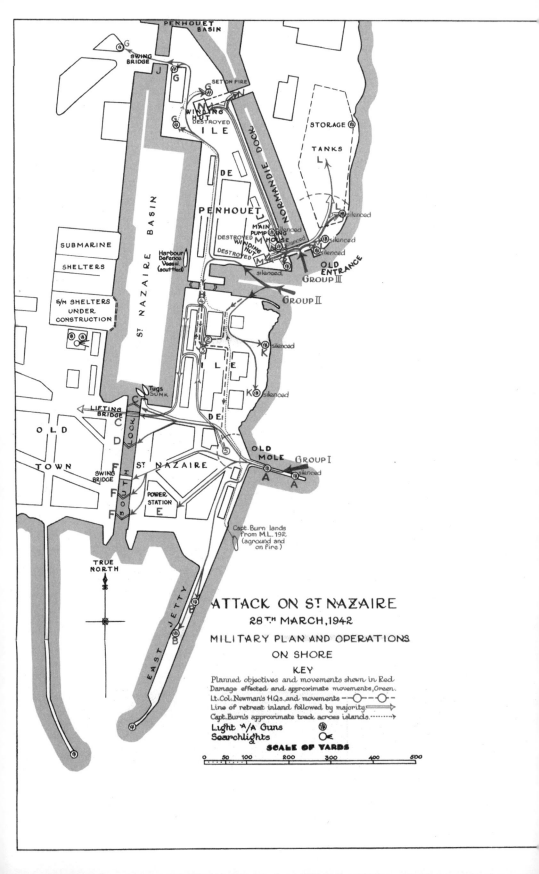

ATTACK ON St. NAZAIRE
28TH MARCH, 1942
MILITARY PLAN AND OPERATIONS
ON SHORE

KEY
Planned objectives and movements shown in Red.
Damage effected and approximate movements, Green.
Lt. Col. Newman's H.Qs. and movements --O---O--
Line of retreat inland followed by majority
Capt. Burn's approximate track across islands. ·········▸
Light A/A Guns   ⑱
Searchlights   O✦

SCALE OF YARDS
0   50   100   200   300   400   500

searchlights. The enemy at once opened fire with short range weapons, then attempted to ram, and as she drew away engaged her with main armament at about 50 yards range. With but one Oerlikon – the remainder of her armament had been put out of action up river – and two Lewis guns manned by Commandos, M.L.306 put up a gallant fight against overwhelming odds; in a few minutes her Commanding Officer had been killed and the remainder of her Officers and nearly everyone onboard wounded. In this desperate situation, Sergeant Durrant, R.E., though hit in many places and mortally wounded, continued to engage the enemy with his Lewis gun to the last, earning the admiration of both friend and foe. Eventually, with nearly all onboard incapacitated and no means of continuing the fight, there was nothing left for it but surrender. The survivors were taken off by one of the torpedo boats,[43] which then continued to the eastward and an hour later fought a brief engagement with the *Tynedale* and *Atherstone*.[44]

These two actions were seen from M.G.B.314, though at the time it was of course not known who were engaged.

At dawn[45] the atmosphere cleared and the visibility became extreme; Commander Ryder reduced speed to 8 knots and ordered M.L.270 to open to 3 miles. Another motor launch was sighted some way astern and M.G.B.314 had just altered course to close her, when the *Tynedale* and *Atherstone* appeared over the horizon.

Opposite, Plan 6

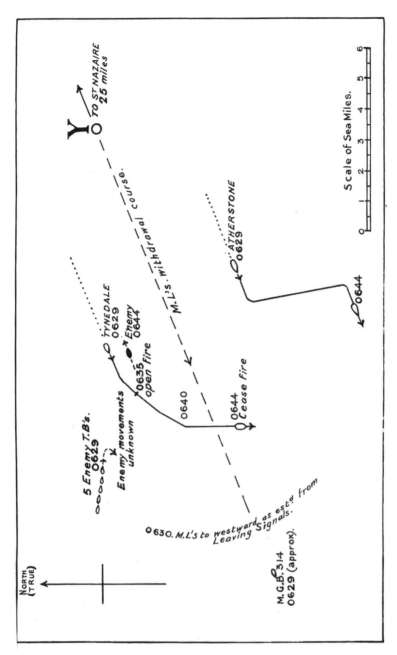

Plan 7 Action between H.M. Ships *Tynedale* and *Atherstone* and 5 German torpedo boats 0630 28 March 1942

N.B. No track chart is available: movements shown are conjectural only

Destroyer Action
(Plan 7)

After parting company at 2200/27, the *Tynedale* and *Atherstone* had patrolled[46] to the north-westward of position Z until 0420/28, when course was shaped for the 0600 rendezvous in position Y. Nothing was sighted, but a report of four destroyers 40 miles to the westward at 2230/27, apparently escorting southbound merchant vessels, was received from aircraft. Between 0218 and 0325/28 "leaving" signals from M.Ls. 6, 7, 8, 12 and 13 were received by the *Tynedale*,[47] and at 0420 the wake of the first motor launch coming out was sighted. Two others passed to the westward at 0430, and yet another pair at 0450.

At 0540 the destroyers were at the rendezvous, and spreading 5 miles apart, steered 248° at 15 knots, the *Tynedale* being to the northward.[48]

As dawn was breaking – at 0630 – the *Tynedale* sighted five enemy torpedo boats 4 miles on her starboard bow, bearing 273°. She at once altered course to port to close the *Atherstone* at full speed and at 0635 the enemy opened fire, to which she replied. The *Atherstone* also turned to port with the object of drawing the enemy away from the motor launches to the westward, and steadied on 170°. Though she could not see the enemy through the *Tynedale*'s smoke she was straddled at a range of 15,000 yards. The *Tynedale* scored a hit on the third ship in the enemy's line herself receiving two hits, which fortunately did little damage. The engagement lasted only nine minutes, for at 0640, the enemy turned away under smoke and firing ceased four minutes later. Their subsequent movements are unknown, but at the time it seemed probable that they would renew the attack, and the *Tynedale* and *Atherstone* therefore steered to the south-westward with the intention of taking off as many of the crews of the motor launches as possible before the enemy returned.

At 0702, two motor launches were sighted ahead, which proved to be M.Ls.270 (No. 7) and 156 (No. 5). The wounded were taken off and the latter was found to be so badly damaged that it was decided she must be abandoned.

The *Atherstone* had just opened fire to sink her when a Heinkel 115 appeared, and she left her to close two other motor craft – M.G.B.314 and M.L. 446 (No. 15) – sighted at that moment (0739). The Heinkel bombed and sank the abandoned M.L.156 some three-quarters of an hour later.

As time went on and the enemy torpedo boats did not re-appear, it became possible to follow the original plan of getting the motor launches home with their crews.

At 0745/28 M.G.B.314 reached the *Atherstone* and was towed alongside in the "glass calm" sea while the wounded were transferred. She had been holed in the forepeak, but it seemed probable she could make the passage home,[49] and her crew – reduced to four seamen – was made up by volunteers from the destroyer.

As soon as these arrangements had been made, Commander Ryder and his staff re-embarked in the *Atherstone*, and with the *Tynedale*, M.G.B.314, and M.Ls.270 (No. 7) and 446 (No. 15), proceeded to the westward to meet the destroyers *Cleveland* and *Brocklesby* which had left Plymouth the previous evening to reinforce the escort for the return passage.

Return Passage
(Plan 3)

The *Cleveland* and *Brocklesby* had reached a position approximately 120 miles W.S.W. of St. Nazaire (lat. 46° 39' N., long. 5° 00' W.), when at 0644/28 they intercepted a signal reporting that the *Tynedale* and *Atherstone* were engaging the enemy torpedo boats. They at once increased to full speed, steering for the position given, then some 80 miles ahead. After half an hour a large trawler was sighted to port. As she wore no colours and altered course away to the north-eastward at increased speed on their approach, she was taken to be an enemy look-out vessel. Seven or eight salvoes were fired at her at 4,000 yards range, leaving her damaged and stopped.

At 0809 M.L.443 (No. 13) was sighted ahead. Her upper deck was crowded with men and she was making slowly to the westward at about 10 knots. When communication had with difficulty been established, she reported that she was leaking, and asked for medical assistance. This, however, could not then be given on account of the urgent necessity of reinforcing the *Tynedale* and *Atherstone*, which, from intercepted signals, were believed still to be in action. Two other motor launches – M.Ls.160 (No. 8) and 307 (No. 12) – which were sighted on the starboard bow a quarter of an hour later were instructed to join M.L.443 (No. 13).

Just before this meeting an enemy aircraft was sighted and engaged; from then until about 1415, shadowing by He.115's and Ju.88's was continuous.

Junction with Commander Ryder's force was effected about 0900/28 in lat. 46° 35' N., long. 3° 49' W., and Commander Sayer (*Cleveland*), who was the Senior Officer, assumed command.

After an exchange of signals it was clear to him that there was no immediate hope of engaging the enemy torpedo boats, which had not been seen for two hours.

It was improbable that there were any more motor launches to the eastward. The three small craft in company were seriously damaged, and a large number of survivors, many of them serious casualties, were onboard the *Tyndale* and *Atherstone*. (Plan 7). He therefore decided to continue the withdrawal by the pre-arranged route, and organised the destroyers in two

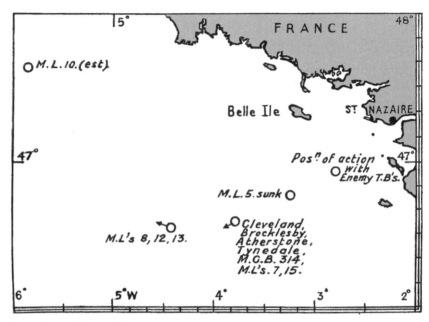

Situation at 0900, 28 March

divisions disposed abeam with the motor launches between them, as being the best formation for A/A defence.

Enemy air activity was increasing, and all ships were frequently in action. Their gunfire was successful in keeping the aircraft at a distance, and no serious attacks developed. At 0942/28, a Beaufighter which had made contact with the *Atherstone* at 0822 shot down a Ju.88 on the port beam, shortly afterwards itself crashing from a very low altitude. No survivors could be found. Another Ju.88 was shot down astern by the *Brocklesby* at 1006 and several others were seen to be hit. Not until 1000 did the air situation permit the medical officers of the *Cleveland* and *Brocklesby* to be transferred to the *Tynedale* and *Atherstone*, where their assistance was urgently required.

Throughout the forenoon the force continued to the westward at a speed dictated by the conditions of the motor launches. From 16 knots this gradually dropped to 10 knots, and even this could not be maintained. All three boats were making water, had serious engine trouble, and were short of fuel. There were signs that a heavy air attack was imminent, and attack by surface vessels was considered not unlikely.

In view of these circumstances, and also of the desirability of getting the critically wounded to port as soon as possible, the question of abandoning the motor craft had to be considered.

Shortly after noon floatplanes diving out of low cloud attacked the *Atherstone* and *Cleveland*, and small bombs fell near both, without inflicting damage or casualties. No British aircraft had been seen since the Beaufighter crashed at 0942/28, but about 1230 another arrived and escorted for some 50 minutes, when it engaged a He.115 and disappeared to the southward. Two Hudsons then made contact, but only remained in company for a few minutes.[50]

The three motor craft were then ordered alongside the *Brocklesby* for examination, as a result of which Commander Sayer reluctantly decided they must be abandoned.[51] The crews and such gear as time permitted were removed, and at 1343/28, M.G.B.314 and the two motor launches were sunk by gunfire – a melancholy end after all they had come through.[52]

At 1350/28, the four destroyers continued their passage to the westward at 25 knots, hoping to overtake the three motor launches sighted by the *Cleveland* in the early morning. Nothing was seen of them, however, and at 1530/28, course was altered to the northward. At 1850, a mutilated signal was intercepted from M.L.443 (No. 13) giving her 1545 position as 46° 55' N., 7° 07' W., and asking for immediate help. This position was 85 miles 210° from the *Cleveland* and Commander Sayer immediately decided to detach the *Atherstone*, and *Tynedale* with the wounded to Plymouth, while the *Cleveland* and *Brocklesby* swept towards M.L.13's estimated position.[53] They parted company at 1900/28, and Commander Ryder then sent a brief report to the Commander-in-Chief, who was still entirely ignorant of the course of events.[54] The remainder of the passage was without incident, and the *Atherstone* and *Tynedale* passed the Eddystone at 0125/29.

Soon after parting company, the *Cleveland* and *Brocklesby* intercepted further signals from M.L.443 (No. 13) indicating that she was making for the Scilly Islands through lat. 47° 07' N., long. 7° 50' W., with the other two motor launches in company; the sweep was organised accordingly, but nothing was seen of the motor launches.

In the morning, the destroyers *Fernie*, *Albrighton* and *Kujawiak* joined the *Cleveland*, and the search was continued till 1315/29, when all destroyers were recalled to harbour by the Commander-in-Chief, the three missing motor launches having arrived at Falmouth that forenoon. Their passage home had not been without incident.

After passing the *Cleveland* at 0830/28, M.Ls.160 and 307 had joined M.L.443. The Senior Officer was Lieutenant Platt, who had been rescued by M.L.160 (No. 8) when M.L,447 (No. 9) was disabled at the Old Mole.

Having shifted to M.L.443 (No. 13),[55] he decided, as there was no sign of British aircraft or destroyers, to run out to 8° W. before making to the northward.

At 1525/28, a Heinkel circled the three motor launches, and after flashing the correct British challenge, came in from astern, and was shot down by rapid fire. A couple of hours later a Blohm and Voss seaplane was observed shadowing. This aircraft attacked at 1800, and was driven off after dropping one bomb. He again came in to attack half an hour later when he was apparently hit and flew off to the westward. It was then that Lieutenant Platt sent a message requesting an escort.

Course was held to the westward till sunset,[56] and then altered up the 8th meridian. At 0130/29, *Ushant* being abeam by dead reckoning, course was altered for the Scilly Islands which, however, had not been sighted by 0900/29. A signal was sent asking for a D/F bearing, but before this came through the Lizard was sighted, and they proceeded into Falmouth.

The remnant of the gallant 10th A/S Striking Force was once more at home. Of the 18 small craft which had sailed three days previously, 10 had been sunk by the enemy, four by their own side during the return passage, and only four remained. Thirty-four officers (55 per cent) and 157 ratings (53.5 per cent) out of 62 officers and 291 ratings were missing[57] or killed; but their task had been brilliantly accomplished, and – in the words of the Commander-in-Chief – "taking into consideration the extreme vulnerability of the coastal craft, neither the losses in men or material can be considered as excessive for the results achieved."

Results and Lessons

It was not possible to estimate the full results of the raid, but enough was known to regard it as a distinct success. The main object was to disable the large lock, and this was achieved. In addition to the destruction of the outer caisson by the *Campbeltown*,[58] the pumping station and operating mechanism of both outer and inner caissons were destroyed. Other port facilities, including possibly the caisson at the Old Entrance were also destroyed; the enemy suffered considerable casualties, partly by their own fire, and at least two ships in the harbour were damaged.

The moral effect must have been considerable, and may well have caused a diversion of troops and armament to Biscay ports.

To these gains there could be added damage to a U-boat and the destruction of a number of enemy aircraft by the British forces – naval and air – on their way back.

Commenting on the operation, the Commander-in-Chief, Plymouth, remarked that for success, surprise was essential. The unseen passage to the Loire was due partly to favourable weather conditions, and partly to careful routeing to keep the force clear of the track of enemy reconnaissance flights. The prompt action of the *Tynedale* which resulted in the probable sinking of the U-boat on the morning of 27/3 was an important contribution to the success of this part of the operation.

In the later stages the large measure of surprise achieved was due to the stratagems employed by Commander Ryder, which the Commander-in-Chief described as "admirable and carefully worked out beforehand". It was fortunate that no patrols were met in the shoal waters of the approach. That surprise was not complete was principally owing to the bombing policy adopted. The weather – always a doubtful factor – prevented accurate location of targets by the bombers, which consequently did not drop their bombs, but their presence overhead was sufficient to put all the enemy defences on the alert and when the alarm was given they were able to concentrate their fire on the motor launches within a few seconds. In the light of this experience the Commander-in-Chief remarked that "bombing unless heavy and continuous, should not take place... If any chances exist of achieving complete surprise, it would be better to have no bombing at all on the night of the operation."

With regard to the actual attack, he pointed out that the landing plan was not sufficiently flexible to take advantage of any "soft spot." Such a spot existed near the outer caisson of the large lock and the Old Entrance, This, or the *Campbeltown* herself, might have been used when it was found the landings at the Old Mole were impossible.

The great difficulty experienced in putting out of action guns sited on the tops of buildings has already been mentioned.

Though their disabilities were, of course, known before, the Commander-in-Chief commented on the unsuitability of the motor launches for operations of this nature; they were set on fire very easily, they provided little or no protection to the personnel embarked, and they were very noisy.[59]

In conclusion, he regretted that little could be told of the "admirable work ashore of the Commando troops, because unfortunately, none who took part has returned to tell the tale; nor is there any officer from HMS *Campbeltown* to give the full story of her gallant exploit.

"Results must be the silent witnesses of their achievement."

Appendix A

Organisation of Naval Forces

Ship	Flotilla Number	Commanding Officer
		Headquarters Boat
		(carrying S.N.O. and Military Commander)
M.G.B.314[60]	0	Lieut. D. M. C. Curtis, R.N.V.R.
		Motor Launches
		1st Flotilla
M.L.192[61]	1	Lieut-Commander. W. L. Stephens, R.N.V.R. (S.O., M.Ls.).
M.L.262[61]	2	Lieut. E. A. Burt, R.N.V.R.
M.L.267[61]	3	Lieut. E. H. Beart. R.N.V.R.
M.L.268[61]	4	Lieut. A. D. B. X. Tillie, R.N.V.R.
M.L.156[60]	5	Lieut. L. Fenton, R.N.V.R.
M.L.177[61]	6	Sub-Lieut. M. F. Rodier. R.N.V.R.
M.L.270[60]	7	Lieut. C. S. B. Irwin, R.N.R
M.L.160	8	Lieut. T. W. Boyd, R.N.V.R.
		2nd Flotilla
M.L.447[61]	9	Lieut. T. D. L. Platt, R.N.R.[63] (S.O., 2nd Flot.)
M.L.341	10	Lieut. D. L. Briault, R.N.V.R.
M.L.457[61]	11	Lieut. T. A. M. Collier, R.N.V.R.
M.L.307	12	Lieut. N. B. Wallis, R.A.N.V.R
M.L.443	13	Lieut. K. Horlock, R.N.V.R.[63]
M.L.306[62]	14	Lieut. I. B. Henderson, R.N.V.R.
M.L.446[60]	15	Lieut. H. G. R. Falconar, R.N.V.R.
M.L.298[61]	16	Sub-Lieut. R. Nock, R.N.V.R.

Motor Torpedo Boat

M.T.B.74[61]   17   Sub-Lieut. R. C. M. V. Wynn, R.N.V.R.

Blockship

Campbeltown   Lieut.-Commander S. H. Beattie, R.N.

Escorting Destroyers

Tynedale   Lieut.-Commander H. E. F. Tweedie, R.N.
Atherstone   Lieut.-Commander R. S. Jenks, R.N.

Reinforcements for Return Passage

Cleveland   Commander G. B. Sayer, R.N.
Brocklesby   Lieut.-Commander M. N. Tufnell, D.S.C., R.N.

Appendix B

Summary of Experiences of Motor Launches

1st Flotilla

M.L.192   Lieut. Cdr. Stephens.

(No. 1)   Hit while going up river in formation and set ablaze. Ran on out of control, and, sheering across bows of Port Column, hit the Old Mole.

M.L.262   Lieut. Burt.

(No. 2)   Ran past Old Entrance and tuned by Aircraft Carrier *Joffre* (on slip). Came down stream close inshore, passed under stern of *Campbeltown*, and landed troops in Old Entrance. Troops repulsed and re-embarked. Embarked second party withdrawing. Backed out and proceeded down stream. Went alongside M.L.457 (No. 11) disabled and under heavy fire off Old Mole. Was hit then, and after drifting was hit again and blew up.

M.L.267   Lieut. Beart.

(No. 3)   Missed Old Entrance; turned by the *Joffre*. Went alongside dredger and attacked with grenades; then landed troops in Old Entrance, but they were repulsed and re-embarked. Backed out and started down river, but was soon hit and abandoned.

M.L.268   Lieut. Tillie.

(No. 4)   Turned in towards Old Entrance, but was hit before reaching shore and blew up.

M.L.156   Lieut. Fenton.

(No. 5)   Steering gear hit and one engine put out of action when about half a mile short of objective. C.O., 1st Lieutenant and many of crew and troops wounded. Withdrew on one engine. Crew transferred to *Atherstone* next morning and M.L. abandoned; subsequently bombed and sunk by a Heinkel.

M.L.177 Sub-Lieut. Rodier.

(No. 6) Landed troops alongside Old Entrance and then proceeded to port quarter of *Campbeltown* and took off about half of crew. Started down river but was hit after about 10 minutes, and burnt for 4 hours. Survivors rescued by German trawler.

M.L.270 Lieut. Irwin.

(No. 7) Stationed ahead with M.G.B.314 and M.L.160. At 0140 received direct hit by heavy shell aft, which wrecked the steering and auxiliary steering gear. Withdrew and subsequently transferred crew to *Brocklesby*, when M.L. was scuttled.

M.L.160 Lieut. Boyd.

(No. 8) Stationed ahead with M.G.B.314 and M.L.270. Successfully engaged flak positions allotted to her and silenced them. Fired torpedo at a ship, believed to be a warship, lying alongside one of the south breakwaters. Then to the rescue of M.L.447 (No. 9) off Old Mole in a very gallant manner and withdrew at 0220 on one engine. Returned to England in company with M.Ls. 443 (No. 12) and 307 (No. 13), and with them shot down a Heinkel III on passage.

1st Flotilla

M.L.447 Lieut. Platt.

(No. 9) Leading M.L., Port Column. Unable to get alongside the Old Mole owing to shoal water. Heavily fired on and pelted with grenades; many casualties. Set on fire, backed out and sank. Survivors, including C.O., rescued by M.L.160 (No. 8).

M.L.341 Lieut. Briault.

(No. 10) Did not get up river due to engine trouble. Transferred troops to M.L.446 (No. 15) at 2030/27, and followed at best speed – 11 knots – but lost contact and returned to England alone. Sighted one Focke Wolfe about 100 miles west of Ushant, but was not attacked.

M.L.457.   Lieut. Collier.

(No. 11)   The only M.L. to land her troops successfully at the Old
Mole. Circled round and came back alongside, but was fired
on. Went astern to mid stream but then hit and drifted off Old
Mole. Refused offer of assistance from M.L.262 (No. 2); hit
again later and blew up.

M.L.307   Lieut. Wallis.

(No. 12)   Third ship in Port Column. Closed close in to Old Mole,
passing M.L.447 (No. 9) as she backed out, and killed at least
four Germans who were throwing hand grenades down on
her, but suffered many casualties and went aground. After
consultation with O.C. troops, backed out, went over to
eastern bank of river and engaged batteries and searchlights
there. Withdrew at 0230, shooting up a merchant ship on the
way out. Met M.L.160 (No. 8) and stood by her. Returned
to England with her and M.L.443 (No. 13); assisted to shoot
down Heinkel III on passage.

M.L.443   Lieut. Horlock.

(No. 13)   Was blinded by searchlights and missed the Old Mole, going a
good way further up the river. Returned, but was unable to get
alongside, and returned to Falmouth in company with M.Ls.
307 (No. 12) and 160 (No. 8); assisted to shoot down Heinkel
III on passage.

M.L.306   Lieut. Henderson.

(No. 14)   Made attempts to berth on both sides of the Old Mole, but
found each blocked by burning M.Ls. Circled round twice
before withdrawing. When 45 miles out, intercepted by
German torpedo boats, and surrendered after suffering many
casualties, including C.O. killed, in unequal fight.

M.L.446 Lieut. Falconar.

(No. 15) At 2030/27 took onboard troops from M.L.341 (No. 10) and overtook force when they were passing the *Sturgeon*. Overshot the Old Mole in the glare of the searchlights, and found herself near the *Joffre*. Returned to attempt landing, but finding most of the troops wounded, including both Officers and the sergeant, withdrew and transferred casualties to the *Atherstone* next morning, the M.L. being subsequently scuttled.

M.L.298 Sub-Lieut. Nock.

(No. 16) No troops carried. Passed the Old Mole and circled to give covering fire. Went alongside in Old Entrance but found no troops there. Went close in to the Old Mole; backed out into mid-stream. Caught fire passing through burning petrol. Was hit when one mile out and eventually blew up.

Appendix C

Armament of British Forces

	4" HA/ LA 4" LA	12-pdr.	3-pdr.	2-pdr	Twin Lewis	Stripped Lewis	Lewis	Oerlikon	0.5-in
M.G.B.314				1	1				4
M.L.192					2	2		2	
M.L.262			1				6	2	
M.L.267							2	1	
M.L.268			1				4	2	
M.L.156			1		1	2			
M.L.177			1		1	2			
M.L.270			1				10		
M.L.160			1		1	2			
M.L.447							8	2	
M.L.341			1	1	2	2			
M.L.457					2	2			
M.L.307			1	1	2	2			
M.L.443			1	1	2	2			
M.L.306			1		1	2		2	
M.L.446					1	2		2	
M.L.298				1	1	2		2	
M.T.B.74						10			
Campbeltown	3	1							2
Atherstone	4			1			2	2	
Tynedale	4			1			2	2	
Cleveland	4			1			2	2	
Brocklesby	4			1			2	2	

75

Appendix D

Material Results achieved by Raid

(From German Sources)

(1) Normandie Dock.

Outer gate completely destroyed.

Inner gate damaged by explosive charges, but still served to hold the water from flooding the dock.

Pumping station and caisson operating machinery completely destroyed.

(2) East Lock.

Outer gate completely destroyed by explosion about 1520, 30 March. Inner gate held firm against the rush of water, despite damage sustained in an air raid a few days previously.

(3) Ships.

Slight damage to tankers *Schledstadt* and *Passat*, which were in the Normandie dock at the time of the explosion, broke loose from their moorings and collided.

Tugs *Champion* and *Pornic* sunk by British troops in St. Nazaire Basin alongside inner gate of the South lock.

Harbour Defence Vessel lying near East Lock in the St. Nazaire basin scuttled by her C.O.,[64] lest it should fall into British hands.

(4) Wharf Installations.

Workshops opposite the Normandie Dock (Forges de l'Ouest) burned down after fires had been started either by gunfire or explosive charges. Efficiency impaired for a long time afterwards.

(5) German Losses in Personnel.

42 killed.

Over 100 missing.

127 wounded.

Appendix E

Eye-Witness[65] Account of the Aftermath of the Raid on St. Nazaire – 28 March–3 April, 1942

The following information as to events subsequent to the raid was obtained from a French electrical mechanic employed at the main electrical and radio workshop in the dockyard. The day after the raid 28 March, he was unable to work as the whole port area was closed to the public, but from a house in the town he heard firing punctuated with explosions till about 1000, when there was quiet for a couple of hours. About noon a particularly violent explosion shook the whole city and broke every window within a very large radius.

The next day, 29 March, was a Sunday, and the informant remained at home. A B.B.C. broadcast to which he listened gave the story of the lockgate and the *Campbeltown* (which was said to have exploded in the early morning), but made no mention of the explosion at noon.

On 30 March he proceeded to work as usual, but instead of entering the workshop, which was situated just east of the large lock, he passed on to look at the lockgate reported destroyed. No one stopped him as he walked on beyond his factory.

The lockgate was certainly destroyed, and there was no sign of HMS *Campbeltown* beyond some metal debris, but what surprised him most was the surrounding carnage. The whole of the corner on both sides of the lock was littered with legs, arms, heads and entrails. From the scattered pieces, he could see that they belonged to Germans. Military working parties were shovelling the remains together and scattering sand over the ground, in a dazed, disorganised way.

He returned to his workshop, where he learned what had happened from some of the German workmen employed there. The *Campbeltown* had crashed into the main gate and was firmly lodged there. She was still there at daybreak, and later a strong cordon of troops had been thrown round the area on both sides of the lock. Meanwhile an inspection party of some 40 senior officers, including the S.N.O. (informant thinks an Admiral), had boarded the ship to see how best she could be moved.[66] Many German soldier sightseers had swelled the numbers round the ship. When she went up they were all wiped out, including the officers onboard. Apparently the officer death roll had been heavy on shore as well as onboard, and this had a large bearing on subsequent events. The most conservative estimate put this death roll at 300, but many people believed that the figure was nearer 400. Informant believes the higher figure judging from the vast quantity of human remains which on Monday morning still covered the ground.

Work in his factory continued haltingly that day, and in the afternoon informant went over to a ship south of the graving docks to do some W/T repairs. At 1630 hours the port area was shaken by another heavy explosion and everyone rushed back towards the lock to see what had happened. A friend of informant had been working on an electric pylon near the old harbour entrance, and had been thrown off his perch into the water by the explosion. He guessed that a delayed action torpedo had gone off in that lockgate.

At 1730 hours a second explosion shattered the remains of this entrance. Pandemonium broke out. Together with all the other workers in his area informant rushed to the bridge over the remaining lockgate. It was packed full of workmen, both French and German, but the exit was barred by sentries. The workmen overpowered them and rushed on to the bridge throwing bicycles over the barrier. The German sentries opened fire, and this was the signal for general firing to break out all over the port. Machine guns were turned on to the crowds of Frenchmen trying to leave the port. In all 280 French workmen were killed in this indiscriminate slaughter.

Informant had his mate killed by his side, and himself succeeded in taking cover in a trench 100 yards to the north-west of the bridge. Here he stayed till nearly midnight, waiting for the firing to die down. He lay there in the centre of it all. Every kind of gun was being fired at a non-existent enemy. The German soldiers having lost so many of their officers in the Saturday mid-day explosion, completely lost their heads and saw British commandos round every corner. Especially they picked on anyone dressed in khaki.

In the port area there was a great number of O.T.[67] men employed on various building jobs. These Germans joined the general panic and were mowed down by machine guns. Their khaki uniforms were mistaken for the British battle dress. Many were killed under our informant's eyes as they ran. Many others were killed in the Penhouet neighbourhood as they left their work. When informant some days later visited this area he found all the houses facing the Avenue de Penhouet – the road north of Penhouet

Basin – pockmarked by bullets and shell holes. A heavy battle had obviously been fought here against the imaginary enemy and German O.T. (labour parties) casualties were severe. After darkness the battle continued between the German soldiers themselves, who returned each others' fire to good effect. When after several days, things returned to normal, informant gathered that some 300-400 Germans, O.T. workmen and soldiers had been killed in this evening battle.

Informant in due course heard the B.B.C. accounts of how the French population had risen and fought the Germans for two or three days after our raid. This was not the case. On the actual morning of the raid, probably less than 50 Frenchmen took up arms. The French in any case had very few arms. Informant knows personally only one Frenchman who fought with us. He was the Sous-chef de la gare at the port goods station. He drew a revolver and was killed in the fighting. The heavy firing from the port area which was heard, and reported as being continued French resistance, was nothing more than this panicky slaughter of unarmed workmen which followed the explosion of the delayed action torpedoes. Informant thinks this would not have happened had the officer death roll not been so heavy on the Monday morning.

From Tuesday till Thursday of that week the whole harbour area was closed and informant could not get to work. During these days, the whole population of the old town of St. Nazaire was evacuated to Chateaubriand, and this area was still clear of civilians when informant left St. Nazaire on 15 April. He heard that about 100 hostages were taken from the French population after the raid, but he believes that none was executed. The Germans were satisfied with the wanton massacre of the 280 French workmen.

All the British prisoners were taken by lorry to La Baule. The wounded were dumped in these lorries without medical attention. Only German wounded were taken away in ambulances. This story is borne out by another informant, who states on the authority of a French doctor that the British wounded at St. Nazaire did not receive any medical attention till four days after the attack, when they were taken to the Royal Hotel, La Baule. They spent one day at this hotel, and were then moved to Rennes to the Hopital Complimentaire E.P.S., Rue Jean Mace, Rennes. In this hospital they were treated by French doctors only and their nurses were male Senegalese. The source of this information was a doctor of Rennes, who knew well all the staff of the hospital.

Endnotes

1   Admiral of the Fleet Sir Charles Forbes, C.-in-C., Plymouth, in his remarks on the operations states definitely that he regards the attack on St. Nazaire as more difficult than that on Zeebrugge.

2   The Normandie dock, aslo known as the "Forme Ecluse", is the largest dock in the world; 1148 ft. long and 164 ft. wide, it could accommodate a ship of over 85,000 tons. Its caissons measured 167 ft. long, 54 ft. high and 35 ft. thick.

3   See Appendix A.

4   HMS *Campbeltown* was fitted out at Devonport for her task of destroying the lock gate, and the Commander-in-Chief, Plymouth, remarks that the work done was admirably quick and efficient. The arrangements for detonating the explosives were devised by Lieutenant N. T. B. Tibbits, R.N., of HMS Vernon. Lieut. Tibbits accompanied the expedition in the *Campbeltown*, and was among those who lost their lives. He was awarded the D.S.C. for his services. The endurance of M.G.B. 314 was not great enough for her to accomplish the return journey under her own power, but Commander Ryder found it possible to increase it sufficiently by fitting additional fuel tanks.

5   The possible alternative of the *Campbeltown*, being a steel ship, bearing the brunt of the fire while the light craft came in under her shelter was discussed, but rejected. The plan finally adopted envisaged sacrificing everything, if necessary, in order to get the *Campbeltown* in.

6   The entrance of the River Loire is about 6½ miles wide, narrowing to a mile at St. Nazaire. The deep water channel – 300 yards wide – follows the north-western shore at a distance of 2 or 3 cables, the remainder of the estuary being occupied by shoals. It was over these shoals, shortly before high water, that the approach was to be made. (See Plan 4).

7   At St. Nazaire:–

    Sunset, 27/3, 1931; end of nautical twilight, 2040.

    Sunrise, 28/3, 0701; beginning of nautical twilight, 0553.

    Moon rise, 27/3, 1405; 1st quarter, 25/3.

    Moonset, 28/3, 0452; 1st quarter, 25/3.

    Low water, 27/3, 1944; high water, 28/3, 0123; height 13½. ft.

    All times are B.S.T. (Zone–1).

8   This route passed through the lettered positions shown in Plan 3.

9   First sighted by the 2nd officer of the watch, Mr. S. W. J. Ford, Gunner, R.N., bearing 037°, 7½ miles distant.

10 During the passage all white ensigns were hauled down and the destroyers wore the colours of the Third Reich.

11 One hit is believed to have been obtained.

12 G.M.T., i.e., 0720 B.S.T.

13 Group Command West subsequently explained that owing to the late reception of the

U-boat's message and the lack of air-reconnaissance forces, the opportunity for an attack on the British force was missed.

14 M.L. No. 10 (341) had developed a defect in her port engine at 1830/27, which reduced her speed to 10.8 knots. Strenuous efforts failed to remedy this, and her troops were transferred to one of the spare M.Ls. – No. 15, M.L.10's engine was not repaired till 2222/27. It being then too late for her to take part in the assault, she returned independently to Falmouth.

15 The Commander-in-Chief, Plymouth, had arranged with Bomber Commmand for an air attack to be carried out.

16 Commander Ryder remarks that the use of R.D/F in the M.G.B. as a navigational aid was invaluable in working their way up the estuary. A considerable set to the northward was experienced during the approach. The *Campbeltown* grounded lightly twice – at about 0045 and 0055. This possibility had been foreseen, as no accurate charts were available, but she could not be lightened further.

17 In actual fact the force had been sighted ten minutes previously (at 0115) when a little over 4 miles from the lock gate by the lookout post on the headland of St. Marc. It was not, however, recognised as being hostile.

18 H.M. The King approved the award of the Victoria Cross to Lieut.-Commander S. H. Beattie for his "great gallantry and determination" on this occasion in command of HMS *Campbeltown*. The citation goes on to say "Under intense fire directed at the bridge from point-blank range of about 100 yards, and in the face of the blinding glare of many searchlights, he steamed her into the lock gates, and beached and scuttled her in the correct position.

This Victoria Cross is awarded to Lieut.-Commander Beattie in recognition not only of his own valour but also of that of the unnamed officers and men of a very gallant ship's company, many of whom have not returned." - *London Gazette*.

19. The ship ran about 35 ft. into the lock, which was 34 ft. wide, the stem buckling and the forecastle deck running over the top and projecting a foot or so over the other side. This brought the explosive charge, the foremost end of which was 36 ft. from the stem, into an excellent position.

20 A summary of the narratives of the individual M.Ls. will be found in Appendix B.

21 This apparent slackening of the firing may have been due to commandos who had disembarked from the *Campbeltown* silencing the positions in her immediate vicinity.

22 M.L.457 had closed up on the leader when M.L.341 (originally No. 10) developed her defect at 1830/27.

23 M.L.477 (No. 9) to the north and M.L.192 (No. 1) to the south. This led to the opinion immediately after the operation that some of the M.Ls. had mistakenly gone to the south side of the Old Mole instead of the north side, as ordered. Under this impression the C.-in-C. Plymouth remarked "this unfortunate misunderstanding certainly reduced the number of troops who got ashore according to the plan and therefore hindered the complete overcoming of local resistance which had been hoped for..." It is now (1947) known that no such mistake occurred, and that any M.Ls. seen to the southward of the Mole got there due to circumstances beyond their control.

24 M.L.177 was hit about 10 minutes after she started down river, set on fire, and burned for

four hours. The survivors, among whom was Lieut.-Com. Beattie, were eventually rescued by a German trawler

25 This was all that was known for many months about the work of the troops on shore, since none who landed was able to re-embark. Some account of how they fared, based on reports received after the conclusion of the war, will be found in pages 52-59.

26 M.T.B.74's two torpedoes each contained 1,800 lb. of explosive, and was fitted with an improvised delay action device, set to explode 2½ hours later. Actually they did not go off till some 36 hours had elapsed.

27 This was the last seen of M.T.B.74, whose fate was unknown for some time. It has since been established that she was set on fire and burnt while attempting to assist one of the burning M.Ls. on her way out. Her C.O., Lieut. Wynne, was gallantly rescued by Chief Motor Mechanic Lovegrove, to whom the C.G.M. was subsequently awarded.

28 It was found extremely difficult to knock out the positions sited on the housetops.

29 The posthumous award of the Victoria Cross to Able Seaman W. A. Savage was approved by H.M. The King for his "great gallantry, skill and devotion to duty as gunlayer of the pom-pom in a motor gunboat. Completely exposed and under heavy fire, he engaged positions ashore with cool and steady accuracy...

This Victoria Cross is awarded in recognition not only of the gallantry and devotion to duty of Able Seaman Savage, but also of the valour shown by many others. unnamed, in motor launches, motor gunboats and motor torpedo boats, who gallantly carried out their duty in entirely exposed positions against enemy fire at very close range."-*London Gazette*.

30 The withdrawal signals were to have been given by special 35 star red and green rockets. These rockets, however, together with part of Colonel Newman's H.Q. Staff, had been sunk in M.L.267. Actually at this time the withdrawal on shore was in progress, but Commander Ryder had no means of knowing this.

31 H.M. The King approved the award of the Victoria Cross to Commander R. E. D. Ryder "for great gallantry in the attack on St. Nazaire. He commanded a force of small unprotected ships in an attack on a heavily defended port and led HMS *Campbeltown* under intense fire from short range weapons at point-blank range. Though the main object of the expedition had been accomplished in the beaching of the *Campbeltown*, he remained on the spot conducting operations, evacuating men from the *Campbeltown*, and dealing with strong points and close range weapons while exposed to heavy fire for one hour and 16 minutes, and did not withdraw till it was certain that his ship could be of no use in rescuing any of the Commando troops who were still ashore. That his motor gunboat, now full of dead and wounded, should have survived and should have been able to withdraw through an intense barrage of close-range fire was almost a miracle."-*London Gazette*.

32 There were 4 dock gates and 2 swing bridges across the South entrance and 1 lifting bridge at the north end of St. Nazaire Basin to be dealt with. In addition were the lock gates of the Normandie dock, but these were not to be destroyed till later.

33 Letters in brackets refer to Plan 6.

34 The destruction of these vessels by some of the Commando troops was subsequently confirmed by captured German documents.

35 M.Ls. No. 262 (No. 2) and 276 (No. 3), having missed the Old Entrance at the first attempt, succeeded in landing their troops there later on: but they were repulsed and forced to re-embark.

36 This party had never got ashore, having been blown up in M.L.268.

37 Colonel Newman's Narrative.

38 Colonel Newman's Narrative.

39 Colonel Newman believed that the Germans in their excitement had forgotten to lower their sights.

40 H.M. The King approved the award of the Victoria Cross to Lieut.-Colonel A. C. Newman when the full story of the raid became known.

"...Although Lieut.-Colonel Newman need not have landed himself, he was one of the first ashore, and during the next five hours of bitter fighting, he personally entered several houses and shot up the occupants and supervised the operations in the town, utterly regardless of his own safety, and he never wavered in his resolution to carry through the operation upon which so much depended.

An enemy gun position on the roof of a U-boat pen had been causing heavy casualties to the landing craft and Lieut.-Colonel Newman directed the fire of a mortar against this position to such effect that the gun was silenced. Still fully exposed he then brought machine gun fire to bear on an armed trawler in the harbour, compelling it to withdraw and thus preventing many casualties in the main demolition area.

Under the brilliant leadership of this officer the troops fought magnificently and held vastly superior enemy forces at bay, until the demolition parties had successfully completed their work of destruction.

By this time, however, most of the landing craft had been sunk or set on fire and evacuation by sea was no longer possible. Although the main objective had been achieved Lieut.-Colonel Newman, nevertheless, was now determined to try and fight his way out into open country and so give all survivors a chance to escape.

The only way out of the harbour area lay across a narrow iron bridge covered by enemy machine guns, and although severely shaken by a German hand grenade, which had burst at his ft., Lieut.-Colonel Newman personally led the charge which stormed the position and under his inspiring leadership, the small force fought its way through the streets to a point near the open country when, all ammunition expended, he and his men were finally overpowered by the enemy.

The outstanding gallantry and devotion to duty of this fearless officer, his brilliant leadership and initiative, were largely responsible for the success of this perilous operation which resulted in heavy damage to the important Naval base at St. Nazaire."- *London Gazette*, 15 June, 1945.

41 This was believed at the time, but it has since been established that the *Campbeltown* did not blow up till shortly before noon that day, (according to German sources, at 1146 B.S.T.). A search of the ship for explosives by the German mine-disposal squad had been prevented owing to a misunderstanding on the part of the officer who had the ship cordoned off. At the moment of the explosion, there was a large number of people onboard, some of them officials searching for secret documents, etc., and others merely sightseers. The casualty roll was heavy, with over 100 missing. See Appendix E.

42 H.M. The King approved the posthumous award of the Victoria Cross to Sergeant Thomas Frank Durrant, R.E. (attached Commandos) for "gallantry, skill and devotion to duty when in charge of a Lewis gun in HMS M.L.306 in the St. Nazaire raid.

M.L.306 came under heavy fire while proceeding up the River Loire towards the port. Sergeant Durrant in his position abaft the bridge, where he had no cover or protection, engaged enemy gun positions and searchlights on shore. During this engagement he was severely wounded in the arm, but refused to leave his gun.

The motor launch subsequently went down river and was attacked by a German destroyer at 30 to 60 yards range and often closer. In this action, Sergeant Durrant continued to fire at the destroyer's bridge with the greatest coolness and with complete disregard of the enemy's fire. The motor launch was illuminated by the enemy searchlights and Sergeant Durrant drew on himself the individual attention of the enemy guns and was again wounded in many places. Despite these further wounds, he stayed in his exposed position, still firing his gun, although after a time only able to support himself by holding on to the gun mounting.

After a running fight, the Commander of the German destroyer called on the motor launch to surrender. Sergeant Durrant's answer was a further burst of fire at the destroyer's bridge. Although now very weak he went on firing, using drums of ammunition as fast as they could be replaced. A renewed attack by the enemy vessel eventually silenced the fire of the motor launch, but Sergeant Durrant refused to give up until the destroyer came alongside, grappled the motor launch and took prisoner those who remained alive. Sergeant Durrant's gallant fight was commended by the German officials on boarding the motor launch.

This very gallant non-commissioned officer later died of the many wounds received in action."- *London Gazette*, 15 June, 1945.

43 See pages 61-62.

44 Sunrise, 0700, 28 March.

45 Before settling down to the patrol, the *Atherstone* carried out a short search for the motor launch which had broken down – M.L.341 (No. 10) – but failed to find her in the dark.

46 0217. From M.L.270 (No. 7) Still in.
0220. From M.L.177 (No. 6) Leaving, 15 knots.
0220. From M.L.160 (No. 8) Leaving, one engine only.
0221. From M.L.307 (No. 12) Leaving, 15 knots.
0222. From M.L.270 (No. 7) Steering broken down.
0316. From M.L.270 (No. 7) Leaving, 12 knots.
0320. From M.L.160 (No. 8) to M.L.270 (No. 7) "Whatchur, chum."
0323. From M.L.307 (No. 12) Leaving, 12 knots.

47 The C.O. HMS *Atherstone* points out that by the time the destroyers arrived at the rendezvous there was an unknown number of M.Ls. in an unknown condition to seaward of them, and suggests that it would have been better if they had steered for the R/V on receipt of the first leaving signals, so as to check up on the M.Ls. as they came out, and give the earliest possible assistance with casualties.

48 She had received five hits in one petrol tank, which did not catch fire as it was full.

49 These were the only British aircraft sighted by the destroyers but the Commander-in-Chief, Plymouth, remarks that "aircraft of No. 19 Group, R.A.F. did much useful work in covering the withdrawal of the forces from St. Nazaire. Twenty sorties occupying 105 flying hours, were carried out during which one H.E.111 and two He.115 were encountered, and one enemy aircraft was destroyed."

50 The Commander-in-Chief, Plymouth, regretted this decision, with which he did not agree.

51 This was in lat. 46° 38' N., long, 4° 52' W. (about 110 miles W.S.W. of St. Nazaire) according to the *Cleveland*'s reckoning. The *Atherstone* put it about 6 miles to the northward.

52 Thereby anticipating the wishes of the Commander-in-Chief, Plymouth, who, at 1926 ordered him to detach two destroyers to the assistance of the motor launches, and at the same time informed him that two Hudsons were proceeding to locate them.

53 It had been intended to send this report early in the forenoon, the position of the force being then known to the enemy from air reconnaissance. Just then a signal was received from the Commander-in-Chief imposing stricter W/T silence. A Hudson aircraft sent for the purpose of receiving the report by visual failed to make contact. During the afternoon, when the force was nearing the Brest Peninsula and shadowing aircraft had apparently been shaken off, it seemed even more necessary to maintain W/T silence. The progress made by 1900 and the desirability of requesting air search for the missing M.Ls. decided Commander Sayer to break it, and the signal was sent at 1946/28.

54 Lieut. Platt had been transferred from M.L.443 (No. 13), on leaving Falmouth, to M.L.447 (No. 9), in order to relieve her C.O. – Lieut. Wood, who had fallen sick – as S.O., 2nd Flotilla.

55 About 1905 B.S.T.

56 About 55 per cent of these, including Lt. Com. Beatty, V.C. proved to have been taken prisoner and returned to the United Kingdom on the conclusion of hostilities. The final figure for killed or missing was 85 officers and men.

57 Photographs taken from the air at 1650/29/3 showed the seaward entrance of the lock dock open, the gate apparently missing, and the dock flooded. Two 450ft. tankers previously seen were still in the lock dock, the outermost emitting smoke, and the innermost with a slight list. There was much oil on the surface in the dock and harbour.

58 On a still night their engines were clearly audible at a distance of 3 miles.

59 Considered unfit for return journey and sunk by own forces.

60 Sunk in action.

61 Captured.

62 Lieut. Platt took over as S.O., 2nd Flotilla, after the order for proceeding had been made on 26/3, Lieut. Wood, R.N.V.R., the Senior Officer, having fallen sick. The spare C.O., Lieut. Horlock, relieved Lieut. Platt in M.G.3B.44 (No. 13).

63 This Officer was killed later in the action.

64 Informant's grade – C.

65 There were a number of reports that two British Officers gave their lives to accompany the Germans onboard the *Campbeltown* in order to allay suspicions that she might blow up. These reports have never received confirmation, and it is believed that they had no foundation in fact.

66 Todt organisation.

PART II

B.R. 1736 (22) (48)

BATTLE SUMMARY No. 29

THE ATTACK ON THE TIRPITZ BY MIDGET SUBMARINES (OPERATION 'SOURCE')
22 September, 1943

NOTE:– The contents of this book, as revised, are based on information available up to and including December, 1947

T.S.D. 21 /45
TACTICAL, TORPEDO AND STAFF DUTIES DIVISION
(HISTORICAL SECTION),
NAVAL STAFF ADMIRALTY, S.W.I.

Battle Summary No. 29, the Attack on the *Tirpitz* by Midget Submarines
(Operation 'Source'), was originally completed at the end of December,
1944. It was chiefly based on two reports by the Admiral, Submarines,[1]
Report on Operation 'Source' dated 8 November, 1943, and Further Report
on Operation 'Source' dated 2 February, 1944. Since all the survivors of
the midgets who succeeded in carrying out the attacks were at that time
prisoners-of-war, many of the details of this epic affair did not become
known until after their return to the United Kingdom on the conclusion
of the war in 1945. It then became "evident that some of the information
and many of the inferences" contained in the reports referred to above
"were, in fact, incorrect,"[1] and a final Report was compiled by the Admiral,
Submarines dated 26 July, 1945.

In addition to the information obtained from returned prisoners-of-war
translations of captured German documents have become available.

The ensuing revision contains amendments and additions to the original
Battle Summary, rendered necessary by the new sources of information
mentioned above.

This edition cancels the previous edition of Battle Summary No. 29,
B.R. 1736 (22), 1945, all copies of which should be destroyed.

T.S.D./H.S.
December, 1948.

CONTENTS

Introduction

On 9 April, 1940 the Germans invaded Norway, and by June the occupation was virtually complete. From that time the enemy proceeded to maintain naval forces, including capital ships, in Norwegian ports, where they were well placed to break out into the Atlantic, and subsequently to threaten the Russian convoys. In any case their presence was sufficient to contain the Home Fleet, and the Admiralty was faced with the old problem of how to get at enemy main units in heavily defended and inaccessible anchorages. Something more potent than the fireships of our ancestors was required, and attacks by aircraft or submarines seemed to offer best prospects of success, but the nearest British bases were about 1,000 miles distant and the dire effects of the pre-war policy of "appeasement" had not yet been overcome; neither Royal Air Force long range bombers nor carrier borne naval aircraft were available for this purpose. Nor would the ordinary submarine meet the need. Improvements in A/S devices and defences rendered it impossible for them to emulate the exploits of our submarines in the Dardanelles and the Baltic in the last war.

To solve the problem "midget" submarines were introduced.[2] The prototype in the British Navy – X3 – completed successful trials early in 1942, and a contract was placed with Messrs. Vickers Armstrongs on 12 May that year for six craft of a new and improved design intended to attack capital ships in a defended harbour by means of explosive charges to be laid on the bottom and fired by time fuses. At the same time, volunteers for "special and hazardous service" were called for, and training commenced, using the prototype X craft (X3) and the second prototype (X4).

This battle summary gives some account of the first attack carried out by these novel craft.

Preparations

The six midget submarines[3]– known as X5–X10 – were delivered by mid-January, 1943, and it was hoped that it would prove possible to use them to attack the German ships in the Norwegian fjords in the early spring, before the hours of daylight became too long. This hope was not fulfilled. 9 March was considered the latest suitable date and, as this did not allow sufficient time for training, the attempt had to be deferred till autumn.

On 17 April 1943, the 12th Submarine Flotilla was formed under Captain. W. E. Banks, D.S.C., R.N., to co-ordinate, under the Rear-Admiral Submarines,[4] "the training and material of the special weapons"; and to this flotilla X5–X10 were attached, with the *Bonaventure* (Acting Captain P. Q. Roberts, R.N.) as their depot ship.

The limiting factor of their activities was the endurance of their crews, and for this reason each midget was provided with two crews – one to man her on passage and one for the actual operation. During the summer of 1943 they carried out intensive training at Loch Cairnbarn, just north of Loch Ewe (west coast of Scotland), under Commander D. C. Ingram, D.S.C., R.N.,[5] which included realistic exercises against capital ships of the Home Fleet surrounded by nets and equipment specially supplied by the Boom Defence Organisation.

During this period, too, was solved the problem of transporting the X craft to within striking distance of their target. After various experiments it was decided that the best method was to tow them there by operational submarines, and six submarines were accordingly earmarked for this purpose. Special security measures were instituted at Loch Cairnbarn and, after 1 September, were increased in stringency. No leave was given, none but specially selected officers and ratings were allowed to leave the area, and all ships were retained in the port till after the completion of the operation.

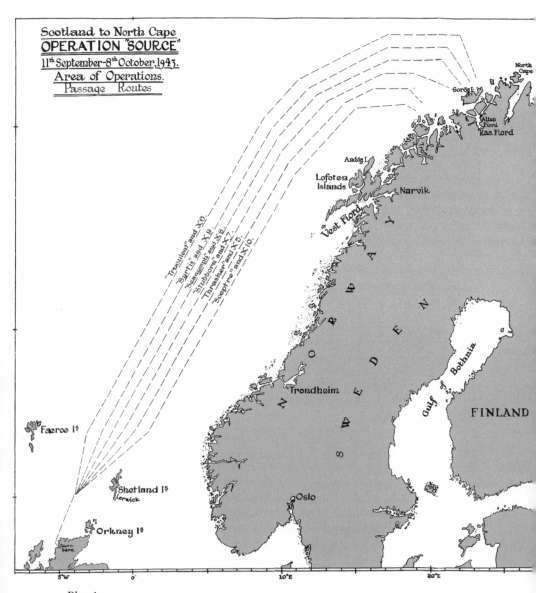

Scotland to North Cape
OPERATION "SOURCE"
11ᵗʰ September-8ᵗʰ October, 1943.
Area of Operations.
Passage Routes

"Truculent" and X.6.
"Syrtis" and X.9.
"Seanymph" and X.8.
"Stubborn" and X.7.
"Thrasher" and X.5.
"Sceptre" and X.10.

North Cape

Sorög I.

Alten Fiord
Raa Fiord

Andög I.

Lofoten Islands

Narvik

Vest Fiord

N O R W A Y

S W E D E N

Gulf of Bothnia

FINLAND

Trondheim

Faeroe Iˢ

Shetland Iˢ
Lerwick

Orkney Iˢ
Cairn-
barn

Oslo

5°W   0°   10°E   20°E

Plan 1

Plan of Operation

Meanwhile detailed plans for the operation were being prepared by the Staff of the Rear-Admiral, Submarines. In order to complete the operation before winter weather conditions were likely to set in, it was decided that the attack should take place at the earliest date on which the hours of darkness permitted. A certain amount of moonlight was necessary to assist the X craft in the navigation of the fjords, and as the period 20-25 September 1943, with the moon in the last quarter, fulfilled these conditions, D Day – the day on which the midgets were to be slipped by their towing submarines – was fixed provisionally for 20 September.

Alternative operation orders were prepared for attacks on Alten Fjord in the extreme north (Operation 'Funnel'), on the Narvik area – between lat. 67° and 69° N. (Operation 'Empire'), and on Trondheim – between lat. 63° and 65° N. (Operation 'Forced') so that operations could be directed against the enemy in whichever area he might be located. In the event this proved to be Alten Fjord (Operation 'Funnel').

Preliminary photographic reconnaissance of the anchorages, especially the net defences, and last minute reconnaissance of the targets were essential to success. As the Alten area was outside the range of home based photo reconnaissance aircraft, arrangements were made for a British photographic unit to be based at Murmansk[6] and a shuttle service by Mosquito aircraft was planned between the United Kingdom and North Russia for the preliminary reconnaissances; for the last minute sorties Spitfires were based at Vaenga (Kola Inlet). In addition Catalinas would be available to run a shuttle service with photographs.[7]

The plan had to cover three distinct phases, viz., the passage of over 1,000 miles to the area of operations, the attack, and the recovery of X craft and return passage.

Briefly, it was as follows (see Plan 1):–

Six operational submarines with the X craft in tow were to proceed independently to a position 75 miles west of the Shetlands and then to follow routes some 20 miles apart until about 150 miles from Alten Fjord, when they were to steer for positions from which to make their landfalls. The operational crews were to take over the X craft from the passage crews at any time convenient after D Day–3 (17 September).

Each operational submarine was allocated to a sector (FAA-FFF) to seaward of the declared mined area off Soroy Sound in which she was to patrol after making her landfall (see Plan 3). The X craft were to be slipped in positions 2 to 5 miles (SA–SF) from the mined area after dusk on D Day (20 September), when they would cross the mined area on the surface and proceed via Stjernsund to Alten Fjord, bottoming during daylight hours on 21 September. All were to arrive off the entrance to Kaa Fjord at dawn 22 September, and then, entering the Fleet anchorage, attack the targets for which they had been detailed. These would be allocated by signal during the passage, in the light of the most recent intelligence.

As soon as the X craft were slipped, the operational submarines were to return to their patrol sectors, and to remain in them during the operations of the X craft in the fjords.

To facilitate the recovery of the midgets, each operational submarine had been supplied with three infra-red transmitters and the X craft with special type receivers. Those which were able to withdraw after the attack were to endeavour to contact a submarine in one of the sectors, in each of which a "Recovery" position (FA–FF) had been established. Should this fail they were to make for one of the bays on the north coast of Soroy, which, circumstances permitting, would be closed and examined by some of the operational submarines on the nights of 27/28 and 28/29 September.

As a further alternative, the commanding officers of any X craft which might not be recovered from the vicinity of Soroy were at liberty to make their way to Kola Inlet, and arrangements were made with the Senior British Naval Officer, North Russia, to maintain a minesweeper looking out for them in the offing from 25 September to 3 October.

Preliminary Movements

On 30 August 1943, HMS *Titania* (Commander W. R. Fell, O.B.E., D.S.C., R.N., ret.) arrived at Loch Cairnbarn to act as depot ship for the operational submarines taking part, and H.M. Submarines *Thrasher*, *Truculent*, *Stubborn*, *Syrtis*, *Sceptre* and *Seanymph* followed within 48 hours. These submarines had all been previously fitted with special towing equipment; two others, similarly fitted – the *Satyr* and *Seadog* – were held at 24 hours' notice at Scapa as reserves.

Towing trials, transfer of passage and operational crews at sea, recovery of X craft and so forth, were carried out between 1 and 5 September; then, after final swinging for adjustment of compasses, all X craft were hoisted inboard of the *Bonaventure* for the fitting of side charges, storing, final preparations and the full "briefing" of their crews and the commanding officers of the towing submarines by Commander G. P. S. Davies, R.N., the officer on Rear-Admiral Barry's Staff who had been mainly responsible for the planning. At this stage, of course, it was by no means certain where the enemy would be found,[8] but the indications were that Alten Fjord was the most probable spot, and in order to reach this area by D Day it was necessary for the submarines to leave 11/12 September.

On 10 September Rear-Admiral Barry arrived at Cairnbarn to see the crews before they sailed on their hazardous adventure. The next day the operational crews of the X craft embarked in the towing submarines, the X craft were manned by the passage crews and that evening they put to sea.

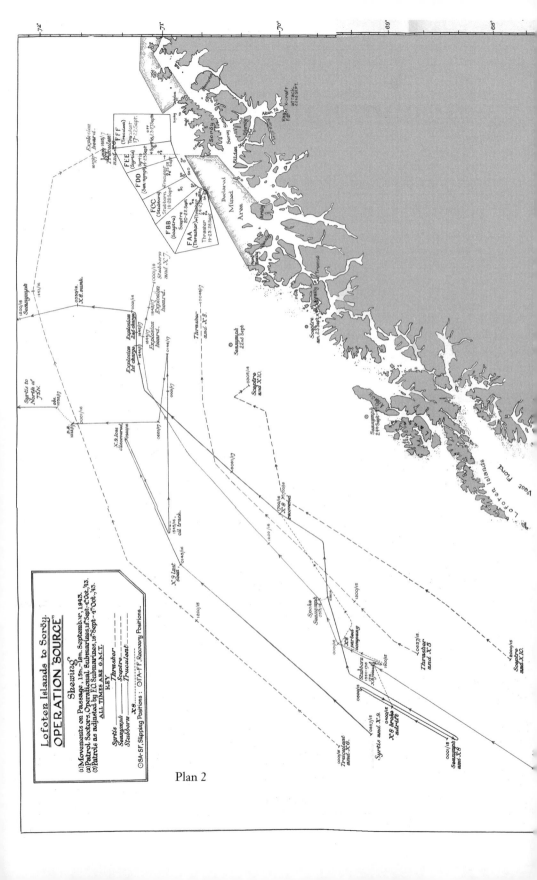

Lofoten Islands to Sorõy.
OPERATION 'SOURCE'
Shewing
(1) Movements on Passage, 15th.-18th. September, 1943.
(2) Patrol Sectors, Operational Submarines, 18th Sept.-4th Oct. '43.
(3) Patrols as adjusted by F.O. Submarines, 18th Sept.-4th Oct. '43.
ALL TIMES ARE G.M.T.
KEY
Syrtis ————— Thrasher — ― — ―
Seanymph ―――― Sceptre — ― — ―
Stubborn X.8. .... Truculent — — — —
○SA-SF, Slipping Positions :: OFA-FF, Recovery Positions.

Plan 2

Passage to Norway
(Plan 3)

At 1600,[9] 11 September, the *Truculent*[10] towing X6, and the *Syrtis* with X9, sailed from Loch Cairnbarn, followed at intervals of about two hours by the *Thrasher* with X5, the *Seanymph* with X8, and the *Stubborn* with X7. The *Sceptre* with X10 did not sail till 1300, 12 September.

From 11–14 September the passage was uneventful. Fine weather prevailed and the submarines with their submerged X craft in tow made good progress.[11] The X craft surfaced to ventilate three or four times every 24 hours for periods of about 15 minutes, during which the speed was reduced.

On 14 September the arrival in the United Kingdom of the Spitfires' photographs from Russia enabled the Rear-Admiral, Submarines, to signal details of net defences and positions of enemy ships in Alten Fjord. "Target plan No. 4" was ordered, which allocated X5, X6 and X7 to the *Tirpitz*, X9 and X10 to the *Scharnhorst* (both in Kaa Fjord), and X8 to the *Lutzow* (then in Langefjord).[12]

Early on 15 September the first hitch occurred. At 0100 the telephone communication between X8 (Lieutenant Smart) and the *Seanymph* (Lieutenant Oakley) failed, and at 0400 the tow parted. Their speed at the time was 8 knots; X8 surfaced five minutes later, but could see nothing of the *Seanymph*, though visibility seemed to be about 5 miles, and at 0430 she set course 029°, speed 3 knots, on her main engines, from an estimated position lat. 69° 04' N., long. 8° 14' E. In the *Seanymph* the parting of the tow was not discovered till some two hours later, when X8 was due to surface for ventilation; at 0600 she reversed her course, and spent the remainder of the day in a vain search for the lost midget.

Meanwhile the *Stubborn* (Lieutenant Duff) – on the adjacent route – had sighted what she took to be a U-Boat at 1213 in estimated position lat. 68° 51' N., long. 8° 34' E., and dived, surfacing again at 1323; in the light of after events, her Commanding Officer was of the opinion that this was quite possibly X8. Two and a half hours later (1550) X7 (Lieutenant Philip) broke adrift from the *Stubborn*; she surfaced immediately and the auxiliary tow was

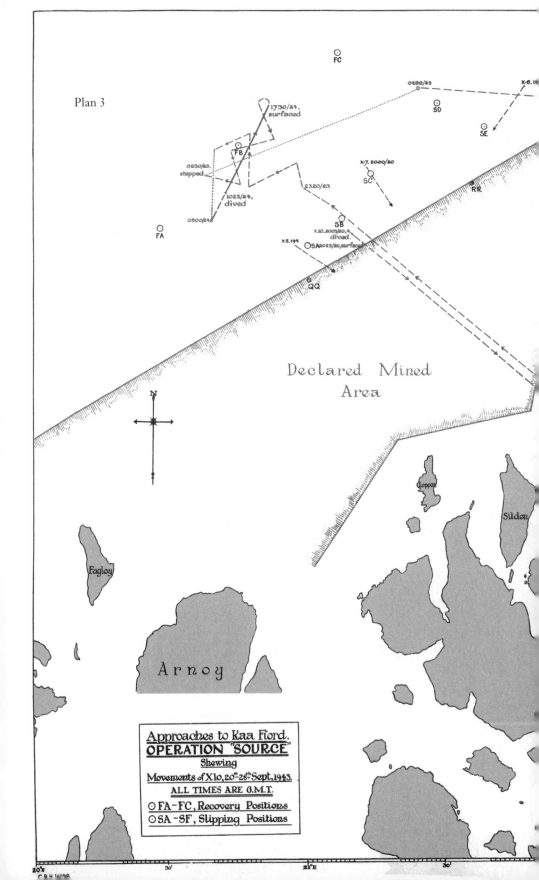

Plan 3

FC

0450/25   X·6·18

SD

SE

1730/24,
surfaced

FB

0230/25,
stopped.

X·7. 2000/20

SC

RR

2320/23

1025/24,
dived

FA

0500/24   SB
                 X.10, 2000/20, &
                 dived.
X·5·19?   SA 2025/20, surfaced

QQ

Declared   Mined
Area

N

Copp??

Silden

Fugloy

Arnoy

Approaches to Kaa Fiord.
OPERATION "SOURCE"
Shewing
Movements of X10, 20ᵗʰ-28ᵗʰ Sept., 1943.
ALL TIMES ARE G.M.T.
⊙ FA-FC, Recovery Positions
⊙ SA-SF, Slipping Positions

20'   30'   21°E   30'

C.B.H.1609B.

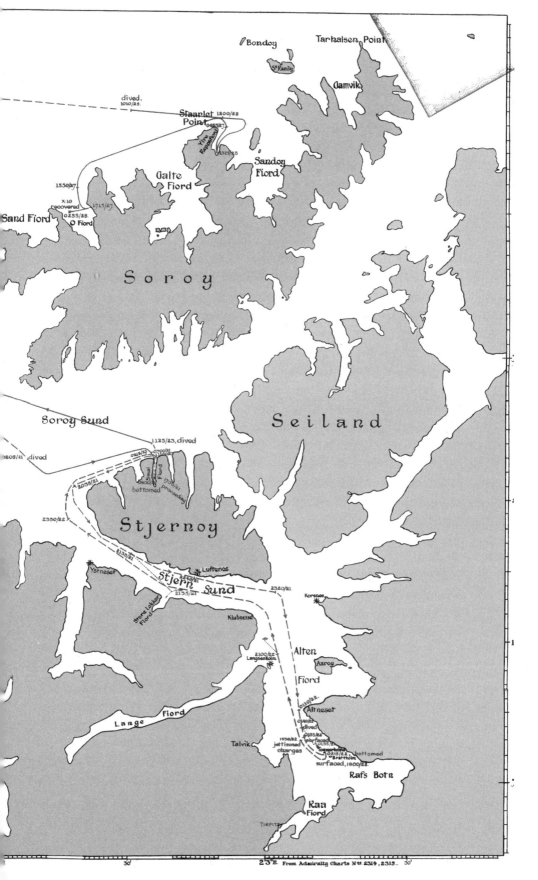

Bondøy
Tarhalsen Point
S.ᵗ Ramöy
Damvik
dived, 1010/23
Staarlet Point 1800/23
Ytre Rammefjord
1325/23
Sandøy Fiord
Galte Fiord
1550/27
X.10 recovered
1715/27
0255/28
O Fiord
Sand Fiord
S o r o y
Soroy Sund
1125/23, dived
0800/21
0700/21
0315/23
0803/21 bottomed
1700/21 proceeding
Smal Fiord
0805/21 dived
2035/21
2350/22
S t j e r n o y
2130/21
Ysnaset
Luftenes
Stjern Sund
1815/21
2320/21
Korsnes
2155/21
Store Lakkar Fiord
Klubnesset
S e i l a n d
2100/22
Langneskolm
Alten
Aaröy
Fiord
0110/22
Altneset
0140/22 dived
Lange Fiord
0155/22 surfaced
Talvik
1050/22 jettisoned charges
0210/22
0135/22
Tommerholm
Brattholm bottomed
surfaced, 1800/21
Rafs Botn
Raa Fiord

TIRPITZ

30'   23°E. From Admiralty Charts Nᵒˢ 2514, 2315..   30'

passed. While this was being done X8 sighted them and closed, and at 1718 the *Stubborn*, with X7 again in tow and X8 in company, proceeded to search for the *Seanymph*. No contact was made, however, and at dusk (1900) course was altered to the northward and the situation reported to the Rear-Admiral Submarines,[13] who lost no time in passing the information to the *Seanymph*. X8 remained in company with the *Stubborn* and X7 till midnight, 15/16 September, when contact was lost; the reason was explained at 0400, when it was found that owing to a phonetic error in passing orders for the course, X8 had been steering 146° instead of 046° throughout the middle watch.

At 0300, 16 September, dawn revealed to the *Stubborn* that X8 had disappeared, but a quarter of an hour later, in position lat. 69° 35' N., long. 10° 16' E. a submarine was sighted which proved to be the *Seanymph*; after giving her all relevant information, the *Stubborn* and X7 set course to the northward and the *Seanymph* once again started to search for her errant charge, which she eventually found at 1700 that afternoon. As the weather was then favourable the opportunity was taken to transfer to her the operational crew; by 2005 X8 was once more in tow and the two submarines continued their interrupted passage to the northward.

The troubles of the *Seanymph* and X8 were at an end for the time being, but in the meanwhile there had been another instance of tow parting, which ended unhappily. The *Syrtis* (Lieutenant Jupp) and X9 (Sub-Lieutenant Kearon) had had an uneventful passage till the early hours of 16 September, though a telephone defect which had developed the previous day prevented communication between them when either was dived. At 0120, 16 September, X9 dived after a period on the surface for ventilating and charging. She was never seen again. After she dived, speed was gradually increased in the *Syrtis* to 8½ knots and an east-north-easterly course steered till 0855, when speed was reduced and a few minutes later under-water exploding signals were fired for X9 to surface. At 0920 the tow was hauled in and found to have parted. The *Syrtis* turned to the reciprocal course at 0955 to return to the vicinity where it seemed most likely X9 had broken adrift; log readings and fuel consumption indicated that this had probably occurred between 0145 and 0300 – some seven or eight hours previously. As she turned a wave carried a bight of the tow over the side, which threatened to foul the propeller. The rope took some time to clear, and it was not until 1145 that she was able to proceed at full speed, course 245°. Shortly afterwards fog was encountered, the visibility varying between 2 cables and 2 miles.

A well-defined oil track running in a direction 088° to 090° – the direct
course for the slipping position, 200 miles distant – was sighted at 1545,
but subsequent search revealed no sign of X9 and at 0143, 17 September,
the *Syrtis* regretfully abandoned the search and, strict wireless silence being
in force in the area, steered to the northward to report what had occurred
from a position north of latitude 73° N.

Meanwhile the remaining five submarines had proceeded with their
X craft in tow, and the *Truculent* (Lieutenant Alexander) and *Thrasher*
(Lieutenant Hezlet), neither of which had any difficulties, both made
their landfalls during 17 September. The *Seanymph* and *Stubborn*, which
had sighted each other in the early morning, fell in with each other and
exchanged signals between 1447 and 1508 that afternoon, much to the relief
of all in the *Stubborn*, who until then were unaware of the fate of X8.

X8, however, was by this time again in trouble. This had started at
0725 when difficulty was experienced in maintaining trim. The trim
became worse as the day wore on; air could be heard escaping from the
starboard side charge, and the ship took up a list to starboard. At 1630,
with the compensating tank dry and No. 2 main ballast tank fully blown,
the Commanding Officer (Lieutenant MacFarlane) decided to jettison the
starboard charge, which was set to "safe" and released at 1635. In spite of
the "safe" setting, however, the charge exploded a quarter of an hour later,
when about 1,000 yards astern of X8 in tow of the *Seanymph*, both vessels
being dived at the time. The explosion was loud, but did no damage to
either.

After the release of this charge, X8 took up a list to port, indicating that
the port charge also had flooded buoyancy chambers, and it was decided that
this charge must be jettisoned also. Before doing so Lieutenant McFarlane
surfaced and, distrusting the "safe" setting, set the charge to fire two hours
after release, and let it go at 1655. At 1840 – 1 ¾ hours later – by which time
X8 was 3 ½ miles distant,[14] the charge detonated astern with tremendous
force flooding the "wet and dry" compartment in X8, distorting its doors,
fracturing pipes and generally causing so much damage to the craft as to
incapacitate her from diving.[15] When the *Seanymph* – which was dived at the
time and also suffered minor damage from the explosion – surfaced about an
hour later, she "found X8 on the surface, signalling, in heavy weather. After
hours of trying to read each other's signals,"[16] the Commanding Officer
of the *Seanymph* gathered something of her plight, and stood to seaward

till dawn, when he decided that she must be scuttled in the interests of the security of the whole operation.[17] Her crew having been successfully taken off, X8 was sunk at 0350, 18 September, in approximate position lat. 71° 41' N., long. 18° 11' E., and the *Seanymph* proceeded submerged to the northward to reach a position from which she could safely report the situation.

Some two hours before the sinking of X8 the *Syrtis* had arrived to the northward of lat. 73° N., where she spent from 0128, 18 September, to 0554 trying to report the loss of X9 to the Rear-Admiral, Submarines. Failing to get any acknowledgment, she finally broadcast the signal[18] and then steered for her patrol area to the northward of Soroy (see Plan 3).

During 18 September the remaining four X craft continued their passage in tow of their submarines. It had been intended to transfer the operational crews to them on 17 September, but this was prevented by deterioration of the weather. This somewhat improved on 18 September and the *Stubborn* successfully transferred X7's operational crew that evening in lat. 70° 57' N., long 20° 35' E.; the other three submarines, however, waited till the next day. On going ahead after the changeover, the *Stubborn* parted the tow; the main tow had already parted on 15 September, and with the auxiliary tow also gone, it was necessary to extemporise with a 2 ½-in. wire spring. Considerable difficulties were experienced and it was not until 0125, 19 September, that they were able to go ahead. The *Seanymph*, meanwhile, had arrived north of lat. 73° N., and her signal (timed 2156A, 18 September) reporting the scuttling of X8 was acknowledged by Iceland W/T at 0525, 19 September, and reached the Rear-Admiral, Submarines, two and a half hours later, who thereupon decided to use the *Seanymph* to intercept any German units which might leave Alten Fjord to the southward as a result of the attack, and ordered her to patrol in the vicinity of lat. 70° 25' N., long. 17° 16' E., until 21 September, when she was to proceed to her pre-arranged patrol sector to assist in the recovery of X craft.[19]

During 19 September the *Sceptre* (Lieutenant McIntosh) and *Syrtis* made their landfalls from the vicinity of their ordered landfall positions, the latter at 1843, when in position lat. 71° 03' 40' N., long. 22° 13' E., sighted a submarine which dived five minutes later, and was probably a U-Boat, as none of our own submarines seem to have been in the neighbourhood at the time.

By the early hours of D Day – 20 September – the situation was as follows. The operational crews of the four remaining X-Boats had all been transferred successfully. The *Truculent*, *Thrasher*, *Sceptre* and *Syrtis* – the latter with no X-Boat – had made successful landfalls and were in their sectors. The *Seanymph*, with both crews of X8 onboard, was on patrol some 60 miles to the westward of Alten Fjord, and the *Stubborn*, which had been delayed by parting tows, was closing the land to make her landfall with X7 manned by her operational crew, in tow. While thus employed, they had an alarming experience. At 0105, 20 September, when in position lat. 70° 45' N., long. 21° 03' E., the *Stubborn* sighted a floating mine. "The mine itself passed clear of *Stubborn*, but the mooring wire caught in the tow astern and slid down the tow until it became impaled on the bows of X7. This brought the Commanding Officer of X7 (Lieutenant Place) on to the casing, where by deft footwork he was able to clear this unpleasant obstruction, remarking as he did so that this was the first time he had kicked a mine away by its horns." After this providential escape the *Stubborn* made her landfall off Soroy without further incident and set course for her slipping position.

A couple of hours later (0300) the *Syrtis* sighted a submarine on the surface in position lat. 71° 00' N., long. 22° 10' E., steering 235° 9 knots at a distance of 3,500 yards. This was soon identified as a U-Boat, but "in order not to compromise the operation in any way, submarines had been forbidden to attack anything below capital ships while on passage out to, or in their patrol areas off Alten, and the Commanding Officer of HMS *Syrtis* had no option but to let this tempting target pass by at 1,500 yards range and a sitting shot."[20] The U-Boat, which had originally seemed to be making for the entrance of Soroy Sound, altered course to 105° at 0315, and disappeared in the direction of Tarhalsen Point[21] (the north-east point of Soroy).

In the course of the day the weather improved considerably; the wind dropped to a south-easterly breeze, the sea went right down, and the visibility was good, enabling all submarines to fix their positions accurately. By the afternoon all was staged to slip for the attack; the crews of all four X craft according to their towing submarines, were "in great spirits and full of confidence" and between 1830 and 2000, 20 September, they were slipped from the *Thrasher*, *Truculent*, *Stubborn* and *Sceptre* in their respective slipping positions and headed independently for Soroy Sound, the operational submarines withdrawing to seaward within their patrol areas.[22]

Scotland to North Cape
OPERATION "SOURCE"
11th September-8th October, 1943.
Area of Operations.
Return Passage
H.M.S. Stubborn & X10.
29th Sept – 5th Oct, 1943.
ALL TIMES ARE G.M.T.
Symbols ⟁ shew positions
at noon, 3rd October.....

Plan 4

The Attack on the *Tirpitz*
(Plans 4, 5, 6)

Of the four X craft which entered Soroy Sound that September evening –
X5 (Lieutenant Henty-Creer), X6 (Lieutenant Cameron), X7 (Lieutenant
Place) and X10 (Lieutenant Hudspeth) – only X10 returned, and she, owing
to a succession of mishaps, was prevented from carrying out her attack on
the *Scharnhorst*.[23] Much, therefore, remained unknown about the operations
of X5, X6 and X7 – all of which, it will be remembered, had been detailed
to attack the *Tirpitz* – until the return of the survivors of X6 and X7 on the
conclusion of the war. From X5 no one survived; she was last seen off Soroy
at 2315, 20 September, by X7, with whom shouts of "Good hunting" were
exchanged; thereafter, she passes out of the picture till her destruction by
the enemy on 22 September.

After crossing the declared mined area off Soroy on the surface during
the night of 20/21 September, the commanding officers had intended to
proceed submerged up Stjernsund during daylight on 21 September,
reaching Alten Fjord by dusk, and then to proceed to the southward to
charge batteries in the vicinity of the Bratholme group of islands, about four
miles from the entrance to Kaa Fjord. All three were to be at the entrance to
Kaa Fjord shortly after daylight on 22 September. To reach the *Tirpitz* they
would then have to negotiate an anti-submarine net at the entrance to the
fjord and a triple line of anti-torpedo nets closely surrounding the ship. It
was expected that these latter nets would not extend downwards more than
about 50 ft., which in 20 fathoms of water would give the X craft plenty of
room to dive under them.

In order to allow all X craft ample time to reach their objectives, and to
guard against the loss of surprise through one of them attacking prematurely,
they had all been forbidden to attack before 0100, 22 September, but they
were free to do so at any time after that, setting their charges to explode in
accordance with a "firing rules table" given in the operation orders. Actually,
the commanding officers mutually agreed to make their attacks between
0500 and 0800, laying their charges set to fire at 0830, by which time it was
hoped they would have been able to withdraw from the area.

The difficulties and hazards which these three X craft had to encounter in penetrating to Kaa Fjord were successfully overcome. The minefields reported off Soroy were negotiated on the surface without incident, though X6 sighted a patrol vessel at 2200.

X6 and X7 both dived between 0145 and 0215, 21 September, each of them experiencing difficulties in trimming. These were overcome, however, but soon afterwards while passing through Stjernsund, X6 developed a defect in her periscope "which was to prove a major handicap throughout, but a triumph of mind over matter to her crew."[24] The passage through the fjords was accomplished without difficulty. An occasional A/S patrol vessel and a solitary aircraft had to be dodged, and X7's report mentions sighting a large vessel "believed to be *Scharnhorst*" under the lee of Aaroy Islands at 1630. The two craft reached their waiting billets about a mile to the northward of Bratholme, X6 arriving first at 1845, and the night was spent in charging batteries, making good defects and dodging traffic. Neither of them made contact with any other X craft, as had rather been hoped, though this was unnecessary from an operational point of view.

At 0045, 22 September, X7 (Lieutenant Place) left the Bratholme Islands and shaped course for the Kaa Fjord defences. X6 (Lieutenant Cameron) followed an hour later. It was a desperate venture, but one thing they had in their favour; the weather was ideal for their purpose, with the sky dull and overcast, and a fresh breeze raising white horses to assist an unseen attack.

By 0400 X7 was safely through the gate in the A/S boom at the entrance to Kaa Fjord, but, meeting an outward bound motor launch, she was forced to go deep shortly afterwards. This temporary blindness resulted in her getting caught in an unoccupied square of A/T nets, formerly used to protect the *Lutzow*. There she remained for about an hour, eventually getting clear at the expense of breaking surface – fortunately unseen – and putting the trim pump and gyro compass out of action. By 0600, after fouling another wire with the periscope standard, she was able to proceed, precariously trimmed at periscope depth, towards the target.

X6, following later, was suffering increasing trouble with her periscope. After dodging a small ferry boat and an A/S patrol vessel, she passed through the A/S boom gap at 0505. Lieutenant Cameron then took her to 60 ft., in order to strip and clean his periscope, while proceeding by dead reckoning towards the western end of the fjord. On coming to periscope depth again, he found himself so close to the *Nordmark* that he had to alter course to avoid fouling her buoy. To add to his difficulties the periscope again clouded over and its hoisting motor brake burnt out; from then on manual control had to be resorted to. Despite this most serious handicap he pressed on, and by 0705 X6 was safely through the boat entrance of the A/T net defence of the *Tirpitz* and within striking distance of her target. Five minutes later (0710) Lieutenant Place in X7 also reached the A/T enclosure and dived to 75 ft. to pass under the net.

So far no suspicions on the part of the enemy had been aroused and life in Kaa Fjord was pursuing its normal course. Hands had been called, the usual A/A defence and anti-sabotage watch ashore and afloat set, the boat gate in the A/T nets opened for shallow draught traffic, and work in the hydrophone listening office had ceased – all at 0600; the normal harbour routine was in progress.[25] Then suddenly events moved quickly.

At 0707[26] a "long black submarine-like object" was sighted on the port beam of the *Tirpitz*, some 20 yards from the shore; it quickly disappeared and though reported no action was taken as it was suspected of being merely a porpoise. It was in fact X6, which after passing through the gate ran aground on the north shore and broke surface. Five minutes later, in backing and filling to get clear of the shore and pointed in the right direction, she again broke surface about 30 yards abeam of the *Tirpitz* and was correctly identified. By this time her gyro compass had been put out of action by the grounding and subsequent violent angles on the boat, and the periscope was completely flooded; Lieutenant Cameron could only grope his way blindly in what he imagined to be the right direction, hoping to fix his position by the shadow of the battleship. After 5 minutes X6 got caught in an obstruction which was taken to be the A/T net on the far (starboard) side of the *Tirpitz*, but which was probably something hanging down from the ship herself or one of the craft alongside. Lieutenant Cameron manoeuvred clear of this obstruction and surfaced close on the port bow of the *Tirpitz*. He was greeted by a brisk fire from small arms and hand grenades, but was too close to the ship for any of the main or heavy A/A armament to bear. Realising that escape was impossible, Lieutenant Cameron destroyed the most secret equipment, backed his craft down until the stern was scraping the *Tirpitz*'s hull abreast B turret, released his charges and scuttled the craft. As she started to sink, a power boat from the battleship came alongside, took off the crew and tried to take X6 in tow, but without success and she quickly followed her explosives to the bottom.[27]

Onboard the *Tirpitz* and in Kaa Fjord the alarm had by this time been raised with a vengeance. The attack had come as a complete surprise and, from entries in the battleship's log, the enemy would seem to have been somewhat nonplussed. Although the first sighting of X6 had occurred at 0707, it was not till nearly a quarter-of-an-hour later (0721) that A/A guns crews were closed up and the order given to close watertight doors. These were reported closed at 0736, by which time hands were at action stations and steam was being raised. Divers had already been ordered to examine the hull for limpet mines, and the ship was then prepared for sea "in order to leave the net enclosure before the time-fused mines detonate."[28] This intention was not carried out, however, for the discovery of the presence of X7 at 0740 – the first intimation that more than one midget was concerned in the attack – presented the Germans with a picture so little to their liking of an unknown number of submarines lurking in the fjord that they decided to keep the *Tirpitz* inside her nets. The gate was accordingly closed, and the ship's position shifted by heaving in on her starboard cable and veering port, in order to get as far as possible from the spot where X6 had sunk.

Meanwhile X7 had also carried out her attack. As mentioned previously, Lieutenant Place had decided to pass under the close A/T nets. Here he had an unpleasant surprise; instead of the expected gap under them, he found that they extended practically to the bottom. At the first attempt X7 got caught at 75 ft.; going full speed astern and blowing to full buoyancy, she broke clear, but turned beam on to the net and broke surface close to the buoys.[29] She dived again immediately and once more fouled the net, this time at 95 ft.; "after about five minutes of wriggling and blowing"[30] she started to rise. By this time the compass was useless as the result of her violent movements, and Lieutenant Place was by no means sure of his position; he therefore stopped his motor and allowed her to come right up to the surface with very little way on for a look round. What happened next is best told in the words of Lieutenant Place's subsequent report:–

> By some extraordinary lucky chance we must have either passed under the nets or worked our way through the boat passage, for on breaking surface the *Tirpitz*, with no intervening nets, was sighted right ahead not more than 30 yards away. Forty ft. was ordered and X7 at full speed struck the *Tirpitz* at 20 ft. on the port side approximately below B turret, and slid gently under the keel where the starboard charge was released

in the full shadow of the ship. Here, at 60 ft., a quick stop trim was caught – at the collision X7 was swung to port so we were now heading approximately down the keel of the *Tirpitz*. Going slowly astern the port charge was released about 150 to 200 ft. further aft – as I estimated, about under X turret. I am uncertain as to the exact time of release, but the first depth charges were heard just after the collision, which, from Lieutenant Cameron's report, would fix the time at 0722.

After releasing the port charge, 100 ft. was ordered and an alteration of course guessed to try and make the position where we had come in. At 60 ft. we were in the net again. Without a compass I had no exact idea of where we were, the difficulties we had experienced and their air trimming had used two air bottles and only 1,200 lb. were left in the third. X7's charges were due to explode in an hour – not to mention others which might go up any time after 0800.

A new technique in getting out of nets had by this time been developed. The procedure was to go full ahead blowing economically and then go full astern, the idea being to get as much way on the boat as the slack of the nets would allow and thus have a certain impetus as well as the thrust of the screws when actually disengaging from the net. In about the next three-quarters of an hour X7 was in and out of several nets, the air in the last bottle was soon exhausted and the compressor had to be run. Once at about 40 ft., 0740, X7 came out while still going ahead and slid over the top of the net between the buoys on the surface. I did not look at the *Tirpitz* at this time as this method of overcoming net defence was new and absorbing, but I believe we were at the time on her starboard bow – we had certainly passed underneath her since the attack. We were too close, of course, for heavy fire, but a large number of machine gun bullets were heard hitting the casing.

Immediately after passing over the nets all main ballast tanks were vented and X7 went to the bottom in 120 ft. The compressor was run again and we tried to come to the surface or periscope depth for a look so that the direction indicator could be started and as much distance as possible put between ourselves and the coming explosion. It was extremely annoying to run into another net at 60 ft. Shortly after this there was a tremendous explosion (0812). This evidently shook us out of the net and on surfacing it was tiresome to see the *Tirpitz* still afloat...

This last excursion into the nets apparently took place well on the *Tirpitz's* starboard bow and from outside the enclosure. After getting clear, Lieutenant Place took X7 to the bottom to survey the damage. She appeared to have suffered but little structurally, but compasses and diving gauges were out of action and the craft was impossible to control. More than once she broke surface, and on each occasion fire was opened from the *Tirpitz*, causing damage to the hull, depth charges were being dropped indiscriminately about the fjord, though up till then not particularly near to X7, and Lieutenant Place decided to surface to give his crew a chance of escaping. She came up close to a target, allowing Lieutenant Place to step on to it, but before the remainder of the crew could escape, X7 sank at 0835.[31] Sub-Lieutenant Aitken the third officer, was able to get out by the use of D.S.E.A. at 1115, but the two remaining members (Sub-Lieutenant Whittam and Engine Room Artificer Whitley) lost their lives.[32]

Lieutenant Place and Sub-Lieutenant Aitken, were picked up by the Germans and taken onboard the *Tirpitz*, where they found the crew of X6 being questioned by officers of the Admiral's staff. All of them were well treated and given hot coffee and schnapps; great admiration for their bravery was expressed by the enemy.

Of the attack as seen from the German side, some interesting details were obtained a few months later from a survivor from the *Scharnhorst*, who was onboard the *Tirpitz* at the time.[33] This prisoner was in an office on the upper deck level of the control tower when at about 0700, 22 September, a small submarine[34] was seen on the surface inside the anti-submarine nets about 13 yards on the port bow of the *Tirpitz*. The alarm was given and hand grenades were thrown at the submarine, which submerged; almost immediately (sic) the order was given to close all watertight doors in the *Tirpitz*. Shortly afterwards four men were seen swimming in the water, and they were quickly brought onboard. The prisoner described how a rating came rushing into his office. "Have you ever seen an Englishman?" he asked, "because there are four standing outside the regulating office at the moment." The prisoner went up to have a look at them and noticed they were peering at their watches. Then suddenly, about half-an-hour (sic) after the submarine was first sighted, there was an exceedingly heavy explosion. The "whole great ship heaved several ft. out of the water and bounced down again with a slight list." All the electric lights went out immediately. Doors jammed, gear of all sorts fell down, fire extinguishers wrenched from the bulkheads started belching foam, and glass from broken scuttles and mirrors was everywhere. Ratings who had been standing up were flung off their ft.[35] In a moment the whole ship was in an uproar.

Up on the bridge the Captain flared into a rage and ordered the four Englishmen to be shot at once as saboteurs, to change his mind when it was pointed out to him that they were only "soldiers doing their duty."

The electric lights soon came on again, and then a periscope was sighted outside the anti-submarine net and the 5.9-in. guns opened fire at maximum depression. A man on the upper deck was blown overboard and killed by the blast. The alarm in the fjord was by this time general, and every available craft was pressed into the service to hunt for submarines and drop depth charges. Two further midgets were reported sunk, one opposite the small River Smornes and one outside the inner anti-submarine net in Kaa Fjord. About an hour after the explosion, the same informant saw two men come to the surface outside the net round the *Tirpitz*. They were picked up by a patrol boat and brought onboard.

From his shipmates he learnt that there had been two explosions, one underneath the *Tirpitz* on the starboard side amidships, and another off the port side which flung up a gigantic column of water as high as the mast.[36]

Apart from the shambles of fallen gear below decks, immediate damage was not apparent. The mast on the after director platform was leaning drunkenly festooned with broken wireless aerials, but otherwise there was no sign of serious damage and the prisoner stated that the ship's company only learned of the full effect of the explosion a good deal later.[37]

Of the part played by X5 (Lieutenant Henty-Creer) little is known. The Germans reported sighting a third midget at 0843, then some 500 yards outside the nets. The *Tirpitz* opened fire and claimed to have sunk this craft, and depth charges were dropped in the position where she disappeared. Some time after the attack divers found wreckage, presumably from this craft, but no bodies or personal gear, and there was no trace of any survivors. Whether she was on her way out at the time, after laying her charges, or whether she was waiting to go in during the next attacking period (i.e. after 0900) will probably never be known.[38]

Narrative of X10
(Plan 4)

Meanwhile the fourth midget, X10 (Lieutenant Hudspeth), had been the victim of a succession of mishaps, which finally compelled her to abandon her attempt on the *Scharnhorst*.[39] On taking over the craft on 19 September the operational crew had accepted defects in her periscope hoist motor and the motor of her "wet and dry" pump, besides a slight gland leak, all of which they were confident they could put right.

X10 was slipped from the *Sceptre* in lat. 70° 40' N., 21° 07' E., at 2000 20 September, and proceeded on the surface at full speed across the mined area in the direction of Stjernsund. At daylight, 21 September, she dived, being then five miles from the west point of Stjernoy Island. Difficulty was experienced in trimming, and the defect in the periscope motor had become worse. Other electrical defects developed and the gyro compass failed, so Lieutenant Hudspeth decided to effect repairs in Smalfjord on the north coast of Stjernoy, where he judged the risk of detection would be less than in one of the small fjords in Stjernsund in which it had been intended to bottom during daylight, 21 September.

X10 arrived at Smalfjord at 0700, 21 September, and bottomed at the head of the fjord on a sandy bottom; by 1705 the defects – though by no means cured – had been sufficiently overcome to warrant proceeding, and X10 got under way. At 2035 she entered Stjernsund, through which she had an uneventful passage, keeping close to the northern shore. All shore lights were burning normally, and nothing was seen of any enemy patrol activity. Apart from one small ship which was sighted with her navigation lights burning at 2135, and disappeared in the direction of Storelokker Fjord, there was no sign of life. By 2320, 21 September, X10 was clear of Stjernsund and altered course to the southward through Alten Fjord on the last lap of her long passage.

So far all had gone well, and there seemed no reason to doubt that daylight would find her off the entrance to Kaa Fjord, ready for the attack. Then things began to go awry.

The first sign of trouble occurred at 0110, 22 September, when it was realised that the gyro compass was wandering. Half an hour later X10 dived to avoid being sighted by a vessel approaching from ahead; it was then found that the damping bottles of the gyro compass were not working, and on raising the magnetic compass the light failed to function. As this light could only be replaced by taking off the top cover from outside, X10 was left with no compass at all. Worse was to follow.

At 0150 she came to periscope depth, and on attempting to raise the periscope a fire developed from the periscope hoisting motor, and Lieutenant Hudspeth was obliged to surface to ventilate and clear her of fumes. Dawn was then breaking, and X10 was almost within sight of the entrance of Kaa Fjord. Clearly, with no compass and with no means of raising or lowering her periscope, she was in no condition to carry out the attack, and Lieutenant Hudspeth decided to bottom before daylight set in.[40] This he did at 0215 in 195 ft. of water 100 yards south-east of Tommerholm Island. As she dived the entrance of Kaa Fjord could be seen 4 ½ miles off, lit up by what appeared to be low powered flood lights.[41]

There X10 remained during the daylight hours of 22 September, while efforts were made to make good her defects. At 0830 – the exact time at which the charges of the other attacking X craft might be expected to explode – two very heavy explosions were heard at intervals of a few seconds. Five minutes later, nine further heavy explosions were heard at short, irregular intervals. These were followed between 0900 and 1000 by a burst of about 12 lighter explosions, which were repeated – this time louder and closer – at about 1100.

Sunset, 22 September, was at 1634, and by that time the defects in X10 had still not been overcome. The explosions which had been heard during the day had convinced Lieutenant Hudspeth that the attack had been carried out, and, as he was unaware of the loss of X8 and X9 on passage, he had reason to hope that all five had got in. In these circumstances he reluctantly decided to give up any idea of attacking,[42] and at 1800 surfaced and made for deep water. At 1825 both charges, set to "safe", were jettisoned in 135 fathoms, and X10 then proceeded on main engines out of Alten Fjord. A darkened vessel was sighted at about 2100 off the entrance to Lange Fjord, but was lost to sight in a snow squall, and the western end of Stjernsund was reached by 2350. This did not allow time to get across the declared mined area before daylight, so X10 again made for Smalfjord, where she arrived at 0215, 23 September. As the fjord was completely deserted and snow squalls frequent, Lieutenant Hudspeth remained on the surface and secured alongside the shore with his grapnel, considering the risk of detection negligible with ship and shore covered with snow.

At 1100, 23 September, after the light in the projector compass had been replaced and with her periscope lashed in the "up" position, X10 left Smalfjord and dived towards the southern end of the minefield. Surfacing at 1800, she crossed the declared area at full speed and reached the recovery position (FB) at about 2300, 23 September, where it was hoped to meet one of the operational submarines. X10 remained in this vicinity for about 30 hours, searching with R.G. gear by night, and surfacing by day in the hope of being sighted; no contact, however, was made, and at 0430, 25 September, she set course for Sandoy Fjord, on the northern coast of Soroy Island. This was reached at noon, and by 1525, 25 September, X10 was secured alongside the beach in Ytre Reppafjord (on the north-west of Sandoy Fjord). This bay was completely deserted, and here she remained till the morning of 27 September, while the crew got some much needed rest.

On 27 September Lieutenant Hudspeth decided to move to Ø Fjord, which a submarine was expected to close that night. X10 reached Ø Fjord at 1550, and R. G. search was carried out across the entrance after dark. At 0055, 28 September, an I.R. beam was sighted and closed; five minutes later contact was made with the *Stubborn* and by 0150 X10 was in tow. It was by this time getting light and too late for her crew to be taken onboard the *Stubborn*; the weather was deteriorating, and it was not until 2200, 29 September, that the transfer could be effected. By this time the operational crew had been onboard their craft for almost exactly 10 days. They had been subjected to much hardship, discomfort and disappointment, but were none the worse for their experience.

Opposite, Plan 5

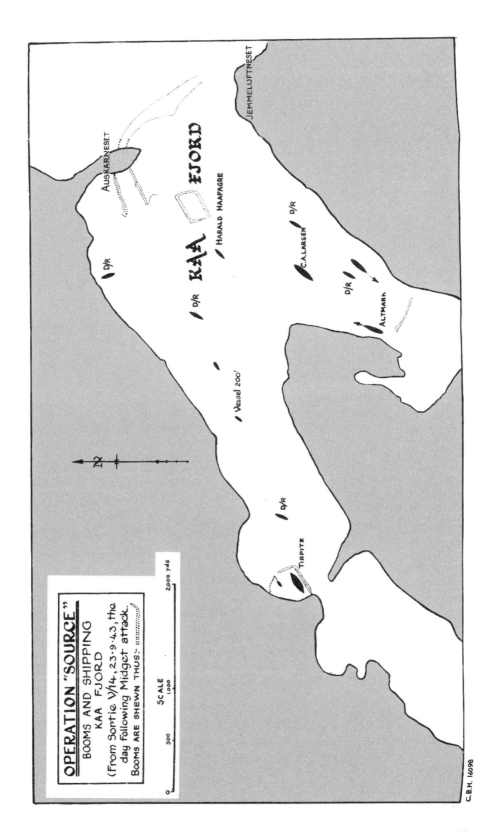

OPERATION "SOURCE"

BOOMS AND SHIPPING
KAA FJORD

(From Sortie V/14, 23·9·43, the
day following Midget attack.
Booms are shewn thus:-)

SCALE

0   500   1,000   2,000 yds

KAA FJORD

AUSKARNESET

JEMMELUFTNESET

D/R

HARALD HAAFAGRE

D/R

C.A.LARSEN

D/R

ALTMARK

Vessel 200'

D/R

TIRPITZ

C.B.H. 16098

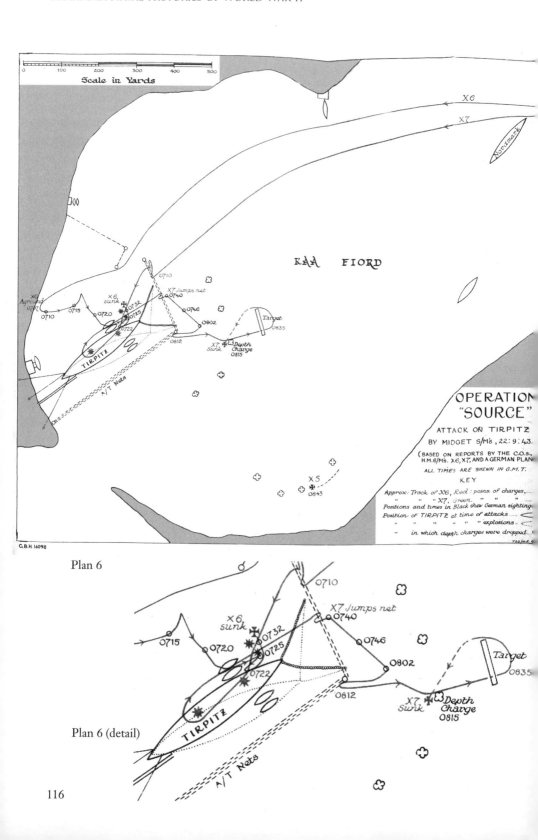

Scale in Yards

KAA FIORD

OPERATION
"SOURCE"

ATTACK ON TIRPITZ
BY MIDGET S/Ms, 22:9:43.

(BASED ON REPORTS BY THE C.O.s,
H.M.6/Ms. X6, X7, AND A GERMAN PLAN

ALL TIMES ARE SHEWN IN G.M.T.

KEY

Approx: Track of X6, Red : posns of charges,
"   "   " X7, green. "   "   "
Positions and times in Black shew German sighting
Position of TIRPITZ at time of attacks ......
"   "   "   "   explosions .
"   in which depth charges were dropped.

C.B.H. 16098

Plan 6

Plan 6 (detail)

Movements of Operational Submarines
(Plan 3)

To return to the operational submarines.

After slipping the X craft on the evening of 20 September, the *Thrasher*, *Truculent*, *Stubborn*, and *Sceptre* established patrols in their respective sectors. The *Syrtis* was already in her sector, and the *Seanymph* had been ordered to patrol in lat. 70° 25' N., long. 17° 16' E. (some 60 miles to the westward); her sector was therefore left vacant.

On 21 September, the Rear-Admiral, Submarines, ordered the *Seanymph* to shift her patrol to the vicinity of lat. 69°, 11' N., long. 15° 27' E. (off Andoy), proceeding so as to arrive there after dark on 22 September, with the object of attacking main enemy units proceeding from Alten Fjord to Narvik.[43] The next day, 22 September – the day of the attack – he took further steps with the same end in view. No reports to the contrary (except the *Seanymph*'s) having been received, it was assumed that the attack would take place as planned, in the early hours of that morning, and it seemed probable that German heavy units capable of moving would vacate Kaa Fjord shortly afterwards. In any event, the *Lutzow* could hardly be a casualty, since with the loss of X8 she was not liable to attack.

Rear-Admiral Barry decided that should information of a major enemy movement be received in time[44] he would send one of the T Class submarines into Soroy Sound, accepting the risk of crossing the declared mined area, and for this purpose the *Thrasher* was ordered to close to the south-east of her area (to position FA) and to charge her batteries full out after dark.[45] The *Truculent* was ordered to the *Seanymph*'s vacant sector so as to be closer at hand in case of need,[46] and the *Sceptre* was ordered to leave her patrol sector and proceed to lat. 69° 44' N., long. 17° 43' E. (some 80 miles to the south-westward, off Kvaloy) arriving there as soon as possible after daylight, 23 September.[47]

These instructions reached the *Sceptre* just after noon, 22 September, and she at once set course for the patrol ordered. Unfortunately, she had been set some 15 miles to the eastward[48] of her patrol sector, and this delayed her arrival in her new position just sufficiently to make her miss sighting the *Lutzow* on her expected passage south.

On 23 September the four submarines left on patrol off Alten Fjord for the recovery of X craft were predisposed so as to cover the sectors left vacant by the *Seanymph* and *Sceptre*, and on 25 September the *Syrtis*, *Truculent* and *Stubborn* were ordered to proceed to the three eastern sectors on 27 September – if no contact with X craft had been made by daylight that morning – and to close the north coast of Soroy on the nights of 27/28 and 28/29 September, as laid down in the operation orders.[49]

These patrols were carried out without incident from 23–27 September. Nothing was seen of any of the X craft, nor of any anti-submarine or air activity by the enemy.[50]

After dark on 27 September, the search off the coast of Soroy was commenced. The *Syrtis* (Lieutenant Jupp) and *Truculent* (Lieutenant Alexander) examined the north-eastern end of the island between Bondoy Island and Staarlet Point. They sighted each other and exchanged signals at 2150, but no X craft was located and they withdrew to seaward and continued their patrols during daylight hours of 28 September. The search was repeated that evening; on this occasion the *Truculent* closed to within 2½ miles of Staarlet Point, but again the search was fruitless. In any case the weather had got so bad that the recovery of an X craft would have been well nigh impossible, and at 2030 she set course for Lerwick (Shetland Islands) followed by the *Syrtis* – which had also failed to find any X craft in her area – at 0215, 29 September.

Meanwhile the *Stubborn* (Lieutenant Duff), working at the south-western end of the island, had closed Ø Fjord on the evening of 27 September. Snow and hail squalls frequently blotted out the land, and land marks, whitened with snow, were hard to identify when seen, but the navigational difficulties were overcome and there she found X10 (see pages 119-121). The *Stubborn* had lost her towing gear on the outward passage, but an extempore tow was passed and both craft withdrew to seaward. The *Stubborn* had not yet covered Sandfjord, which was on her beat, and during 28 September she tried to communicate with the *Truculent* intending to request her to do so that night. In this she was unsuccessful, but by the evening the weather – wind force 6 from the west, sea and swell 5-6 – decided the Commanding Officer not to attempt to close the land again. To have done so might well have entailed the loss of X10, and at 0600, 29 September, the *Stubborn* with X10 in tow set forth on her 1,000 mile passage to Lerwick.[51]

Return Passage

The morning of 29 September saw the *Thrasher*, *Truculent*, *Syrtis* and *Stubborn* – the latter with X10 in tow – starting their return passage.[52] The *Sceptre* and *Seanymph* remained on patrol off Andoy.

It was still blowing strong from the westward, but during the afternoon the wind dropped and went round to ENE., and at 2130 the passage crew of X7 (Lieutenant Philip) which was onboard the *Stubborn* was able to take over X10 from the operational crew. The transfer was completed by 2200, 29 September and the passage was resumed at 7 knots.

During the early part of 30 September the wind was light from the ENE., but a stern sea was getting up and at 0500 speed was reduced to 5 knots on this account. This speed was maintained throughout the day until 2330, when the tow parted. X10 surfaced immediately; after considerable difficulty another tow was improvised, and at 0340, 1 October, course was set to the southward at 3 knots. During the forenoon the *Stubborn*'s own towing pendant was broken out from the casing and passed aft. The tow was lengthened by shackling this pendant to the 2½-in towing wire, and it was then considered safe to proceed at 5 knots.

The *Stubborn* had been trying, without success, to report her situation to the Rear-Admiral, Submarines, since 2337, 29 September. Her signal,[53] which included brief details of X10's experiences and of her hearing heavy explosions[54] on the morning of the attack, eventually reached him at 2154, 30 September. The almost complete depletion of the *Stubborn*'s towing equipment was not realised at the time, but next day (1 October) the *Truculent* and *Syrtis* were ordered to keep pace with her and the *Stubborn* was ordered to report progress on crossing lat. 65° N., or if the tow parted.[55]

Meanwhile a fleet operation was impending which would take surface forces across the routes of the submarines, and at 1804, 1 October, they were ordered to be south of lat. 66° N. by 1800, 3 October, or, if this was not feasible, to remain north of lat. 68° 20' N. till 1800, 4 October.[56]

At 0300/2 October, the *Stubborn* reported herself in lat. 69° 13' N., long. 90° 22' E., steering 223°, 4.5 knots. It seemed doubtful whether she could reach lat. 66° N. in time. An attempt to do so might result in the loss of X10, and after consultation with the Commander-in-Chief, Home Fleet,[57]Rear-Admiral Barry cancelled the instructions of the day before, and ordered her to proceed at her best speed for Lerwick.[58]

During the morning of 2 October there was an improvement in the weather and by 0800 the swell and sea had moderated sufficiently for the *Stubborn* to increase to 6 knots. This speed was maintained until 1230 the next day (3 October) when X10 again broke adrift. The tow had parted just short of the join between the *Stubborn's* towing pendant and the 2½-in. wire. After the towing pendant had been hauled inboard in the *Stubborn* the Commanding Officer and 1st Lieutenant of the operational crew (Lieutenant Hudspeth and Sub-Lieutenant Enzer) returned to X10 in the rubber dinghy. Working on the casing in a heavy swell, these two officers and Lieutenant Philip succeeded, with the help of the *Stubborn's* two spare periscope wires, in recovering the 2½-in. wire, which was then got onboard the *Stubborn* and again shackled to her towing pendant. The work was completed in 4½ hours and at 1700 the *Stubborn* went ahead at 3½ knots.

About an hour later (1807) a signal was received in the *Stubborn* from the Rear-Admiral, Submarines, warning Lieutenant Duff that a gale was expected and directing him to embark the passage crew and to scuttle X10 at his discretion.[59] The *Stubborn* was still some 400 miles from Lerwick; the chances of towing her there without a crew onboard were slight and Lieutenant Duff decided to sink her.[60] It was a hard decision to take after all they had been through together. By 2040 the three officers remaining in X10 were embarked, and five minutes later she sank in lat. 66° 13' N., long. 4° 02' E.[61]

Little more remains to be told. The expected gale did not materialise till 6 October and by that time the four submarines on passage had arrived at Lerwick – the *Thrasher* on 3 October, the *Truculent* and *Syrtis* on 4 October, and the *Stubborn* on 5 October. The *Seanymph* and *Sceptre* maintained their patrol off Andoy without incident until 4 October, when in compliance with directions from the Rear-Admiral, Submarines, they withdrew from the area and after an uneventful passage arrived at Lerwick on 7 October.

Conclusion

With the arrival of the operational submarines at Lerwick, operation 'Source' may be considered to have come to an end.

Of the six midget submarines which had left Loch Cairnbarn nearly four weeks before, not one had survived. Three had been sunk in the attack and three had succumbed to the vicissitudes of the long sea passages. Happily, the loss of life was not proportionate to the loss of X craft. Out of the 42 officers and men who formed their crews, 33 survived; three had been lost on passage and six by enemy action.

For some time after the attack little was known of the results and details. Gradually, as reports were received and pieced together, the story of the attack emerged and it became apparent that the *Tirpitz* had sustained very considerable damage to the hull, machinery and armament. Temporary repairs were still in progress in February, 1944, and it was unlikely that they would be completed for one or two months.

Summing up, Rear-Admiral Barry remarked that the success of the operation was "the culmination of many months spent in developing and perfecting the new weapon, in the intensive training of the crews for the hazardous enterprise, and in detailed and careful planning for the actual operation."

That so many of the X craft were able to reach their destination in good condition after the long passage was attributable to the skill and perseverance in overcoming many difficulties shown by the officers and men responsible alike for technical development in the early stages and for the preparation of the craft immediately prior to the operation.

After stressing the importance of the training carried out by Commander Ingram[62] the Rear-Admiral remarked that the skill and seamanship of the commanding officers of the towing submarines played a most important part in the operation, and to this was due in no small measure the safe and timely arrival at the slipping positions of four out of the six X craft which set out. The passage crews of the X craft, too, showed fine seamanship, determination and endurance; during the long and arduous passage these crews managed to keep their craft in a high state of efficiency, which largely contributed to the final success of the operation.

"Finally," to quote the Rear-Admiral, "I cannot fully express my admiration for the three commanding officers, Lieutenants H. Henty-Creer, R.N.V.R., D. Cameron, R.N.R., and B.C.G. Place, D.S.C., R.N., and the crews of X5, X6 and X7 who pressed home their attack and who failed to return. In the full knowledge of the hazards they were to encounter, these gallant crews penetrated into a heavily defended fleet anchorage. There, with cool courage and determination and in spite of all the modern devices that ingenuity could devise for their detection and destruction, they pressed home their attack to the full... It is clear that courage and enterprise of the very highest order in the close presence of the enemy was shown by these very gallant gentlemen, whose daring attack will surely go down to history as one of the most courageous acts of all time."

Appendix A

Nominal List of Officers and Ratings of X Craft
taking part in Operation 'Source'

Operational Crew		Passage Crew
	X5[63]	
Lieut. H. Henty-Creer, R.N.V.R.[63]		Lieut. J. V. Terry-Lloyd, S.A.N.F.
Mid. D. J. Malcolm, R.N.V.R.[63]		A/Ldg. Sea. B. W. Element
Sub-Lieut. T. J. Nelson, R.N.V.R.[63]		Sto. 1 N. Garrity
E.R.A. 4 R. J. Mortiboys[63]		
	X6[63]	
Lieut. D. Cameron, R.N.R.[65]		Lieut. A. Wilson, R.N.V.R.
Sub-Lieut. J. T. Lorimer, R.N.V.R.[65]		Ldg. Sea. J. J. McGregor
Sub-Lieut. R. H. Kendall, R.N.V.R[65]		Sto. 1. W. Oxley
E.R.A. 4 E. Goddard[65]		
	X7[63]	
Lieut. B. C. G. Place, D.S.C., R.N.[65]		Lieut. P. H. Philip, S.A.N.F. (V)
Sub-Lieut. L. B. C. Whittam, R.N.V.R.[63]		A. B. J. Magennis
Sub-Lieut. R. Aitken, R.N.V.R.[65]		Sto. 1 F. Luck
E.R.A. 4 W. M. Whitley[63]		
	X8[64]	
Lieut. B. M. McFarlane, R.A.N.		Lieut. J. Smart, R.N.V.R.
Lieut. W. J. Marsden, R.A.N.V.R.		A/Ldg. Sea. W. H. A. Pomeroy
Sub-Lieut. R. X. Hindmarsh, R.N.V.R.		Sto. 1 J. G. Robinson
E.R.A. 4 J. B. Murray		
	X9[64]	
Lieut. T. L. Martin, R.N.		Sub-Lieut. E. Kearon, R.N.V.R.[64]
Sub-Lieut. J. Brooks, R.N.		A.B. A. H. Harte[64]
Lieut. M. Shean, R.A.N.V.R.		Sto. 1 G. H. Hollett[64]
E.R.A. 4 V. Coles		
	X10[64]	
Lieut. K. R. Hudspeth, R.A.N.V.R.		Sub-Lieut. E. V. Page, R.N.V.R.
Sub-Lieut. B. E. Enzer		E.R.A 4 H. J. Fishleigh
Mid. G. G. Harding, R.N.V.R.		A/P.O. A. Brookes
E.R.A. 4 L. Tilley		

Appendix B

German Security Measures, etc., Kaa Fjord, September, 1943

A. Defence Obstacles

(1) Across the mouth of Kaa Fjord, from Auskarneset, on the north side, to Jemmeluftneset, on the south side, stretched a wide-meshed anti-submarine net, with a depth of 48 m.. There was a 400 metre-wide gap in it at the extreme southern end, which, since the summer of 1943, could be closed by a movable boom of loosely interlocked wire network suspended by buoys to a depth of 10 m., and secured to the bank at Jemmeluftneset; owing to the continuous traffic passing to and from Alta and Bossekop, this gap was only closed in the event of a submarine alarm at Altenfjord or its approaches and was protected by depth charge throwers.

(2) A small boat, either an A/S vessel or patrol-boat, fitted with hydrophone apparatus, was constantly stationed some 600 m. E.S.E. of the gap, checking all ships passing through.

(3) The net enclosure at Barbrudalen, where the *Tirpitz* lay, consisted of a double air-torpedo net, with a 15 metre depth, and a secondary net, 36 m. deep. A 20-metre wide gap had been left in the side nearest the mouth of the fjord – which placed it on the port bow of the battleship – and could be closed by a baffle, to which was attached a net with a depth from 11 m. to 36 m.. Whenever this gap was left open at night, a special boat was put to guard it, while a watch was also kept on it from the *Tirpitz*.

(4) An identical set of net defences surrounded the *Scharnhorst* at Auskarneset, with the 10 metre-wide gap in the north-west edge of the enclosure.

(5) At the time of the attack, the German repair ship *Neumark* was in Kaa Fjord, lying in Kvaenvik Bay; she was protected to the north-east by a double air-torpedo net, from 15 to 18 m. deep.

(6) Stjern Sund and Varg Sund were both guarded by a patrol boat, the

security measures for the area being in the hands of the Sea Defence Commandant, Hammerfest.

B. Disposition of Defence Personnel

(1) The boat which stood guard over the gap in the big anti-submarine net at Jemmeluftneset maintained its hydrophone in constant use, and was supported in its task by the other ships in the vicinity with hydrophone apparatus. All vessels entering or leaving were halted and checked.

(2) (a) The gap in the *Tirpitz* enclosure at Barbrudalen was immediately closed at night after the last ship had passed through, and it was not until morning when the traffic again commenced that the baffle was removed. If it were left open during the hours of darkness, a boat with a guard-party from the *Tirpitz*, equipped with small arms and hand grenades, kept watch over it. During darkness the ship's hydrophones were manned without break.[66]

(b) Further security measures taken were:–

The watches on deck ("security posts"), were strengthened.

A special security officer was on duty on the A.A. operational position. Shore-patrols were started.

A sharp check was kept both on all vessels coming alongside and on everyone coming onboard.

(3) Security measures for the enclosure at Auskarneset (*Scharnhorst*) were the same as those at Barbrudalen. The gap, however, was only shut in special instances.

Appendix C

Damage Suffered by the *Tirpitz* in X Craft Attack, 22 September, 1943

Reports of the damage immediately after the attack did not supply a clear idea of its extent, in particular those from the engine-room. At 2000 on 22 September, 1943, the Gunnery Officer was able to report that all the main armament was in order, and the only defect to the secondary armament was in Port Turret 3, which was jammed; the L.A. fire-control was also undamaged. One of the control positions of the heavy A/A guns was "unstabilised"[67] but repair work was well in hand. The range-finding gear was in working order only in the foremast, Turret B, and the secondary armament. The possibility of repairing the sets in Turret D and forward position was regarded as doubtful. On 27 September an engine-room report was made which finally gave a fairly clear picture of the damage to the *Tirpitz*.

(1) All three main engines out of order.[68] Generator-room 2 out of order; dynamo control room 2 now in order. Approximately 200 cm. of water in the ship.

(2) All the compartments of the ship had either temporarily or permanently been made water-tight.

(3) The pumping-out of the double-bottoms in compartments 8 to 10 had been started.

(4) The 8 main turbines had to be opened up, as damage to the blades was suspected. and this was con firmed in one of them.

(5) Rudder installation 2 out of order; Rudder 2 damaged; the possibility of their being repaired was then not determinable.

(6) 6 shaft-bearing covers were broken.

(7) The boilers were in order with the exception of Starboard 1 and 2, which had only minor defects.

The German Naval War Staff considered it possible that the *Tirpitz* might never regain operational efficiency; it was at least certain, however, that she would be out of action for several months, and April, 1944, was reckoned as the earliest date for her to be again fit for service.

Endnotes

1. Admiral, submarines, Final report on Operation 'Source', 26/7/45.
2. Successful attacks had been carried out by the Italians with somewhat similar craft on the *Queen Elizabeth* and *Valiant* at Alexandria, 19 December, 1941, and a Japanese version of the craft had taken part in the attack on Pearl Harbour on day 7 of that month. A Japanese midget torpedoed the *Ramillies* at Diego Suarez, 30 May 1942, and another attacked shipping in Sydney Harbour on 1 June, 1942.
3. Brief details of the craft were as follows:–

Length	51 ft.
Beam	8 ½ ft.
Overall height	10 ft.
Surface draught	7 ½ ft.
Weight	35 tons
Diving depth	300 ft.
Maximum surface speed on main engines	6 ½ knots
Range (limited by human endurance)	1500 miles at 4 knots
Maximum submerged speed on main motors	5 knots
Submerged endurance (without recharging batteries)	80 miles at 2 knots
Human endurance	10-14 days

   Armament – Two detachable saddle charges, each containing 2 tons of Amatex, dropped on the bottom under the target, and fired by clock time fuses

   Crew – Operational – 3 officers (including 1 qualified diver), 1 E.R.A.

   Passage – 1 officer, 1 able seaman (L.T.O.), 1 stoker.
4. Rear-Admiral C. B. Barry, D.S.O.
5. Rear-Admiral Barry subsequently remarked:– "By his leadership and ability Commander D. C. Ingram, D.S.C., R.N., as officer in charge of training, inspired all officers and ratings alike and achieved that high standard of training and fitness which was so essential. He was responsible that the crews were at the peak of their efficiency at the time the operation began."
6. This unit was sent in the destroyers *Musketeer* and *Mahratta* and arrived in Kola Inlet 31 August.
7. Owing to bad weather the Mosquito aircraft was not able to carry out its part of the plan. Three Spitfires arrived at Vaenga on 3 September. Rear-Admiral Barry remarks, "The subsequent reconnaissances flown by this unit were invaluable. Full details of the dispositions of the enemy units and net defences were signalled from Russia, and given to all the personnel taking part before they left harbour. The first photographs taken by this unit did not arrive until a few hours after the X craft had sailed; but this did not in fact matter, as the relevant information was complete in the signalled report."
8. On 3 September Soviet reconnaissance had located the *Tirpitz*, *Scharnhorst* and *Lutzow* in the Alten area, but on 7 September the first Spitfire sortie showed only the *Lutzow* present, and the *Tirpitz* and *Scharnhorst* were later reported off Ice Fjord, Spitzbergen. However, visual reconnaissance at 1000 A, 10 September, confirmed the return of the two ships to Alten Fjord, and later the Senior British Naval Officer, North Russia, signalled their exact positions in berths in Kaa Fjord.
9. G.M.T. is used throughout except where otherwise stated.

10. *Truculent*   Lieut. R. L. Alexander, D.S.O., R.N.
    X6   Lieut. D. Cameron, R.N.R.(O);
                Lieut. A. Wilson, R.N.V.R.(P).
    Syrtis   Lieut. M. H. Jupp, D.C.S., R.N.
    X9   Lieut. T. L. Martin, R.N.(O);
                Sub-Lt. E. Kearon, R.N.V.R.(P).
    Thrasher Lieut. A. R. Hezlet, D.S.C., R.N.
    X5   Lieut. H. Henty-Creer, R.N.V.R.(O);
                Lieut. J. V. Terry-Lloyd, S.A.N.F.(P).
    Seanymph Lieut. J. P. H. Oakley, D.S.C., R.N.
    X8   Lieut. B. M. McFarlane, R.A.N.(O);
                Lieut. J. Smart, R.N.V.R.(P)
    Stubborn Lieut. A. A. Duff, R.N.
    X7   Lieut. B. C. G. Place, D.S.C., R.N.(O);
                Lieut. P. H. Philip, S.A.N.F.(P).
    Sceptre   Lieut. I. S. McIntosh, M.B.E., D.S.C., R.N.
    X10   Lieut. K. R. Hudspeth, R.A.N.V.R.(O);
                Sub-Lt. E. V. Page, R.N.V.R. (P).
    (O) = Operations; (P) = Passage Commanding Officer.
    For list of X craft crews see Appendix A.

11. The average speed made good over this period was approximately:– "T" class submarines, 10 knots; "S" class, 8 ½ knots.

12. See Plan 4.
    Tirpitz, battleship, 45,000 tons; 8 15-in., 12 5.9-in., 16 4.1-in. HA/LA. guns.
    Scharnhorst, battlecruiser, 32,000 tons; 9 11-in., 12 5.9-in. HA/LA., 14 4.1-in. HA. guns.
    Lutzow, pocket battleship, 10,000 tons; 6 11-in., 8 5.9-in., 6 4.1-in. HA. guns.

13. As all signals between Rear-Admiral, Submarines, and the submarines taking part in the operation were made in individual one-time pads, this signal could not be deciphered by anyone except Rear-Admiral, Submarines.

14. From log readings and revolutions taken by the *Seanymph*.

15. Rear-Admiral, Submarines, subsequently remarked:– "It is not clear why the second explosion caused such damage at an apparent range of 3½ miles while the first explosion only 1,000 yards away did none. Both charges had been dropped in approximately the same depth of water (180 fathoms). It may be that only partial detonation occurred in the first charge, which had been set to "safe". Whatever the reason, the force of the second explosion would appear to have illustrated the efficiency of the charges. I find it hard to believe that the explosion was in fact 3½ miles away; but whatever the horizontal range was, there is no doubt about the depth of water, so that in any event the result of the explosion was indeed remarkable."

16. HMS *Seanymph*. Report of Sixth War Patrol.

17. In anticipation of the possibility of just such a situation, the Rear-Admiral, Submarines, had signalled to the *Seanymph* and *Stubborn* on 16 September:– "Should at any time you consider it necessary to sink X8 in order not to prejudice the operation, this step would have my full approval. 162208A." Rear-Admiral Barry subsequently remarked:– "I consider that the Commanding Officer of X8 acted correctly in releasing the side charges when it became apparent that they were flooded, and that the Commanding Officer, HMS *Seanymph's* decision to sink X8 to avoid compromising the operation, was the correct one."

18. This signal was never received by the Rear-Admiral, and it was not until the evening of 2 October that it was known that X9 had broken adrift and consequently had not taken part in the attack.

19. The loss of X8 would leave the *Lutzow* unattacked, but the Rear-Admiral decided to

accept this and not to alter the targets for the other X craft.

20. Admiral, Submarines: Report on Operation 'Source'.

21. This may have been the same U-Boat sighted by the *Syrtis* in the evening of the previous day. Rear-Admiral Barry subsequently remarked:– "It reflects credit on the look-out kept by our submarines that with six of them in the vicinity, and four of them with X craft in tow, none were sighted. A single sighting might have compromised the operation.... "

22. Commenting on the passage. Rear-Admiral Barry remarked:– "That four out of the six X craft which set forth... should have made these passages, varying between 1,000 and 1,500 miles, in tow of submarines, without major incident, to be slipped from their exact positions at the time ordered ten days later, was more than I had ever anticipated... I consider this passage a fine example of seamanship and determination by all concerned."

23. For the operations of X10. see Sec. 7.

24. Admiral, Submarines. Final Report on Operation 'Source', 26 June, 1945.

25. See Appendix B.

26. A note in the *Tirpitz'* log states that times between 0705 and 0730 are not accurate.

27. His Majesty the King approved the award of the Victoria Cross to Lieutenant Cameron, the D.S.O. to Sub-Lieutenants Lorimer and Kendall, and the C.G.M. to Engine Room Artificer Goddard for this gallant attack.

28. Log of the *Tirpitz*.

29. Fortunately unseen by the enemy. Their attention was probably concentrated on the opposite direction, as X6 would have just been recognised as a submarine on the port beam of the *Tirpitz* at this time.

30. Lieutenant Place's report.

31. X7 was salved, minus her bows, by 1 October, 1943. There is nothing to substantiate a statement made to Lieutenant Place by German interrogators that the bodies of the two missing members of his crew had been recovered and buried with full military honours.

32. His Majesty the King approved the award of the Victoria Cross to Lieutenant Place and the D.S.O. to Sub-Lieutenant Aitken for this gallant attack.

33. See C.B. 04051(98).

34. X6.

35. The violence of the explosion seems to have made a great impression. Men who were onboard the *Tirpitz* at the time who had previously served in the *Scharnhorst* are reported to have said:– "We've had torpedo hits, we've had bomb hits. We hit two mines in the Channel, but there's never been an explosion like that."

36. The *Tirpitz*'s log records at 0812 "two heavy consecutive detonations to port at 1/10 sec. interval... Ship vibrates strongly in vertical direction and sways slightly between the anchors. It is not clear how many of the charges laid off the port bow actually went off; but subsequent examination of the seabed failed to discover any of the charges or even splinters. It seems likely, therefore, that all four charges detonated completely and that only the decision to move the bows of the ship bodily to starboard on her cable saved her from far worse damage and even, perhaps, from destruction. This action took her away from X6 's charges and also from X7's first charge, though at the time the Germans were unaware that a second attack had taken place. She brought up, however, with X7's second charge under the engine room, to which must be ascribed most of the damage.

37. For damage to the *Tirtpitz*, see Appendix C.

38. The Rear-Admiral, Submarines, remarked that it was clear from the position in which X5 was found that Lieutenant Henty-Creer and his crew showed courage of the highest order in penetrating the fleet anchorage and that they lived up to the highest traditions of the Service.

39. According to survivors from the *Scharnhorst* three months later it appears that she had left her anchorage on the afternoon of 21 September to carry out gunnery exercises in Alten Fjord and was returning to Kaa Fjord on the morning of 22 September, when she received

a signal stating that the *Tirpitz* had been torpedoed. She put about and proceeded to Lang Fjord, so it seems that in any case X10 would not have found her quarry.

40. Sunrise, 0405 G.M.T.; nautical twilight (sun 12° below the horizon) commenced 0145/22 September.

41. These may have been for the purpose of illuminating the net across the entrance.

42. This decision was fully endorsed by Rear-Admiral Barry, who remarked:– "I consider Lieutenant Hudspeth's decision to abandon the attack was in every way correct. To have made the attempt without a compass and with a periscope which could not be operated and must remain in the fully raised position would have made any chance of success remote indeed. With the attack already compromised it would have been doomed to failure from the outset and would merely have been an unnecessary loss of valuable lives."

43. F.O. Submarines 1205 A (1105 G.M.T.) of 21 September to *Seanymph*. This signal was made in a general "Out" pad and could thus be read by all submarines taking part. At 1401 all submarines were informed of the sinking of X8.

44. The Senior British Naval Officer, North Russia, had been requested to fly a reconnaissance over the area in the afternoon of 22 September, and it was possible that this reconnaissance might show signs of a move of main units. As things turned out the reconnaissance failed.

45. F.O. Submarines 1541 A (1441 G.M.T.) of 22 September.

46. F.O. Submarines 1139 A (1039 G.M.T.) of 22 September.

47. F.O. Submarines 1255 A (1155 G.M.T.) on 22 September.

48. The *Stubborn* also experienced an easterly set. At 0831/22 September, she found herself inside the declared mine area, having been set 13 miles, 117° in 24 hours. She succeeded in regaining safer waters without mishap.

49. These dispositions were ordered by the following signals from the Flag Officer, Submarines, to submarines taking part in Operation 'Source' timed 1444 A (1344 G.M.T.) 23 September, and 1802 A (1702 G.M.T.), 25 September respectively:– 1) "For recovery of X craft. *Thrasher* cover Sectors FAA and FBB. *Truculent* cover Sector FDD and FEE west of 22° E. *Syrtis* cover Sector FEE east of 22° E. and Sector FFF." During this period the *Stubborn* remained in Sector FCC. (2) "If no repetition no contact has been made with X craft by daylight 27 September submarines assume patrol as follows:– Syrtis Sector FFF. Truculent Sector FEE, Stubborn Sector FDD. These submarines then act as in paragraph 16, Operation 'Funnel'."

50. The fact that no enemy anti-submarine or air activity was encountered indicates that the Germans were unaware of how the X craft had been transported or how they had made their passage. An air raid was carried out on Polyarnoe (Kola Inlet), apparently directed at the submarine base, on 24 September, and it seems possible that the enemy thought the X craft were operated from there.

51. Rear-Admiral, Submarines, remarked:–"The recovery of the sole survivor must be regarded as a fine piece of seamanship on the part of the Commanding Officer, HMS *Stubborn*. The Commanding Officers of *Truculent* and *Syrtis* also made close approaches to an unknown coast in darkness and in bad weather to try and locate any missing X craft. They withdrew their submarines safely to seaward in accordance with their orders when they had satisfied themselves that a proper search had been carried out."

52. The same routes as those laid down for the outward passage were followed in the reverse direction. (See Plan 1.)

53. The *Stubborn*, 1930 A (1830 G.M.T.) of 30 September to F.O., Submarines:– "My position 70° 34' N., 13° 48' E., with X10 in tow. Last tow in use and speed therefore greatly reduced in anything except calm weather. X10 reports defects prevented attack and [charges] jettisoned in Alten Fjord. X10 heard 11 heavy explosions between 0830 and 0840 22 September." The word in square brackets was received corruptly and repeated later.

54. This information was passed to the other submarines without delay. The *Truculent* states that its receipt was "most encouraging". Till then, all they knew of the attack was a signal

from F.O., Submarines on 26 September stating that it was apparent from German broadcast that submarines had attacked main units.

55. F.O., Submarines, 1518 A (1418 G.M.T.) of 1 October to Submarines. The Rear-Admiral subsequently remarked that if he had known that the *Truculent* had onboard a complete towing outfit, steps would have been taken to transfer X10 to her.

56. F.O., Submarines, 1904 A (1804 G.M.T.) of 1 October to *Syrtis, Stubborn, Truculent*.
"...In order to keep clear of own surface forces, *Syrtis* proceed by Route Black, *Truculent* by Route Grey.
All submarines addressed must be south of 66° N. and south-east of a line 230° from 66° 01' N., 4° 20' E. by 1900 A/3.
If unable to comply remain north of 68° 20' N. until 1900/4.
Stubborn report position, course and speed at 0400 A/2."

57. Admiral Sir Bruce Fraser, K.C.B., K.B.E.

58. F.O., Submarines, 1108 A (1008 G.M.T.) of 2 October to *Syrtis, Stubborn, Truculent*.
"...*Stubborn* is to continue at best speed via Route Pink for Lerwick disregarding instructions in paragraphs 2 and 3 of my 011904. *Stubborn* report position, course and speed at 0400, 3 October, and 2000, 3 October. *Truculent* comply with paragraph 2 of my 011904. *Syrtis* comply with paragraph 2 of my 011904 if possible, otherwise paragraph 3, and report position, course, speed and intention forthwith."

59. F. O., Submarines, 1802 A (1702 G.M.T.) to *Stubborn*. "Weather as you proceed south-west expected to deteriorate considerably reaching gale force 8 from SW. If weather now permits, you should embark passage crew and at your discretion scuttle X10."

60. Lieutenant Duff subsequently reported:– "I considered towing X10 on the surface with no crew onboard but in view of (a) the gale warning, (b) the continuing stern swell, (c) the possibility of losing sight of her and not being able to scuttle her if the tow parted, I decided to sink her."

61. Rear-Admiral Barry highly commended Lieutenant Duff for the determination and fine seamanship he displayed both on the outward passage with X7 and in the recovery of X10, and his later efforts to bring her safely to port.

62. See pages 91-92.

63. Lost by enemy action.

64. Lost on passage.

65. Taken prisoner.

66. It is significant that on the night if the attack, 21-22 September, this gap was left open owing to a breakdown in the telephonic communication between the battleship and Bossekop, which necessitated the continual passage to and fro of small craft. Accordingly, the guard-boat was put on watch and the *Tirpitz*'s hydrophones were manned until 0600, 22 September.

67. "Ohne Stabilisierung"

68. "unklar."

PART III

B.R. 1736

C.B. 3081 (20)

BATTLE SUMMARY No. 27

NAVAL AIRCRAFT ATTACK ON THE TIRPITZ (OPERATION 'Tungsten') 3 April, 1944

T.S.D. 759/44

TACTICAL, TORPEDO AND STAFF DUTIES DIVISION
(HISTORICAL SECTION),
NAVAL STAFF, ADMIRALTY, S.W.1.

CONTENTS

Introduction

Monday, 3 April, 1944, was a red letter day for the Naval Air Arm. On that day powerful forces of Bombers and Fighters attacked the German battleship *Admiral von Tirpitz*[1] in her strongly defended anchorage at Kaa Fjord, Norway, mauled her severely and returned to their carriers, having lost but three of their number.

The *Tirpitz* had been damaged by midget submarines the previous September (1943), and since then had not moved from Kaa Fjord, but it was believed that temporary repairs had been effected by March, and though she was probably not 100 per cent fit for operations, she constituted a potential threat to the North Russian convoys. It was therefore "highly desirable to put her out of action again,"[2] and plans were put in hand for an attack by carrier borne aircraft.

Her berth was known to be strongly defended by nets, A/A guns, flak ships and smoke generating apparatus. In addition, five *Narvik*[3] class destroyers were stationed at Alten Fjord (see Plan 2), and a considerable number of submarines – normally employed against the North Russian convoys – were maintained at Narvik, Hammerfest and other northern ports. The air forces based in the immediate neighbourhood were small, but they could be rapidly reinforced in an emergency (see Appendix F). Three routine reconnaissance flights – in the Faeroes, Spitzbergen and Jan Mayen areas – were flown almost daily.

Plans and Preparations
(Plans 1 and 2)

The planning, preparation and execution of the project, which was known as Operation 'Tungsten', was entrusted by the Commander-in-Chief, Home Fleet,[4] to his second-in-command, Vice-Admiral Sir Henry Moore,[5] Captain L. D. Mackintosh,[6] an officer of great experience in Naval air matters, being specially appointed as his Chief of Staff. The following ships[7] were detailed to take part:–

One battleship (*Anson* (Flag, Vice-Admiral Moore)).
Two Fleet carriers (*Victorious*, *Furious*).
Four escort carriers (*Emperor*, *Searcher*, *Pursuer*, *Fencer*).
Four cruisers (*Royalist* (Flag, Rear-Admiral, Escort Carriers[8]), *Jamaica*, *Belfast*, *Sheffield*).
Two Fleet oilers (*Brown Ranger*, *Blue Ranger*).
Fourteen destroyers.

It was originally intended to carry out the operation between 7 and 16 March, but the *Victorious* was delayed in dockyard hands and it had to be postponed for about a fortnight. Even this left very little time for training, especially in the case of the *Victorious*, some of whose squadrons were newly formed.[9]

Vice-Admiral Moore's plan had to cover two distinct phases – the assembly of the surface forces at the flying off position and the details of the air attack. It was framed so as to be readily adaptable to an alternative locality, in case the *Tirpitz* should shift berth, and was sufficiently flexible to permit easily of postponement in event of bad weather. In order to minimise the risk from enemy submarines and also to give the surface forces a good chance of making their approach undetected, it was decided to synchronise the operation with the passage of an outward bound North Russian convoy, which was certain to draw the submarines to the eastward of Bear Island. Convoy J.W.58 was due to leave Loch Ewe for Kola Inlet on 27 March; this was accordingly chosen as "D-Day", and provisional arrangements were made to carry out the air attack on D + 8 Day, 4 April, by which time the convoy would be in the Barents Sea.

Part of the 'Tungsten' force was to be included in the battleship covering force, and for the 1,200 mile passage to Northern Norwegian waters the following organisation was laid down:–

> Force 1, consisting of the *Duke of York* (Flag, Commander-in-Chief), *Anson* (Flag, Vice-Admiral Moore), *Victorious*, *Belfast* and six destroyers, covering convoy J.W.58.

> Force 2, the remainder of the 'Tungsten' force, under Rear-Admiral Bisset, was to meet Force 1 in position "OO", lat. 72° 30' N., long. 13° 00' E. (some 250 miles to the north-westward of Kaa Fjord), at 1800, 3 April, when the Commander-in-Chief intended to part company, leaving the Vice-Admiral to conduct the operation against the *Tirpitz*.

The air attack was to be made by two bombing forces of 21 Barracudas each launched from the Fleet carriers, supported by Wildcats and Hellcats from the *Pursuer*, *Searcher* and *Emperor* Corsairs from the *Victorious*. The first strike was to be carried out by No. 8 (*Furious*) Wing; the second, which was to leave the carriers an hour later, by No. 52 (*Victorious*) Wing.[10] Nine bombers were to be flown off from the *Furious* and 12 from the *Victorious* in each strike.

It was decided to use four different types of bombs, the effect of which would be complementary,[11] and each bombing force was to be armed as follows:–

(a) Eleven aircraft with three 500 lb. S.A.P. each.
(b) Five aircraft with one 1,600 lb. A.P. each.
(c) Five aircraft with three 500 lb. M.C. or 600 lb. A/S each.[12]

As a result of training practices, it was found that bombing errors in range were more than double those in line under conditions of light wind. For this reason the direction of the attack was to be along the length of the target, the bombs being released in a tight stick to give a maximum probability of hitting with at least two bombs in each successful attack. Fighter protection for the Fleet during the attack was to be provided by Seafires from the *Furious* and Wildcats from the *Fencer*.[13] Zero time was fixed for 0415 on whatever day the operation might take place, when the carriers would be approximately 120 miles to the northward of Kaa Fjord (position "PP", lat. 71° 30' N., long. 19° 00' E.).

During the weeks preceding the attack, training was carried out energetically. A full scale bombing and air firing range, representing realistically the *Tirpitz* in Kaa Fjord, and including smoke defence and dummy A/A batteries, was constructed at Loch Eriboll. Ordnance and special target maps of an exactly similar type to those provided for the actual operation were supplied to all air crews; and in spite of unfavourable weather, a large number of practices were carried out by both T.B.R.s and Fighters, which in the event "proved to be of inestimable value".[14] A full dress rehearsal of the whole operation was staged off Scapa, testing the forming up and flying procedure with Loch Eriboll as the target, on 28 March, and two days later the forces left Scapa to carry out the operation.

Passage From Scapa
(Plan 1)

The Commander-in-Chief, Home Fleet, sailed from Scapa with Force 1 (*Duke of York*, *Anson*, *Victorious*, *Belfast*, screened by the destroyers *Onslaught*, *Javelin*, *Piorun*, *Sioux* and *Algonquin*) in the forenoon of 30 March. A full calibre concentration shoot by the battleships and live bombing by the *Victorious* was carried out at Stack Skerry, and course was then shaped to the N.N.W. for position "C" – east of the Faeroes – where the screening destroyers were detached to Skaale Fjord (Faeroes) with orders to fuel and then join Force 2, being relieved by the *Milne*, *Meteor*, *Matchless*, *Marne*, *Ursa* and *Undaunted*, which had fuelled there the day before. Force 1 then steered to the north-eastward to provide cover for convoy J.W.58. By the morning of 1 April it was clear that the convoy, though shadowed intermittently by hostile aircraft, was making satisfactory progress, and had indeed inflicted casualties on both aircraft and U-boats, without itself suffering any damage. No other enemy air reconnaissance, apart from routine meteorological flights,[15] was taking place. This apparent lack of interest in any possible covering force suggested that a sortie by the *Tirpitz* was unlikely. The weather was unusually favourable for air operations, so, following Nelson's maxim never to trifle with a fair wind, the Commander-in-Chief decided to cease covering the convoy and to advance the date of operation 'Tungsten' by 24 hours. This decision he signalled to all concerned at 1121,[16] 1 April, at the same time altering the rendezvous with Force 2 to a position 75 miles 195° from the previous one, in order to give Rear-Admiral Bisset time to reach it by 1900 the next day (2 April).[17]

Force 2 (*Royalist*, *Searcher*, *Emperor*, *Pursuer*, *Fencer*, *Furious*, *Sheffield*, *Jamaica*, with the Fleet oilers *Blue Ranger* and *Brown Ranger*, screened by *Virago*, *Verulam*, *Vigilant*, *Swift* and *Wakeful*) meanwhile had sailed from Scapa at 1900, 30 March, and shaped course to the westward of the Orkneys to pass through positions "C" (off the Faeroes), where it was joined by the *Onslaught*, *Piorun*, *Javelin*, *Sioux* and *Algonquin* from Skaal Fjord, and "D". There was a fresh northerly wind, and the oilers experienced some difficulty in keeping up, being unable to maintain their reputed speed of 13 knots.

At 1435, 1 April, Rear-Admiral Bisset received the Commander-in-Chief's signal advancing the date of operation 'Tungsten'. This necessitated proceeding at once at the Force's maximum speed – 17 knots – the two oilers, with the *Piorun* and *Javelin* as escort, being detached to make for position "QQ", some 300 miles to the north-westward of Alten Fjord, where they were to stand by to fuel destroyers in case of need.

The next day (2 April) there was a slight contretemps which might have had most serious consequences. At 0650 the *Pursuer* had to reduce speed on account of a breakdown of her steering gear. Shortly afterwards the Force was turned by blue pendant to close her, as the visibility was not very good at the time and Rear-Admiral Bisset did not wish to get separated too far. "Then occurred an incident which... showed most clearly the limitations of the Fleet Wave Short Range (210 kc/s) for manoeuvring. The visibility suddenly shut down to nothing in a blinding snowstorm; *Pursuer* and Force 2 were approaching each other on opposite courses, and the signal for Force 2 to turn to the original course could not be got through even to all ships of the original body, quite apart from the screen. Luckily the visibility cleared just in time to avoid a serious incident, and the *Pursuer* joined at 0725."[18]

The junction between Forces 1 and 2 was effected without difficulty in the afternoon, 2 April, and at 1620 the Commander-in-Chief in the *Duke of York*, with the *Matchless* and *Marne*, parted company and proceeded to the north-westward,[19] while Vice-Admiral Moore with the 'Tungsten' forces[20] steered direct for the flying off position ("PP"), which it was intended to reach at 0415[21] the following morning.

"By 0300 on 3 April it appeared that everything was in our favour. So far as we knew we had not been sighted, and flying conditions were perfect for putting the operation into effect. There was a light off-shore wind, and visibility was in fact so good that while landing on the strikes later we sighted the Norwegian coast at a distance of about 50 miles." [22]

Opposite, Plan 1

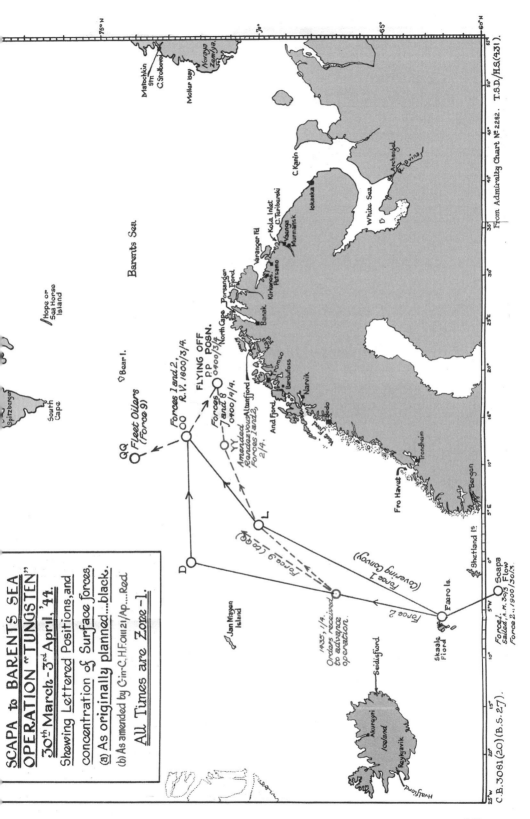

SCAPA to BARENTS SEA
OPERATION "TUNGSTEN"
30th March - 3rd April, '44.
Showing Lettered Positions, and
concentration of Surface forces,
(a) As originally planned....black.
(b) As amended by C-in-C, H.F. on 12/Ap....Red.
All Times are Zone -1.

C.B. 3081(20)(B.S.27).

From Admiralty Chart No 2282. T.S.D./H.S.(431).

141

Departure of First Strike
(Plans 1 and 2)

Meanwhile, in the carriers, final preparations had been in progress since the previous evening.

In the *Victorious* the flying programme was complicated throughout by the fact that she was carrying more aircraft than she had been designed to operate, and this difficulty was enhanced by the necessity of handling two types of aircraft and four types of bombs. All aircraft were fuelled and serviceable by 1700, 2 April, and the Corsair long range tanks fitted, but these were not filled till 0100, 3 April. Bombing up was carried out at 1800.

Anxiety had been felt as to the effect of North Sea winter conditions on the aircraft necessarily parked on deck.[23] These were all allocated to the second strike, and after running their engines at 0200, were struck down to the comparatively warm hangar, while the first strike was ranged on deck.

At 0130, "that ghastly hour when man's stamina is at its lowest,"[24] the air crews were called for last minute briefing. By 0405, 3 April, all aircraft were ready, and their engines were started up; there was not a single failure in any of the carriers – a fine tribute to the work of the maintenance personnel and aircraft handling parties. The air crews were in fine fettle. "Knowing that they were about to attempt an opposed attack of a character which hitherto had not been attempted in the European theatre, they left the carriers' decks in the greatest of heart and brimful of determination, and proceeded through the complicated business of forming up and taking departure to the target exactly as if a parade ground movement. That in fact they met no German Air Force opposition subtracts not one iota from the credit that is due to them."[25]

Zero hour for flying off was 0415, and at 0416 the first of the ten escorting Corsairs took off from the *Victorious*, followed 8 minutes later by the twenty-one Barracudas from her and the *Furious*. The remainder of the Fighter Escort flew off from the escort carriers between 0423 and 0426,[26] and by 0437 "had made a perfect form up with the Barracuda Wing, and at that time took departure[27] for the target on a course of approximately 120°."[28]

Weather conditions were ideal – a good steady breeze of 12 to 14 knots from the southward, maximum visibility with very little cloud in the direction of the coast and no swell.

"It was a grand sight with the sun just risen to see this well balanced striking force of about 20 Barracudas and 45 Fighters departing at very low level between the two forces of surface ships, and good to know that a similar sized force would be leaving again in about an hour's time."[29]

The whole strike was under the command of Lieut.-Commander R. Baker-Faulkner, of the *Furious*, the Senior Officer of the Bombers, under whom Lieut.-Commander F. R. A. Turnbull, of the *Victorious*, commanded the Corsairs, and Lieut.-Commander J. W. Sleigh, D.S.C., of Rear-Admiral Bisset's staff, the Hellcats and Wildcats.

For twenty minutes they flew low over the water, commencing to climb to 10,000 ft. at 0457, when some 25 miles from the Norwegian coast. Two minutes later Loppen Island was identified fine on the port bow, and the coast was crossed at 0508. Passing close west of the head of Lang Fjord[30] they proceeded to the eastward down the snow covered valley towards the head of Kaa Fjord, finally swooping on their unsuspecting quarry from the south-west.

First Strike
(Plan 2)

The attack was carried out almost exactly as planned, and it was soon clear that the enemy had been caught napping. A destroyer and a large merchant vessel in Lang Fjord showed no sign of life, though the Hellcat squadron passed directly overhead. No hostile aircraft were seen, nor was there any interference from flak till the strike was within 3 miles of the target area.

At about 0528 the Force was deployed and began its initial dive from 8,000 ft.; at the same time high angle batteries at the head of the fjord and elsewhere opened a heavy but inaccurate fire, and the *Tirpitz* was sighted in the expected position. Diving to keep hill cover, Lieut.-Commander Baker-Faulkner sent all Hellcats and Wildcats down to "strafe" guns and target, which they did most effectively and "undoubtedly spoilt the *Tirpitz* gunnery,"[31] while the Corsairs patrolled over the whole area at about 10,000 ft. A smoke screen was started all round the fjord as soon as the aircraft were sighted, but it was too late, and a minute afterwards (0529) the bombers dived to the attack, releasing their bombs from heights of between 3,000 and 1,200 ft. Hits were scored immediately, causing heavy explosions and flames, and it was evident that the *Tirpitz* was severely damaged. Exactly 60 seconds after the first bomb had fallen, the attack was over, and the aircraft, leaving the enemy on fire in several places, headed to the north-west for Silden Island, whence they took their departure for the carriers. On the way out the fighters engaged a flak ship, a destroyer and two armed trawlers, leaving the latter on fire. No difficulty was experienced on the return passage to the Fleet, which was sighted at a distance of 40 miles. Only one Barracuda was missing;[32] the remainder, to quote from the *Victorious* report, "returned in flight formation with an unanimous broad grin," landing on between 0619 and 0642. One Hellcat whose hook had been damaged by the enemy landed in the water and was lost, the pilot being picked up by the *Algonquin*.

Second Strike
(Plan 2)

Meanwhile, at 0525 – just as the first strike was attacking – the second strike had commenced flying off the carriers. One Barracuda failed to start, and another, after an apparently successful take off from the *Victorious*, crashed into the sea, all the crew being lost.[33] The remaining 19 with their escort of 45 fighters formed up at between 50 and 200 ft. and took their departure at 0537. The strike was commanded by Lieut.-Commander V. Rance of the *Victorious*, and Lieut.-Commander M. F. Fell of the *Searcher* was senior officer of the close escort.

After crossing the coast the initial approach was made at 10,000 ft. for about 12 miles; this was slowly reduced, and the final attack was commenced from 7,500 to 7,000 ft. A large brown smoke screen, visible 40 miles away, had been laid from generators all round the target area and from the *Tirpitz* herself; "it did not interfere with bombing, but must have hampered close range weapons considerably."[34] Again no enemy aircraft was encountered and the Hellcats went down to attack the heavy gun positions as soon as they opened fire, the Wildcats attacking the *Tirpitz's* exposed personnel just prior to the main attack. She appeared to be on an even keel, and of normal trim and draught, despite the efforts of the first strike; but she had swung across the fjord with her stern nearly aground, and was thought to be drifting. The bombers' final dive was carried out in quick succession, the port column attacking first at 0636; bombs were released at heights of 3,000 ft. or a little less.

There was considerable close range flak, mostly in the form of a box barrage, round the target. One Barracuda was hit,[35] but is believed to have carried out its attack. By the time the last aircraft dived the *Tirpitz* had ceased firing and was burning fiercely amidships. As in the first strike, the attack had lasted just a minute.

The strike withdrew towards Silden Island, the fighters as before engaging targets as they presented themselves, amongst others a 5,000-ton merchant ship – which was left smoking – in Lange Fjord, one of about 3,000 tons in Ox Fjord, and a wireless or direction-finding station.

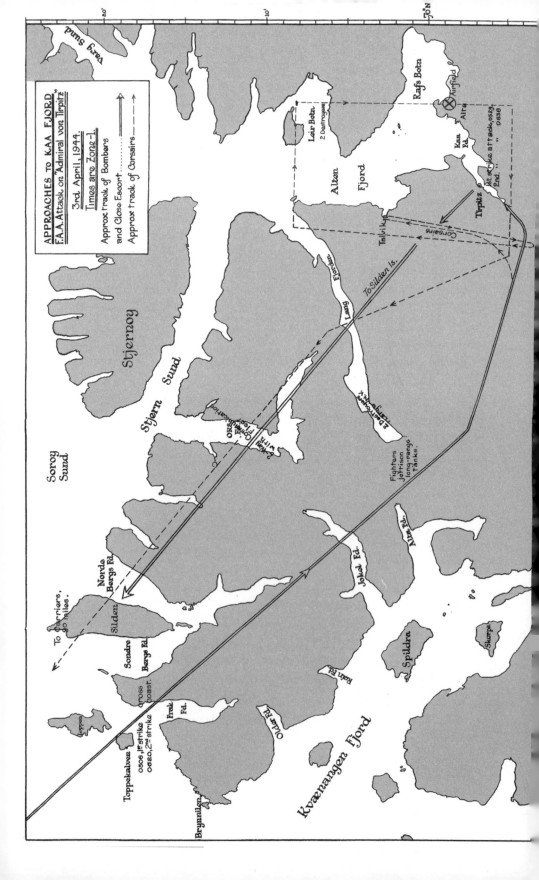

APPROACHES TO KAA FJORD
F.A.A. Attack on "Admiral von Tirpitz"

3rd April, 1944.
Times are Zone-1.

Approx track of Bombers
and Close Escort...........
Approx track of Corsairs ----

Prins Sund

Stjernøy

Soroy Sund

Stjern Sund

Lar Botn
2 Destroyers

Rafs Botn

Airfield

Alten Fjord

Alta

Kaa Fd.

Tirpitz

1st strike attack, 0529
2nd. " " 0556

Corsairs

Talvik

Lang Fiorden

To Silden Is.

2 Destroyers Langnes

To Carriers,
90 miles.

Norde
Bergs Fd.

Silden.

Sondre
Bergs Fd.

2 ships with Fleet
Communication

Fighters
Jettison
long-range
Tanks.

Jøkel Fd.

Alta Fd.

Spildra

Skorpa

Frak
Fd.

across
coast.

Olaz Fd.

Ban Fd.

Toppekalvez
0506, 1st strike
0520, 2nd strike

Bryuniken.

Kvaenangen Fjord

Visibility was still extreme, and the Fleet was found without difficulty; two destroyers which had been sent inshore for air-sea rescue (though fortunately not required for this purpose), were useful as signposts, keeping their forward guns pointed in the direction of the Fleet. By 0758 all aircraft had landed safely on the carriers.[36]

Opposite, Plan 2

Return to Scapa

During the absence of the Air Striking Forces the Fleet had remained in the vicinity of position "PP", fighter protection and anti-submarine patrols being maintained by aircraft from the *Fencer* and *Furious*.[37] After the second strike had landed on, course was shaped to the west-north-westward, while in the *Victorious* reports of the air crews were collected and analysed, photographs of the attack developed and examined, and a preliminary estimate of hits and damage got out. This was signalled to the Vice-Admiral at 1737, 3 April.[38]

Seventeen direct hits, three of them by 1,600 lb. bombs, were judged to have been scored, and the *Tirpitz* was considered to be out of action.

Vice-Admiral Moore had intended to repeat the attack the next morning (4 April), and during the afternoon the re-fuelling of destroyers by the Fleet was started as an urgent evolution, the consequent reduction in anti-submarine protection being accepted.[39] Later, after receiving reports of the serious damage already inflicted on the *Tirpitz*, and also of the "fatigue of the air crews and their natural reaction after completing a dangerous operation successfully,"[40] he decided to cancel further operations, and directed all forces, including the Fleet oilers (Force 9), to return to Base.

Forces 7 and 8 shaped course accordingly at 2100, 3 April, the *Searcher*, which had developed a defect limiting her speed to 12 knots, being ordered to follow under the escort of the *Jamaica*, *Sioux* and *Virago*. The passage was uneventful, and at 1630,[41] 6 April, Forces 7 and 8 entered Scapa Flow, where they were given a rousing reception by the Commander-in-Chief and the ships of the Home Fleet in harbour. The *Searcher*, closely followed by the Fleet oilers, with their respective escorts,[42] arrived safely some ten hours later.

Lessons and Comments

Commenting on the Air side of the operation, Vice-Admiral Moore emphasized the value of the preliminary practices at Loch Eriboll; "the importance of this training cannot be overstressed". He attributed much of the success of the attack to the ideal weather conditions and to the achievement of surprise; and considered it "clear that the 'strafing' by fighters 'softened up' the defence, and later the instantaneously fused bombs reduced it to a negligible quantity." The large number of maps, charts, photographs and scale models which gave the air crews a clear picture of what to expect was a contributory factor to the success.[43]

The air communications worked satisfactorily throughout, but – in spite of strict orders to the contrary – R/T silence was broken by several aircraft before they reached the coast. This might well have prejudiced the success of the whole operation.

With regard to the surface ships, no difficulty was experienced in manoeuvring the two carrier forces, in spite of the inequality of their speeds.[44] Both forces kept in visual signalling touch, both during the flying operations and on passage; if the enemy had attacked by air at any time it would have been possible to provide fighter protection for the whole Fleet with one force of fighters.

Probably the most important point – in its wider application – raised by the operation was the question of the type of ship from which the Senior Flag Officer could most advantageously direct it. During the planning stages, Vice-Admiral Moore had considered shifting his flag to the *Victorious*, but owing to her late arrival and limited accommodation, he decided to remain in the *Anson*. "On the limited experience of this one operation," he subsequently wrote, "I am of the opinion that the Senior Officer of a large force of this nature should not be in a carrier, but that either a junior Flag Officer or the Senior Carrier Captain should be responsible to him for matters concerning flying, thus avoiding overloading the Senior Flag Officer with the more technical side of the operation."

The Commander-in-Chief commented on this point that much would depend on the nature of the operation, and remarked "For a planned operation the Admiral has the advantage in the battleship, since her signalling arrangements are better for manoeuvring the force and the carriers' attention can be devoted to air matters. For operations which are uncertain and where frequent changes of plan may be necessary, the advantage may be with the carrier."[45]

Further experience will no doubt determine the question, but it is perhaps worth noting that on this occasion a considerable amount of signalling was necessary in order to put Vice-Admiral Moore *au fait* with the results of the attack and the air situation, on which depended his decision whether or not to attack next day. This decision could possibly have been reached earlier had he been in direct personal touch with the air situation onboard a carrier.

Opposite, Plan 3

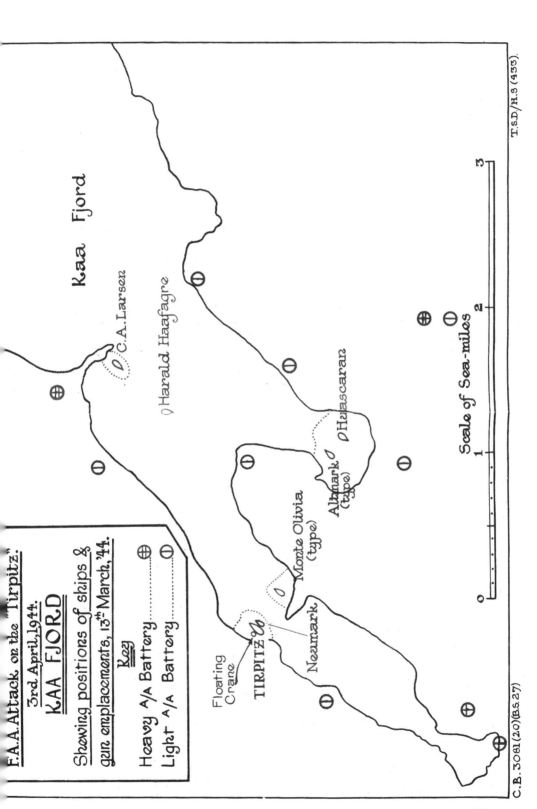

F.A.A. Attack on the "Tirpitz".
3rd April, 1944.
KAA FJORD

Showing positions of ships & gun emplacements, 13th March, '44.

Key

Heavy A/A Battery .... ⊕
Light A/A Battery .... ⊖

Kaa Fjord

C.A.Larsen

Harald Haafagre

Monte Olivia (type)

Neumark

Albnark (type)

Hulascaran

Floating Crane

TIRPITZ

Scale of Sea-miles

0   1   2   3

C.B. 3081 (20) (B.S.27)

T.S.D./H.S (453).

151

Plan 4

F.A.A. ATTACK on **TIRPITZ**, 3rd April, 1944.
Admiralty Assessment of Hits, 3/5/44
This assessment is conservative, and a larger propor-
-tion of hits, particularly with 500 lb. S.A.P. bombs
is regarded as probable.

"ADMIRAL von TIRPITZ"

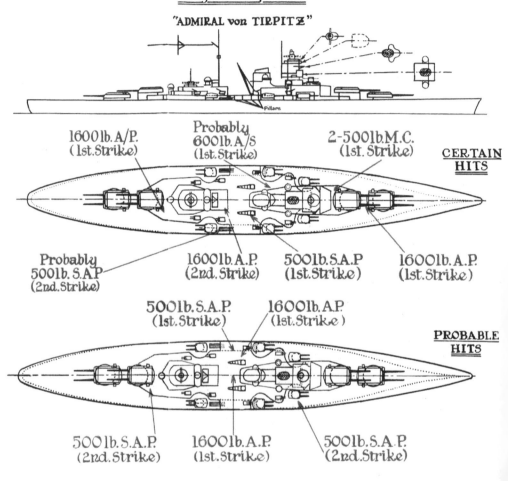

1600 lb. A/P.
(1st. Strike)

Probably
600 lb. A/S
(1st. Strike)

2-500 lb. M.C.
(1st. Strike)

CERTAIN HITS

Probably
500 lb. S.A.P
(2nd. Strike)

1600 lb. A.P.
(2nd. Strike)

500 lb. S.A.P
(1st. Strike)

1600 lb. A.P.
(1st. Strike)

500 lb. S.A.P.
(1st. Strike)

1600 lb. A.P
(1st. Strike)

PROBABLE HITS

500 lb. S.A.P.
(2nd. Strike)

1600 lb. A.P.
(1st. Strike)

500 lb. S.A.P.
(2nd. Strike)

FIRE AND SURFACE DAMAGE

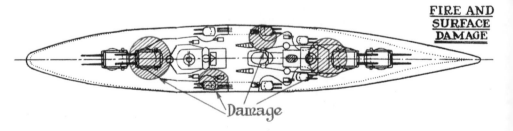

Damage

C.B. 3061 (20) (BS 27)

T.S.D./H.S. (454).

Conclusion
(Plan 4)

It is not possible yet to estimate the full results of the raid[46] with accuracy, but enough is known to regard it is as a distinct success. The smoke from the bursting bombs, as well as the enemy smoke screen, made accurate observation at the time difficult and obscured some of the photographs taken; and the damage caused cannot, of course, be known for certain till enemy records are available. The lowest assessment of hits on the *Tirpitz* allowed eight certain, of which three were by 1,600-lb. bombs, and five probable, a total of at least 13 (see Appendix D). On the basis of the certain hits only, expert opinion deemed that "although temporary repairs sufficient to enable the ship to proceed to sea for an emergency operation could possibly be effected in three months, completely effective repair would take considerably longer." If the probable hits were included, it was considered unlikely that the ship could take part in any form of offensive operation in less than five months.

In addition to the bomb damage to the *Tirpitz*, the fighters left their mark on at least two merchant ships, two flak ships and a destroyer, besides setting on fire two armed trawlers, silencing (temporarily) A/A batteries and shooting up various shore installations.

Nor can it be doubted that the moral effect of the successful attack in the teeth of all the defences, for the loss of two bombers shot down, must have been as depressing for the enemy as exhilarating for the Naval Air Arm. Not that they appeared to need much "exhilarating"; Captain Denny's remarks on the spirit in which they set out on their hazardous task have already been quoted, and their determination to press the attack right home caused a considerable number to drop their bombs at much lower heights than those ordered (which may have detracted from the effectiveness of some of the A.P. and S.A.P. hits obtained). As for the fighters, the following signal from the *Victorious* to the Rear-Admiral, Escort Carriers, shows what the bombers thought of their performance: "Strike leaders and aircrews of both strikes wish to thank the fighter escort for the superb way in which the fighters went down on to the flak. In addition, fighters can claim a burning tanker."

All did well. In Vice-Admiral Moore's words: "Great credit is due to Rear-Admiral A. W. La T. Bisset, Rear-Admiral, Escort Carriers, and the Commanding Officers of the Fleet and Escort Carriers for the efficiency and team work which was achieved in so short a time, and for the smoothness with which the operation was carried out. But above all, I wish to express my admiration for the brilliant and daring attack carried out by the aircrews themselves, most of whom were having their first experience of enemy action." These remarks were endorsed by the Commander-in-Chief, who also paid tribute to the "careful planning, preparation and handling of his forces" by the Vice-Admiral, which was "so largely responsible for the great success of the operation."

Appendix A

Ships Employed in Operation 'Tungsten'

Battleship

Anson	10 14-in., 16 5.25-in. HA/LA. guns.	Flag, Vice-Admiral Sir Henry R. Moore, K.C.B., C.V.O. D.S.O. (Vice-Admiral 2nd-in-Command, Home Fleet). Captain E. D. B. McCarthy, D.S.O., R.N.

Fleet Carriers

Victorious	16 4·5-in. guns. 24 Barracudas. 21 Corsairs.	Captain M. M. Denny, C.B., C.B.E., R.N.
Furious	12 4-in. HA/LA. guns. 18 Barracudas. 15 Seafires.	Captain G. T. Philip, D.S.O., D.S.C., R.N.

Escort Carriers

Searcher	2 4-in. HA/LA. guns. 20 Wildcats.	Captain G. O. C. Davies, R.N.
Emperor	2 4-in. HA/LA. guns. 20 Hellcats.	Act. Captain T. J. N. Hilken, D.S.O., R.N.
Pursuer	2 4-in. HA/LA. guns. 20 Wildcats.	Act. Captain H. R. Graham, D.S.O., D.S.C., R.N.
Fencer	2 4-in. HA/LA. guns. 10 Wildcats. 9 Swordfish.	Act. Captain W. W. R. Bentinck, O.B.E., R.N.

Cruisers

Royalist	8 5·25-in. guns.	Flag, Rear-Admiral A. W. La.T. Bisset (Rear-Admiral, Escort Carriers). Captain M. H. Eveleigh, R.N.
Belfast	12 6-in.,12–4-in. H.A. guns.	Captain F. R. Parham, D.S.O., R.N.
Sheffield	12 6 in., 8 4 in. H.A. guns.	Captain C. T. Addis, D.S.O., R.N.
Jamaica	12 6-in., 8 4-in. H.A. guns.	Captain J. Hughes-Hallett, D.S.O., R.N.

Destroyers

Milne	6 4·7-in., 1 4-in. H.A. guns. 5 21-in. torpedo tubes.	Captain J. M. R. Campbell, D.S.O., R.N. (Capt. (D) 3rd Flotilla).
Ursa	4 4·7-in. guns. 8 21-in. torpedo tubes.	Commander D. B. Wyburd, D.S.C., R.N.
Onslaught	4 4·7-in., 1 4-in. H.A. guns. 8 21-in. torpedo tubes.	Commander The Hon. A. Pleydell-Bouverie, R.N.
Piorun[47]	6 4·7-in., 1 4-in. H.A. guns. 5 21-in. torpedo tubes.	Commander S. Dnienisiwicz, V.M.
Verulam	4 4·7-in. guns. 8 21-in. torpedo tubes.	Lt.-Com. W. S. Thomas, D.S.C., R.N.
Meteor	6 4·7-in., 1 4-in. H.A. guns. 5 21-in. torpedo tubes.	Lt.-Com. D. J. B. Jewitt, R.N.
Undaunted	4 4·7-in. guns. 8 21-in. torpedo tubes.	Lt.-Com. A. A. MacKenzie, R.D., R.N.R.
Vigilant	4 4·7-in. guns. 8 21-in. torpedo tubes.	Lt.-Com. L. W. L. Argles, R.N.
Virago	4 4·7-in. guns. 8 21-in. torpedo tubes.	Lt.-Com. A. J. R. White, R.N.

Swift	4 4·7-in. guns. 8 21-in. torpedo tubes.	Lt.-Com. J. R. Gower, R.N.
Javelin	6 4·7-in. guns. 10 21-in. torpedo tubes.	Lt.-Com. P. B. N. Lewis, D.S.C., R.N.
Wakeful	4 4·7-in. guns. 8 21-in. torpedo tubes.	Lt.-Com. G. D. Pound, R.N.
Algonquin[48]	4 4·7-in. guns. 8 21-in. torpedo tubes.	A/Lt.-Com. D. W. Piers, D.S.C., R.C.N.
Sioux[48]	4 4·7-in. guns. 8 21-in. torpedo tubes.	A/Lt.-Com. E. E. G. Boak, R.C.N.

Appendix B

Particulars of Aircraft Taking Part in Operation 'Tungsten'

Type of Aircraft	Crew	Armament /Rounds per Gun	Load Carried	Speed	
				Maximum	Cruising
Barracuda II	3	2x.303-in/500 2x.303-in/500 (free)	1x1,600-lb. A.P. or 3x500-lb. M.C. or 3x500-lb. S.A.P. or 2x600-lb. A.S.	188 knots at 2,000 ft.	145 knots at 5,000 ft.
Corsair	1	6x.5-in/200		352 knots at 23,000 ft.	216 knota at 20,000 ft.
Hellcat	1	6x.5-in/200		342 knots at 23,000 ft.	212 knots at 20,000 ft.
Wildcat V	1	4x.5-in/400		273 knots at 21,000 ft.	184 knots at 15,000 ft.
Wildcat VI	1	4x.5-in/240		270 knots at 21,000 ft.	184 knots at 15,000 ft.
Seafire III	1	2x20-mm./135 4x.303-in/350 2x20mm./13500		306 knots at 12,000 ft.	190 knots at 20,000 ft.

Nominal List of Air Crews Taking Part in the Attack
1. Fighter Support Supplied by *Victorious* (Corsairs)

Fighter Wing Leader – Lt.-Com. F. R. A. Turnbull, R.N.
Lt.-Com. (A) P. N. Charlton, R.N.

Ty. Sub-Lt. (A) G. A. Rawstron, R.N.Z.N.V.R.   Ty. Sub-Lt. (A) W. H. Rose, R.N.V.R.
Ty. Sub-Lt. (A) J. S. Bird, R.N.V.R.   Ty. Sub-Lt. (A) W. Knight, R.N.V.R.
Ty. Sub-Lt. (A) M. C. Kelly, R.N.V.R.   Ty. Sub-Lt. (A) V. A. Fancourt.
Ty. Sub-Lt. (A) J. F. R. Ball, R.N.V.R.   Ty. Sub-Lt. (A) E. Hill, R.N.V.R.
Ty. Sub-Lt. (A) C. H. D. Grayson, R.N.V.R.   Ty. Sub-Lt. (A) J. W. Mayhead, R.N.Z.N.V.R.
Lt.-Com. (A) C. C. Tomkinson, R.N.V.R.   Ty. Sub-Lt. (A) D. J. Sheppard, R.N.V.R.
Ty. Sub-Lt. (A) L. D. Durno, R.N.V.R.   Ty. Sub-Lt. (A) A. W. Direen, R.N.Z.N.V.R.
Ty. Sub-Lt. (A) A. J. French, R.N.Z.N.V.R.   Ty. Sub-Lt. (A) M. T. Blair, R.N.V.R.
Ty. Sub-Lt. (A) B. L. Hayter, R.N.V.R.   Ty. Sub-Lt. (A) S. Leonard, R.N.V.R.
Ty. Sub.-Lt. (A) D. Robertson, R.N.V.R.

2. Fighter Support Provided by Escort Carriers

1st Strike

A/Lt.-Com. J. W. Sleigh, D.S.C., R.N.
(of R.A.E.C. Staff, operating from Pursuer).

2nd Strike

A/Lt.-Com. (A) M. F. Fell, R.N. (Searcher).

Searcher (Wildcats)
Ty. A/Lt.-Com. (A) J. Cooper, R.N.V.R.
Lt. Cotching, R.N.R.
Ty. Sub-Lt. (A) K. B. Pearson, R.N.V.R.
Ty. Sub-Lt. (A) J. M. Boswell, R.N.V.R.
Ty. Sub-Lt. (A) P. J. M. Canter,
R.N.Z.N.V.R.
Ty. Sub-Lt. (A) W. S. Smith, R.N.V.R.
Ty. Sub-Lt. (A) C. G. Sanville, R.N.V.R.
Ty. Sub-Lt. (A) F. T. Sherborne, R.N.V.R.

Searcher (Wildcats)
Ty. A/Lt.-Com. (A) G. R. Henderson,
R.N.V.R.
Ty. Lt. (A) R. J. Harrison, R.N.Z.N.V.R.
Ty. Lt. (A) C. G. Cullen, R.N.V.R.
Ty. Lt. (A) W. J. Sheppard, R.N.V.R.
Ty. Sub-Lt. (A) E. F. Hocking, R.N.V.R.
Ty. Sub-Lt. (A) S. W. Edney, R.N.Z.N.V.R.
Ty. Sub-Lt. (A) D. Farthing, R.N.V.R.
Ty. Sub-Lt. (A) H. J. Pain, R.N.V.R.
Ty. Sub-Lt. (A) A. Sharpe, R.N.Z.N.V.R.
Ty. Sub-Lt. (A) C. St. George,
R.N.Z.N.V.R Ty. Sub-Lt. (A) A. R. Duff,
R.N.Z.N.V.R.

Pursuer (Wildcats)
Ty. A/Lt.-Com. D. R. B. Cosh,
R.C.N.V.R
Ty. Lt. H. P. Wilson, R.C.N.V.R.
Ty. Lt. (A) A. G. Woods, R.N.V.R.
Ty. Lt. (A) D. R. Gardner, S.A.N.F.
Ty. Lt. (A) A. N. Pym, R.N.V.R.
Ty. Sub-Lt. (A) D. L. W. Frearson,
R.N.V.R.
Ty. Sub-Lt. (A) N. K. Turner, R.N.V.R.
Ty. Sub-Lt. (A) A. C. Lindsay, R.N.V.R.
Ty. Sub-Lt. (A) A. A. Davison,
R.N.Z.N.V.R.
Ty. Sub-Lt. (A) T. L. M. Brander, R.N.V.R.
Ty. Sub-Lt. (A) M. J. Leeson, R.N.V.R.

Pursuer (Wildcats)
Ty. A/Lt.-Com. (A) L. A. Hordern,
R.N.V.R.
Ty. Lt. (A) A. C. Martin, RN.Z.N.V.R
Ty. Sub-Lt. (A) V. H. Martin, R.N.Z.N.V.R.
Ty. Sub-Lt. (A) D. Symons, R.N.V.R.
Ty. Sub-Lt. (A) A. B. Christie,
R.N.Z.N.V.R.
Ty. Sub-Lt. (A) R. Banks, R.N.V.R.
Ty. Sub-Lt. (A) R. C. Wilkinson, R.N.V.R.[49]
Ty. Sub-Lt. (A) W. Park, R.N.V.R.

Emperor (Hellcats)
Lt.-Com. (A) S. J. Hall, R.N.
Ty. Sub-Lt. (A) J. G. Devitt, R.N.V.R.
Ty. Sub-Lt. (A) J. H. Jellie, R.N.Z.N.V.R.
Ty. Sub-Lt. (A) R. L. Thompson, R.N.V.R.
Ty. Sub-Lt. (A) B. Ritchie, R.N.V.R
Ty. Sub-Lt. (A) R. S. Hollway, RN.V.R.
Ty. Sub-Lt. (A) T. H. Hoare, R.N.Z.N.V.R.
Sub-Lt. C. H. Roncoroni, R.N.R.
Ty. Sub-Lt. (A) S. A. Craig, R.N.V.R.
Ty. Sub-Lt. (A) R. Hooker, R.N.Z.N.V.R.

Emperor (Hellcats)
Lt.-Com. (A) S. G. Orr, R.N.V.R.
Ty. Sub-Lt. (A) G. J. Elger, R.N.V.R.
Lt. O. R Oakes, R.M.
Ty. Sub-Lt. (A) B. F. Brine, R.N.V.R.
Ty. Sub-Lt. (A) A. C. McLennan,
R.N.Z.N.V.R.
Ty. Sub-Lt. (A) G. A. M. Flood, R.N.V.R.
Ty. Sub-Lt. (A) C. D. Spencer, R.N.V.R.
Ty. Sub-Lt. (A) R. A. Cranwell,
R.N.Z.N.V.R.
Ty. Sub-Lt. (A) L. M. Wenyon, R.N.V.R.
Ty. Sub-Lt. (A) D. R. P. Owen, R.N.V.R.

3. Bombers

1st Strike
No. 8 T.B.R. Wing (*Furious*)
Wing-Leader Lt.-Com. (A) R. Baker-Faulkner, R.N.

Aircraft	Pilot	Observer	Air Gunner
		827 Squadron (Flown off from *Victorious*)	
K	Lt.-Cdr. (A) R. Baker-Faulkner, R.N.	Lt. G. M. Micklom, R.N.	Ldg. Air. A. M. Kimberley.
A	Ty. Lt. (A) H. R. Emerson, R.N.Z.N.V.R.	Lt.-Cdr. (A) K. H. Gibney, R.N.	C.P.O. Air C. Topliss.
Q	Ty. Sub-Lt. (A) C. M. Lock, R.N.V.R.	Ty. Sub-Lt. (A) J. Grieveson, R.N.V.R.	Ldg. Air. D. E. Wootten.
C	Ty. Sub-Lt. (A) J. D. Herrold, R.N.V.R.	Ty. Sub-Lt. (A) G. Alexander, R.N.V.R.	Ldg. Air. H. N. Hoyte.
M	Ty. Sub-Lt. (A) I. G. Robertson, R.N.V.R.	Ty. Sub-Lt. (A) H. W. Pethick, R.N.V.R.	Ldg. Air. J. Coulby.
F	Ty. Sub. Lt. (A) D. W. Collett, R.N.V.R.	Lt. G. C. Yorke, R.N.	Ldg. Air. T. Carnell.
G	Ty. Sub-Lt. (A) E. E. Green, R.N.V.R.	Ty. Sub-Lt. (A) L. J. Jouning, R.N.V.R.	Ldg. Air. R H. Lee.
P	Ty. Sub-Lt. (A) J. A. Gledhill, R.N.V.R.	Ty. Sub-Lt. (A) J. McCormick, R.N.V.R	Ldg. Air. N. A. F. Poole.
H	Ty. Sub-Lt.(A) J. Watson, R.N.V.R.	Ty. Sub-Lt. (A) R. D. Smith, R.N.V.R.	Ldg. Air. R. R. Williams.
B	Ty. Lt. (A) P. G. Darling, R.C.N.V.R.	Ty. Sub-Lt. (A) H. E. K. Gale, R.N.V.R.	Ldg. Air. E. Hunter.
R	Ty. Sub-Lt. (A) A. D. Ritchie, R.N.V.R.	Ty. Sub-Lt. (A) K. A. Sellers, R.N.V.R.	Ldg. Air. W. Murray.
L	Ty, Sub-Lt. (A) J. R. Brown, R.N.V.R.	A/Ty. Sub-Lt. (A) D. L. Pullen, R.N.V.R.	Ldg. Air. P. A. Reynolds.
		830 Squadron (Flown off from *Furious*)	
A	A/Ty. Lt.-Com. (A) RD. Kingdon, R.N.V.R	Ty. Lt. (A) J. B. Armitage, R.N.Z.N.V.R.	C.P.O. Air. A. E. Carr.
C	Ty. Sub-Lt. (A) A. E. Browse, R.N.V.R.	Ty. Sub-Lt. (A) A. H. Dobbie, R.N.V.R.	A/Ldg. Air. G. F. Priestley.

B	Ty. Sub-Lt. (A) D. S. Clarabut, R.N.V.R.	Ty. Sub-Lt. (A) E. D. Knight, R.N.V.R.	Ldg. Air. W. A. Ball.
H	Ty. Sub-Lt. (A) J. A. Grant, R.N.V.R.	Ty. Sub-Lt. (A) A. C. P. Walling, R.N.V.R.	Ldg. Air. D. P. Bussey.
M[50]	Ty. Sub-Lt. (A) T. C. Bell, R.N.V.R.	Ty. Sub-Lt. (A) R. N. Drennan, R.N.V.R.	Ldg. Air. G. J. Burns.
F	Ty. Lt. (A) J. B. Robinson, R.N.V.R.	Ty. Sub-Lt. (A) R. L. Eveleigh, R.N.V.R.	A/P.O. Air. S. W. Lock.
G	Ty. Sub-Lt. (A) D. E. Rowe, R.N.Z.N.V.R.	Ty. Sub-Lt. (A) D. A. Brown, R.N.Z.N.V.R.	Ldg. Air. A. C. Wells.
K	Ty. Sub-Lt. (A) J. D. Britton, R.N.V.R.	Ty. Sub-Lt. (A) J. C. Fairclough, R.N.V.R.	Ldg. Air. J. Whyte.
L	Ty. Sub-Lt. (A) R. G. Williams, R.N.Z.N.V.R.	Ty. Sub-Lt. (A) R. D. Burton, R.N.V.R	Ldg. Air. A. H. Thomson.

2nd Strike
No. 52 T. B. R. Wing (*Victorious*)
Wing-Leader, Lt.-Com. (A) V. Rance, R.N.

829 Squadron
(Flown off from *Victorious*)

L	Ty. Lt. (A) M. Meredith, R.N.V.R.	Lt.-Cdr. V. Rance, R.N.	C.P.O. Air. T. L. Cridland.
B	Ty. Sub-Lt. (A) A. Hamersley, R.N.V.R.	Ty. Sub-Lt. (A) E. R Shipley, R.N.V.R.	Ldg. Air. T. Harding.
F	Lt. P. Hudson, R.N.	Ty. Sub-Lt. (A) I. D. C. Cooksey. R.N.V.R.	Ldg. Air. R. T. Knight.
H	Ty. Sub-Lt. (A) S. C. Taylor, R.N.Z.N.V.R.	Ty. Sub-Lt. (A) N. Harrison, R.N.V.R.	Ldg. Air. A. B. Sim.
A	Lt.-Cdr. D. Phillips, R.N.	Ty. Sub-Lt. (A) H. Ashford, R.N.V.R.	C.P.O. Air. E. J. W. Sherlock.
K	Ty. Lt. (A) G. W. Grindred, R.N.V.R.	Ty. Sub-Lt. (A) P. Hollis, R.N.V.R.	Ldg. Air. I. Kitley.
P	Ty. Sub-Lt. (A) M. C. Farrer, R.N.Z.N.V.R.	Ty. Sub-Lt. (A) S. A. Erratt, R.N.V.R.	Ldg. Air. R. Bacon.
G	Ty. Lt. (A) N. B. Hustwick, R.N.Z.N.V.R.	Ty. Sub-Lt. (A) E. Stacey, R.N.V.R.	Ldg. Air. T. Spencer.
R	Ty. Sub-Lt. (A) A. N. Towlson, R.N.V.R.	Ty. Sub-Lt. (A) L. J. Ryan, R.N.Z.N.V.R.	Ldg. Air. W. Firth.
Q[51]	Ty. Sub-Lt. (A) E. C. Bowles, R.N.V.R.	Ty. Lt. (A) J. P. Whittaker, R.N.V.R.	Ldg. Air. C. J. Colwell.

| M[52] | Ty. Sub-Lt. (A) H. H. Richardson, R.N.V.R. | Ty. Sub-Lt. (A) A. G. Cannon, R.N.V.R. | Ldg. Air. E. Carroll. |

831 Squadron
(Flown off from *Furious*)

A	Lt.-Cdr. (A) D. Brooks, R.N.	Ty. Lt. (A) D. S. Miller, R.N.V.R.	P .O. Air. T. W. Halhead.
K	Ty. Lt. (A) C. G. Hurst, R.N.V.R.	Ty. Lt. (A) W. S. Lindores, R.N.V.R.	Ldg. Air. D. Robinson.
G	Ty. Sub-Lt. (A) P. H. Abbott, R.N.V.R.	Ty. Sub-Lt. (A) L. W. Peck, R.N.V.R.	Ldg. Air: V. Gallimore.
C	Ty. Sub-Lt. (A) N. H. Bovey, R.N.V.R.	Ty. Sub-Lt. (A) W. Smith, R.N.V.R.	Ldg. Air. V. Watkins.
F	Ty. Lt. (A) G. Russell Jones, R.N.V.R.	Ty. Sub-Lt. (A) J. Cartwright, R.N.V.R.	Ldg. Air. G. A. McRae.
L	Ty. Sub-Lt. (A) R. N. Robbins, R.N.V.R.	Ty. Sub-Lt. (A) J. Coe, R.N.V.R.	Ldg. Air. T. Ward.
B	Ty. Sub-Lt. (A) T. M. Henderson, R.N.V.R.	Ty. Sub-Lt. (A) V. Hutchinson, R.N.V.R.	Ldg. Air. V. Smyth.
H	Ty. Sub-Lt. (A) M. M. Bebbington, R.N.V.R.	Ty. Sub-Lt. (A) G. J. Burford, R.N.V.R.	Ldg. Air. R. R. Rankin.
M	Ty. Sub-Lt. (A) P. Hunter, R.N.V.R.	Ty. Sub-Lt. (A) E. M. King, R.N.V.R.	Ldg. Air. W. A. Allen.

Appendix C

Bombing Attack: Tactical Details

1st Strike

No. 8 T.B.R. Wing (*Furious*)

Wing-Leader Lt.-Com. (A) R. Baker-Faulkner, R.N.

Aircraft in Order of Drive	Bomb Load	Column	Direction of Attack	Angle of Dive and Height of Release
		827 Squadron (Flown off from *Victorious*)		
K	3 500-lb. M.C.	–	Stern to bow	1,200 ft.
A	1 1,600-lb. A.P.	Starboard	From Green 130°	50°, 3,00 ft.
Q	3 500-lb. S.A.P.	Starboard	–	50°, 2,500 ft.
C	3 500-lb. S.A.P.	Starboard	From Green 120°	50°, 2,500 ft.
M	3 500-lb. S.A.P.	Starboard	From Green 100°	55°, 2,000 ft.
F	1 1,600-lb. A.P.	Port	Stern to bow	45°, 2,500 ft.
G	3 500-lb. S.A.P.	Port	–	55°, 2,000 ft.
P	2 600-lb. A/S	Port	Stern to bow	70°, 1,500 ft.
H	2 600-lb. A/S	Port	From Red 170°	50°, 2,500 ft.
B	3 500-lb. S.A.P.	Starboard	From Green 100°	50°, 2,800 ft.
R	3 500-lb. M.C.	Port	From Red 130°	50°, 2,500 ft.
L	3 500-lb. M.C.	Starboard	From Green 120°	55°, 2,500 ft.
		830 Squadron (Flown off from *Furious*)		
A	1 1,600-lb. A.P.	Port	–	30°, 2,500 ft.
C	3 500-lb. S.A.P.	Port	Port quarter to starboard bow	50°, 2,000 ft.
B	1 1,600-lb. A.P.	Port	Port bow to starboard quarter	45°, 1,200 ft.
H	3 500-lb. S.A.P.	Port	Starboard quarter to port bow	70°, 2,000 ft.
M	3 500-lb. S.A.P.	Shot down		
F	1 1,600-lb. A.P.	Port	–	45°, 2,000 ft.
G[53]	1 1,600-lb. A.P.	Port	Port bow to starboard quarter	45°, 2,700 ft.
K	1 1,600-lb. A.P.	Port	–	45°, 2,000 ft.
L	3 500-lb. S.A.P.	Port	Bow to stern	60°, 2,500 ft.

2nd Strike

No. 52 T. B. R. Wing (*Victorious*)

Note:– One of the aircraft if this strike shown as carrying 500-lb. S.A.P. bombs atually carried 2 600-lb. A/S bombs.

Wing-Leader, Lt.-Com. (A) V. Rance, R.N.

Aircraft in Order of Drive	Bomb Load	Column	Direction of Attack	Angle of Dive and Height of Release
		829 Squadron (Flown off from *Victorious*)		
L	3 500-lb. S.A.P.	Port	–	–
B	3 500-lb. M.C.	Starboard	–	4,000 ft.
F	3 500-lb. M.C.	Port	Across target	2,000 ft.
H	3 500-lb. S.A.P.	Starboard	–	70°, 2,000 ft.
A	3 500-lb. M.C.	Not in information	–	65°, 3,500 ft.
K	3 500-lb. S.A.P.	Port	–	60°, 2,000 ft.
P[54]	3 500-lb. S.A.P.	Port	–	65°, 2,500 ft.
G	1 1,600-lb. A.P.	Port	–	50°, 3,000 ft.
R	1 1,600-lb. A.P.	Starboard	–	65°, 3,500 ft.
Q	1 1,600-lb. A.P.	Crashed in the sea after take off.		
M	Shot down.			
		831 Squadron (Flown of from *Furious*)		
A	3 500-lb. S.A.P.	Starboard	Port quarter to starboard bow	–
K	3 500-lb. S.A.P.	Starboard	Port quarter to starboard bow	3,000-3,500 ft.
G	3 500-lb. S.A.P.	Starboard	Stern to bow	3,000 ft.
C	3 500-lb. S.A.P.	Starboard	From port quarter	–
F	3 500-lb. S.A.P.	Starboard	From port quarter	2,000 ft.
L	3 500-lb. S.A.P.	Starboard	Stern to bow	–
B[55]	3 500-lb. S.A.P.	Starboard	Stern to bow	3,000 ft.
H	3 500-lb. S.A.P.	Starboard	Stern to bow	3,000 ft.
M	3 500-lb. S.A.P.	Starboard	Stern to bow	–

Lenovo
Premium Care
Advanced Support from Real People.
Real Fast.

Congratulations on your new Lenovo device.

Premium Care gives you direct access to **best-in-class technical support** via a dedicated support line. Whatever the problem, Lenovo's **expert technicians** are on-hand to ensure you get the most from your new device.

 REAL PERSON

Available on phone, chat or email, our expert technicians will take care of you.

 HASSLE-FREE

Instantly accessible how-to guides and advice for getting started, for both hardware and software.

 REAL FAST

Real-time solutions at your fingertips, with availability for home or at work visits the next Working Day.

 PC HEALTH CHECK

Free annual PC Health Check that allows our experts to spot issues before they affect you.

To unlock a special promotion, follow these three **simple steps**:

1. Visit www.lenovo.com/supportservices and **select** "Register" or "Purchase a warranty upgrade".

2. Enter your Lenovo device's **Serial Number** and choose your support

3. At checkout use promo code: **SRVC1309**

Need help?
Call for UK: **+441256774577**
for Ireland: **+35315628320**

SN:YX09TEKL

Lenovo

PN: SP41A30007

Bombing Attacks: Air Crews' Reports

First Strike
No. 8 T.B.R. Wing (*Furious*)

Aircraft in order of Dive	Observations
	827 Squadron
A	Flak, both light and heavy, inaccurate. Explosion seen about the bridge superstructure.
Q	One hit abaft funnel by one of first aircraft; one hit forward; smoke puff from after end of ship.
C	Two of Wing-Leader's bombs hit near "A" and "B" turrets, and two other hits about the same time, port side amidships; one bomb fell in water. No enemy opposition.
M	First two bombs hit forward turrets; bomb from Aircraft C hit amidships and bomb from A hit further aft.
F	One hit on forecastle; two hits on "A" turret; a splash 20 yards on port beam. Smoke just started.
G	Aircraft next ahead hit bridge, deep red flash between funnel and bridge on port side; two exploded near ship in mid-air, another hit "X" turret.
P	Both own bombs hit starboard side of bridge. Aircraft ahead's bombs all seemed to be on target; six to seven hits amidships seen before attacking.
H	One hit seen on bow before attack; Aircraft "P" got two hits on port side of bridge and one aft; one bomb astern.
B	Wing-Leader's bombs, at least one, possibly two, hit before bridge, causing smoke and flame.
R	Leader scored two hits, one before bridge, one just further aft.
L	Aircraft "B" caused big explosion amidships; sheets of flame just before funnel. Two near misses, 30 yards to starboard.
	830 Squadron
C	Very large explosion on forecastle; "Pilot yelled that the C.O. (Aircraft."A")... had got a hit" One of own bombs hit amidships; three bombs seen to fall in fjord.
B	Before dropping bombs, at least one 1,600-lb. bomb seen to hit; several smaller explosions. Large column of smoke rose very quickly to about 1,300 ft.
H	Explosion amidships and large column of white smoke; smaller smoke column from bridge area; large explosion and dense white smoke from "B" turret.
F	Steady red glow amidships and smoke pouring up.
G	Bomb hit, producing large sheet of flame forward control position followed by heavy pall of smoke. Ship's flak ineffective. Own bomb (1,600-lb.) failed to release.

K	During din, saw *Tirpitz* constantly hit by various bombs. Aircraft "F" hit amidships with 1,600-lb. bomb, causing large explosion. Target enveloped in large red flames, with smoke amidships. Own bomb (1,600-lb.) hit near the previous one with similar result. *Tirpitz* was stationary, and heading about 330° up Kaa Fjord.
L	Several explosions seen through smoke during run in. Bomb from Aircraft "K" exploded amidships. One near miss 50 ft. from port bow, and several bombs bursting near an oil tank and five smoke generators on beach alongside ship.

829 Squadron

B	Hits seen amidships, starboard side by bridge.
F	Target hit amidships by leader's bombs. Smoke screen over area, but ship visible.
H	Own bombs and another stick missed over. Saw one Barracuda shot down – port wing broken and on fire.
A	Own bombs hit amidships. Fire, a dull red glow about the size of a gun turret.
K	Large explosion amidships; two near misses seen.
P	Smoke obscured everything except target. Red glow amidships, port side, observed. One aircraft, which seemed to have dropped bombs, seen to dive in flames. Own bombs dropped safe, owing to electrical failure.
G	Hit by another aircraft seen abaft funnel, port side; smoke issuing from between two forward turrets. Saw Barracuda with smoke coming from wing.
R	One hit on stern, slightly to port between turrets. A large swirl astern, either near miss or screws turning.

831 Squadron

A	Large fire burning port side by bridge superstructure; second fire broke out in similar position, starboard side.
K	Ship appeared to be adrift with stern almost aground, bow into fjord. Saw two hits amidships; black smoke and flames from funnel. Own bombs, one hit starboard side amidships, two near misses. One Barracuda on fire flying north, apparently under control.
G	Large fire seen amidships; fresh explosion seen just before releasing bombs. Own bombs, one hit after gun turret, one near miss astern.
C	Stern within 30 yards of shore. Fierce fire near "X" turret. Saw two hits a midships, one all either beam, apparently from separate aircraft, and one hit on port side of forecastle.
F	Large orange flame billowing from funnel; an explosion on bows and fire amidships.
L	Saw two hits amidships, fire and belching flames; one hit on forecastle. Own bombs fell short.

B	Fierce fire burning amidships. One of own bombs failed to drop and was subsequently jettisoned over sea.
H	Saw four bomb hits, and one burst on land about 30 yards astern of target.
M	One large explosion just forward of superstructure, followed by an explosion near "B" turret; near miss astern on the coast.

Operation Tungsten: Aircraft Losses

Aircraft	Crew	Remarks
M 830 Squadron (*Furious*)	Sub-Lt. (A) T. C. L, R.N.V.R., Pilot. Sub-Lt. (A) R. N. Drenan, R.N.V.R., Observer.	Damaged in First Strike; seen in controlled glide after the attack, and may have made good forced landing.
Q 829 Squadron (*Victorious*)	Sub-Lt. (A) F. C. Bowles, R.N.V.R., Pilot. Lt. (A) J. P. Whittaker, R.N.V.R., Observer. Ldg. Air. C. J. Colwill, T.A.G.	Crash in sea after successful take-off. Crew all killed.
M 829 Squadron (*Victorious*)	Sub-Lt. (A) H. H. Richardson, R.N.V.R., Pilot. Sub-Lt. (A) A. G. Cannon, R.N.V.R., Observer. Ldg. Air. E. Carroll, T.A.G.	Shot down in flames during second strike. Possibly crew baled out.
Hellcat (1)[56]		
(*Emperor*)	Sub-Lt. T. H. Hoare, R.N.Z.N.V.R.	Hook damaged by enemy. Landed in water; pilot saved by HMS *Algonquin*.

Appendix D

Analysis of Hits Claimed

Notes:– (1) This Appendix is based on V.A.C. 2nd B.S. 128/026 of 10 April, 1944, Appendix I; *Victorious* letter 0137/6206 of 5 April, 1944, Appendices I, II and Enclosure IV, a.nd M.056600/44 containing Admiralty Assessment. In columns (3) and (4) the figures have been adjusted, where necessary to agree with the bomb loads carried as stated in *Victorious* report, and reports of individual aircraft.

(2) The Admiralty assessment states that although the hits shown in columns (7) and (8) are all that can be established from the evidence now (3 May, 1944) in possession of the Admiralty, "it is emphasised that this assessment... is conservative, and that a larger proportion of hits, particularly with 500-lb. S.A.P. bombs is regarded as probable."

Type of bomb	Number carried per aircraft	Number of aircraft to attack	Total bombs dropped	Classified hits separately identified	Other hits supported by photographic evidence	Admiralty assessment Certain	Admiralty assessment Probable
(1)	(2)	(3)	(4)	(5)	(6)	(7)	(8)
First Strike							
1,600 lbs. A.P.[58]	1	7	6	2	1	2	2
500 lbs. S.A.P.	3	8	24	5	2	1	1
500 lbs. M.C.	3	4	12	2	1	2	
600 lbs. A/S	2	2	4	1		1	

Type of bomb	Number carried per aircraft	Number of aircraft to attack	Total bombs dropped	Hits claimed		Admiralty assessment	
				Classified hits separately identified	Other hits supported by photographic evidence	Certain	Probable
Total		21	46	10	4	6	3
Second Strike							
1,600 lbs. A.P.	1	2	2	1		1	
500 lbs. S.A.P.[59]	3	13	38	3	2	1	2
500 lbs. M.C.	3	3	9	1	2		
600 lbs. A/S[58]	2	1	1	1			
Total		19	50	6	4	2	2
Grand Total		40	96	16	8	8	5

Appendix E

Flying Programme

Note:– Fleet protection provided by *Furious* Seafires and *Fencer*. *Fencer* to keep four Wildcats airborne continuously, and to have four more at stand-by on deck.

Time Zero plus. (Zero 0415).	*Victorious*	*Furious*	*Pursuer* *Emperor* *Searcher*
0.00-0.10	Fly off twelve Corsairs.		
0.08-0.20		Fly off two Seafires (A).	Each fly off ten fighters. (First Strike escort).
0.10-0.20	Fly off twelve Barracudas.	Fly off nine Barracudas.	
0.20-1.20	First Strike takes Departure: Proceeds to Target.		
0.20-0.56		Range up nine Barracudas.	
0.20-1.00	Range up twelve Barracudas, twelve Corsairs.		
0.20-0.35			Each range up ten fighters.
1.00-1.20	Fly off Second Strike.		
1.10-1.20			Fly off Second Strike.
1.20-2.20	Second Strike takes Departure: Proceeds to Target		
1.20-1.35	First Strike Attacks.		
1.20-1.30		Range four Seafires (B).	

Time Zero plus. (Zero 0415).	Victorious	Furious	Pursuer Emperor Searcher
1.30-1.35		Fly off four Seafires (B).	
1.35-1.45		Land on two Seafires (C).	
1.35-2.35	First Strike returns to Carriers.		
2.10-2.20		Range four Seafires (C).	
2.20-2.35	Second Strike Attacks.		
2.20-2.25		Fly off four Seafires (C).	
2.25-2.35		Land on four Seafires (B).	
2.35-3.35	Second Strike returns to Carriers.		
2.35-2.55			Land on fighters.
2.35-3.05		Land on nine Barracudas.	
2.35-2.50	Land on twelve Corsairs.		
2.50-3.15	Land on twelve Barracudas.		
3.25-3.35		Land on four Seafires (C).	
3.35-3.55			Land on fighters.
3.35-4.05		Land on nine Barracudas.	
3.35-3.50	Land on twelve Corsairs.		
3.50-4.15	Land on twelve Barracudas.		
4.05-4.15		Range four Seafires (D).	
4.15-4.20		Fly off four Seafires (D).	

Analysis: Flett Carriers' Flying Programme

Note.-Planned times have been adjusted as follows:– Time to and from target, 20 minutes less each way. 15 minutes allowed for attacking has been included in the time to target and counts as time takcn to climb to attacking height.

Zero Time 0415

Planned Time. Zero Plus.	Operational Time. Zero Plus.	*Victorious*	*Furious*
0.00-0.10	0.01-0.08	Off ten Corsairs.	
0.10-0.20	0.09-0.15	Off twelve Barracudas, one Corsair.	
0.08-0.10	0.08-0.09		Off two Seafires (A).
0.10-0.20	0.09-0.13		Off nine Barracudas.
0.20	0.21	First Strike took	
1.15	1.14	Departure.	
1.00-1.1 0	1.00-1.05	First Strike Attack.	
	1.05-1.18	Off ten Corsairs. Off eleven Barracudas.	
1.10-1.20	1.06-1.09		Off nine Barracudas.
1.20	1.23	Second Strikc took Departure.	
1.30-1.35	1.33-1.35		Off four Seafires (B). On
1.35-1.45	1.37-1.42		two Seafires (A).
1.55	1.55	First Strike Returned.	
2.15	2.21	Second Strike Attack.	
1.55-2.35	2.03-2.25	Land on First Strike.	
1.55-2.25	2.03-2.23		Land on First Strike. Off
2.20-2.25	2.54-2.55		four Seafires (C). On four
2.25-2.35	2.57-3.11		Seafires (B).
2.55	3.00	Second Strike Returned. Land on Second Strike.	
2.55-3.35	3.05-3.40		
2.55-3.25	3.13-3.43		Land on Second Strike.

Appendix F

Principal German Air Bases Affecting Operation

Name	Position	Distance from Kaa Fjord	Remarks (a) Normal use. (b) Normal number of Fighters.
1. Alta	69° 59' N. 23° 19' E.	5 miles	(a) Landing ground. (b) Four Me.109.
2. Banak	70° 04' N.	30 miles	(a) T/B base. Meteorological flight. (b) Nil.
3. Kirkenes-Petsamo		85-130 miles	(a) Air attack, North Russian Front (Army co-operation) Barents Sea reconnaissance. (b) Twenty-four Me.109. Nine F.W.190. (Ground attack).
4. Tromsø	69° 41' N. 19° 01' E.	85 miles	(a) Flying boat base. (b) Nil.
5. Bardufoss	69° 03' N. 18° 32' E.	110 miles	(a) Reconnaissance and Meteorological. (b) Nil.
6. Narvik area		190 miles	(b) Five Me.109.
7. Trondheim area		480 miles	(a) Reconnaissance and Meteorological. (b) Twelve F.W. 190.
8. Bergen-Stavanger		900 miles	(a) Reconnaissance; Meteorological; T/B. (b) Thirty to forty Me.109 and Me.110.

Endnotes

1. *Admiral von Tirpitz*, 45,000 tons, 30·25 knots; 8 15-in., 12 5·9-in. H.A/L.A., 16 4·1-in. H.A., 16 37mm., 4 to 6 quadruple 20-mm., some 20-mm. single guns.
2. Vice-Admiral, Second in Command, Home Fleet, operation orders.
3. *Narvik*, 2,400 tons, 39 knots; 5 5·9-in. H.A/L.A., 4 1·46-in. A/A, 5 to 10 0·79-in. A/A. guns.
4. Admiral Sir Bruce Fraser, G.C.B., K.B.E.
5. Vice-Admiral Sir Henry Moore, K.C.B., C.V.O., D.S.O.
6. Captain L.D. Mackintosh, D.S.O., D.S.C., R.N. The Vice-Admiral subsequently wrote: "His knowledge and experience of naval air matters were of great assistance... both in planning and carrying out of the operation."
7. See Appendix A. List of ships, with commanding officers.
8. Rear-Admiral A. W. La T. Bisset.
9. This training was further curtailed by 24 hours owing to the necessity for sailing the *Victorious* with the convoy covering force. Vice-Admiral Moore considered "that the efficiency which they achieved in the short time available was most creditable."
10. This necessitated one squadron of the *Furious* wing being accommodated in and operated from the *Victorious* and vice versa. The alternative was for each carrier to operate its own aircraft and each attack to be carried out by a composite strike composed of a squadron from each carrier. Either method has its objections, but reporting on the operation the Vice-Admiral expressed the opinion that, while aircraft should operate from their own carrier if possible, "the advantage of operating a complete wing as a unit which has been trained together outweighs the disadvantages."
11. The 1,600 lb. A.P. bomb, if released above 3,500 ft., could penetrate the main armour and do vital damage, but offered less chance of hitting, due to the smaller number which could be carried. The 500 lb. S.A.P. bomb, if released above 2,000 ft., which could penetrate the 2-in. weather deck and do serious between-deck damage, could be carried in sufficient numbers to give a reasonable expectation of several hits.
    The 500 lb. M.C. bomb should detonate above the deck or water, and cause casualties by blast and splinters to exposed enemy A.A. personnel, hereby reducing casualties to our bombers. These bombs were to be carried by the first aircraft to attack.
    The 600 lb. A/S. bomb might cause considerable underwater damage by a near miss up to 30 ft., and would detonate on hitting the ship, causing damage to the superstructure and helping to eliminate A.A. fire.
12. This was subsequently modified, and the forces were actually armed as follows:–
    1st Strike.-(a) 9: (b) 7; (c) 5.
    2nd Strike.-(a) 13; (b) 3; (c) 5.
    Only two 600 lb. A/S bombs per aircraft were carried on account of the light wind prevailing at the time.
13. "The air plan was complicated by the employment of three different classes of carrier and five different types of aircraft, three of which were practically untried operationally by us. Also three of the four types of bombs which it had been decided to use in the attack had not previously been used in operations in this country." – Vice-Admiral Moore's report.
14. Vice-Admiral Moore's report.
15. During the forenoon, 1 April, the *Victorious*'s airborne Corsairs could have intercepted the Trondheim *Zenit*, both outward and inward bound; but as the plot showed that it would

not sight the fleet, it was allowed to proceed unmolested, for fear that it might get off a fighter alarm report and thus betray the presence of the fleet.

16. Times throughout, except where otherwise stated, are B.S.T. (Zone-1).

17. From C.-in-C., Home Fleet.   011121/April, 1944.
    To   V.A.2, R.A.E.C., Admiralty,
          S.B.N.O., North Russia, V.A.D., C.S.10.
    Intend operation 'Tungsten' take place on D plus 7 (R) 7. Force 2 amend route to pass through position L and rendezvous with Force 1 in new position YY 195° 75 miles from position OO at 1900A, 2 April.
    Detached Force 9 with two destroyers to proceed direct to QQ.

18. Rear-Admiral Bisset's report.

19. The C.-in-C. cruised within about 200 miles of the 'Tungsten' operating area until news was received of the successful termination of the operation, when he returned to Scapa, as previously arranged, arriving at 0830, 5 April.

20. The 'Tungsten' forces were organised as follows:–
    Force 7 – *Anson* (flag), *Victorious, Furious, Jamaica, Belfast*, 6 destroyers.
    Force 8 – *Royalist* (flag, Rear-Admiral), *Emperor, Searcher, Fencer, Pursuer, Sheffield*, 6 destroyers.
    Force 9 (detached) – *Blue Ranger, Brown Ranger*, 2 destroyers.

21. Sunrise, 3 April, was at 0435; nautical twilight (sun 12° below horizon) commenced 0127. The moon was in the first quarter (full moon 8 April) and set at 0626, 3 April.

22. Vice-Admiral Moore's report.

23. Captain Denny in his report started that the "*Victorious* flight deck is very wet in any weather, and the spray and sleet were freezing on the deck." Vice-Admiral Moore subsequently remarked, "It was realised that for the *Victorious* to carry 45 aircraft would involve the operation of a deck park, which in Northern waters may be undesirable, owing to the risk of unserviceability. Although this would not be acceptable for a long period, it was considered that for the short period involved the increase in striking potential justified this risk, and as it turned out only one Barracuda was unserviceable on the day of the attack."

24. *Victorious* report – Officers had been informed under conditions of strict secrecy of the intended operation some days previously, and were thus able to make themselves acquainted with the large amount of intelligence available. Detailed briefing of squadrons separately was completed at sea on 1 April, when telegraphist air gunners were for the first time given details of the plan. After full briefing on the *Victorious* the two strike leaders were flown over to the *Furious* to co-ordinate briefing of the other half of each strike. Army liasion officers were bombarded in the escort carriers and working in close co-operation with the air staff officers rendered valuable assistance in briefing the fighter pilots.

25. *Victorious* report.

26. A/S patrol and fighter protection for the Fleet were flown off from the *Fencer* and *Furious* with the first strike.

27. The departure point for the strikes had been fixed as four miles from the Fleet carriers in the direction of the escort carrier force.

28. Rear-Admiral Bisset's report. The Rear-Admiral remarked "The forming up of the composite striking force worked so smoothly that I consider the method used should be standardised." With this opinion Vice-Admiral Moore fully concurred.

29. Rear-Admiral Bisset's report. Admiral Bisset added: "It was especially heartening to an ex-carrier captain accustomed for several years to be very short of aircraft (especially fighters) and made one wonder 'what might have been' if the Fleet Air Arm had been adequately supplied with aircraft in the early days of the war."

30. The fighters jettisoned their long range tanks between Alta and Lange Fjords, after 1 hour 5 minutes flying.

31. Report by Lt.-Cmdr. Baker-Faulkner.

32. Aircraft M of 830 Squadron. It was seen after the attack in a controlled glide with its engine stopped at a height of about 1,000 ft., proceeding up Kaa Fjord in a south-westerly direction; "there is every reason to expect that he was able to make a good forced landing." (*Furious* report.) (See Appendix C (2).)

33. Aircraft Q of 829 Squadron, see Appendix C (2).

34. Report by Lieut-Cmdr. Rance.

35. Aircraft M of 829 Squadron. It made its getaway with the remainder and was subsequently seen diving vertically in flames on to the mountain side. (See Appendix C (2).)

36. One Barracuda still had a 600-lb. A/S bomb, which could not be jettisoned owing to an electrical failure. This aircraft was landed on the *Victorious* last of all, the flight deck being cleared in case of mishaps. All, however, went well.

37. A total of 40 Barracudas and 81 Fighters took part in the two strikes; 25 Fighters (Seafires and Wildcats) were retained with the Fleet for its defence and nine Swordfish for A/S patrols. After the attack was over, Corsairs from the *Victorious* relieved the *Furious* Seafires on combat patrol.

38. "To V.A.2 (R) *Furious*.   From *Victorious*.
    Preliminary examination completed and following claims are considered well founded:–
    (1) First strike 827 and 830 Squadrons.
        3-1,600-lb. A.P., 4-500lb. S.A.P., 3-500-lb. M.C. hits.
    (2) *Tirpitz* during 1st strike was in a position shown in Mosaic A. A 1,600-lb hit was obtained vicinity fore superstructure, 3-500-lb. bombs hit amidships and a number forward of bridge. Photographic evidence exists of between-deck bomb detonations. Nevertheless, *Tirpitz* still on an approximate even keel and normal trim and draught.
    (3) Smoke generators started during attack, but were ineffective. Flak was not experienced until just before the attack started and was light and ineffective.
    (4) Second Strike 829 and 831 Squadrons.
        4-500-lb. S.A.P., 2-500-lb. M.C. and 1-600-lb. A/S hits are allocated (a) one hit starboard side of mainmast, which caused large explosion, (b) two hits on forecastle, causing big explosions, (c) one abreast Y turret and three amidships.
    (5) Between strikes *Tirpitz* had shifted berth to position bows 295352, stern 30352 and was shrouded in smoke screen which did not interfere with aiming, but together with bomb smoke made observation of results difficult. Flak was heavy, but ragged in target area, a box barrage being put up over target.
    (6) Those near misses which appear in photographs so far seen are not judged near enough to cause substantial damage.
    (7) *Tirpitz* was left shrouded in smoke with two fires burning amidships, and had ceased fire when last aircraft dived.
    (8) No signs of G.A.F. were observed.
    (9) I believe *Tirpitz* now to be useless as a warship. 031737A."
    For final assessment of hits, see Appendix D and Plan 4.

39. There had been two reports of possible submarines in the area during the forenoon; air search had, however, failed to make contact.

40. This fatigue has been frequently mentioned in United States reports of operations in the Pacific, and a number of accidents have been ascribed to it.

41. M.S.T. (Zone-2).

42. Force 9's escort had been reinforced on 5 April by the *Ulysses* from Scapa, by order of the Commander-in-Chief.

43. The careful briefing of the air crews has already been mentioned (see pages 142-143).

44. This threw a heavy strain on the engine room departments of escort carriers. Rear-Admiral Bisset remarked:– "A special word of praise is due to the engine room departments of the escort carriers. From 1430 on Saturday, 1 April to 1600 on Thursday, 6 April, the ships were for the most part steaming at their full speed of 17 knots with nothing in hand

for station keeping... their total engine room complement amounts to approximately 13 officers and 30 ratings."

45. Opinions from sea on the important point have been called for, and since this operation much experience has been gained. There are both advantages and disadvantages in the Admiral flying his flag in the carrier, and the choice of ship must depend to a large degree upon the type of operation which is being carried out and the type and strength of the enemy's forces.
46. September, 1944.
47. On loan to the Polish Navy.
48. Royal Canadian Navy.
49. Had to return to carrier before taking part in strike.
50. Failed to return from attack.
51. Crashed in the sea after take-off; all crew lost.
52. Shot down.
53. Bomb failed to release.
54. Bombs dropped safe, owing to electrical failure.
55. One bomb failed to release.
57. Rear-Admiral Bisset decided against the risk of landing this aircraft without hook on either of the Fleet Carriers because of the large number of aircraft in repair at the time.
58. One bomb failed to release.
59. Three bombs dropped "safe".

Part IV

B.R. 1736 (22) (A)   RESTRICTED

NAVAL STAFF HISTORY
SECOND WORLD WAR
C.B.4499(A)

TIRPITZ
An Account of the Various Attacks Carried Out By the British Armed Forces and Their Effect Upon the German Battleship

1948

Volume 1
REPORT AND APPENDICES

Admiralty
31 March, 1949

P.03370/47
    C.B. 4499(A) Tirpitz – An account of the various
attacks carried out by British Armed Forces and their
effect upon the German battleship, Volume I. Reports
and Appendices, 1948, having been approved by My
Lords Commissioners of the Admiralty is promulgated
for information and guidance.

This book is invariably to be kept locked up when not in use and is not to be taken outside the ship or establishment for which it is issued without the express permission of the Commanding Officer.

This book is the property of His Majesty's Government.

It is intended for the use of Officers generally, and may in certain cases be communicated to persons in His Majesty's Service below the rank of Commissioned Officer who may require to be acquainted with its contents in the course of their duties. The Officers exercising this power will be held responsible that such information is imparted with due caution and reserve.

Attention is called to the penalties attaching to any infraction of the Official Secrets Acts.

Director of Naval Construction
Admiralty
31 March, 1949

P.03370/47

Brief History

Tirpitz and the ill-starred *Bismarck* were planned during the first years of the Nazi Regime as part of a class of heavy battleships which were to have a standard displacement of 45,000 tons; they followed the 33,000 ton battlecruisers *Scharnhorst* and *Gneisenau* as a further stage in the re-birth of the German Battle Fleet. It was intended to follow *Tirpitz* and *Bismarck* with six super-battleships of 60,000 tons, four large battlecruisers of 35,000 tons, six large fleet aircraft carriers, and all the battlecruisers, destroyers and other attendant craft needed to make a bid for supremacy on the high seas.

Tirpitz was laid down at Wilhelmshaven in October, 1936, launched in April, 1939, and completed in November, 1940. She commissioned on 25 January, 1941, and spent the remainder of the year carrying out extensive trials, overcoming the inevitable teething troubles and working up into an efficient fighting unit. During this period she visited Kiel, Gdynia and Danzig, returning to Kiel at intervals for repairs and adjustments. (See Figure I).

Meanwhile attention was being paid by the Germans to the future employment of their heavy naval units. In spite of the reverses suffered in the loss of, first, the pocket battleship *Graf Spee* and then the battleship *Bismarck* and also the blockading of the *Scharnhorst* and *Gneisenau* which had been at Brest since mid-March, 1941, there still remained formidable operational units for deployment. In August, 1941, Admiral Raeder (Commander-in-Chief of the German Navy) recommended the concentration of heavy ships in northern waters as promising strategic results. In December, 1941, Hitler demanded a concentration of battleships and pocket battleships in northern waters because latest intelligence had firmly convinced him that a British landing in northern Norway was imminent; he was deeply concerned at the possible catastrophic results of such a landing and said "The fate of the war will be decided in Norway". The outcome was that in mid-January, 1942, *Tirpitz* sailed for Norway and approximately a month later *Scharnhorst* and *Gneisenau* made their historic dash through the English Channel in a successful effort to regain German ports.

Tirpitz's first sortie was made from Trondheim in March, 1942, after a Russia-bound convoy had been shadowed by German reconnaissance aircraft. Torpedo carrying Albacores of the Fleet Air Arm made contact with the ship off the Lofoten Islands on 9 March and launched an unsuccessful attack following which *Tirpitz* retired at high speed. She returned to Trondheim and remained in that area until early July, 1942. On 7 July, British reconnaissance aircraft sighted *Tirpitz* off Tromsø and on 8 July the Russians claimed to have attacked her off North Cape with torpedoes fired from a submarine. The ship was next located at Bogen Fjord, near Narvik, where she remained until October, 1942, when machinery defects which had developed during the previous months made it desirable for her to return to Trondheim for repairs before the onset of the Arctic winter.

On 11 January, 1943, Hitler, furious at the failure of an attack on a convoy by *Hipper* and *Lutzow*, announced his intention of decommissioning the large ships. He told Raeder that the present critical situation demanded the application of all available fighting power, personnel and material, and that the large ships must not be permitted to be idle for months. On Hitler's instructions Raeder produced a memorandum on the decommissioning of the large ships; he strenuously contested the decision but to no effect. Following this, Raeder resigned and was succeeded by Dönitz. Decommissioning of certain ships was put into effect, but following strong representations from Dönitz, Hitler agreed to keep *Tirpitz* and *Scharnhorst* in commission; Dönitz reasoned that these heavy units, together with *Lutzow* and six destroyers, would form a fairly powerful task force. On 2 February, 1943, Hitler issued an order for the cessation of work on the building of large ships.

The machinery repairs to *Tirpitz* appeared to have been completed (with spares brought from Germany) by the end of February, 1943, at which time she was reported as undergoing exercises in Trondheim Fjord. She left the Trondheim area in March, 1943, and joined the *Scharnhorst* and *Lutzow* in the Narvik area. The three ships left Narvik in company on 27 March and arrived in the Kaa Fjord, between Tromsø and North Cape, on 2 April. They stayed in this area until 7 September. On 9 September they carried out a raid on the Norwegian Islands of Spitzbergen with the object of destroying Allied bases and installations which were alleged to have been set up there. This raid indicated that the German battleship was likely to become more active and plans were therefore made to attack her with the X-Craft which had just come into operational service.

Three of the six X-Craft which were despatched to make this attack in the Kaa Fjord, to which *Tirpitz* had returned after the Spitzbergen raid, successfully negotiated the inner defences around her on 22 September and two of them laid their explosive charges on the sea-bed under or near the ship before being destroyed. At least two of these charges detonated as intended and the resultant damage immobilised *Tirpitz* for six months. At the end of this period, that is mid-March, 1944, she was reported as running trials in the Altenfjord and arrangements were made to lay on a bombing attack by Fleet Air Arm Barracudas from the Home Fleet Carriers. The first attack was made on 3 April by 40 Barracudas in two waves escorted by ship-borne fighters, just as *Tirpitz* was on the point of leaving her berth to run an extensive series of sea trials to test the repairs. The attack was a complete surprise, 14 hits were scored in spite of very low cloud, a smoke screen and the difficulty of attacking over mountains, and though the material efficiency of the ship was not seriously impaired, the heavy casualties meant that she would not be able to fight an action for some time.

Tirpitz was still in Kaa Fjord when she was again attacked by Fleet Air Arm aircraft on 17 July and 22, 24 and 29 August. Observer posts, which had been set up some distance from the anchorage, were able to give warning of these raids and a thick smoke screen, heavy anti-aircraft fire and low cloud prevented the attacks being pressed well home. Two hits were scored on 24 August but again no vital damage to the ship resulted.

The urgent necessity of releasing for the Far East the capital ships held at Scapa to counter the menace of *Tirpitz* made it imperative to render the ship inoperative at an early date. On 15 September, 1944, she was attacked at her anchorage in the Kaa Fjord with the new 12,000 lb. M.C. bombs (Tallboys) which had been developed primarily for land demolition purposes. 21 Bomber Command Lancasters, operating from a Russian base, found the ship almost completely obscured by smoke. Only one hit (at the fore end) was registered owing to the extreme difficulty of carrying out a high level bombing attack in the poor visibility conditions prevailing, but severe damage was caused and *Tirpitz* was henceforth incapable of being a threat to shipping. However, this fact did not become known to the Allies until the termination of the war, and the attacks continued.

Following this latest damage the Germans held a Conference at which they decided that as it was no longer possible to make *Tirpitz* ready for sea and action again, the ship's remaining fighting efficiency should be utilised as a reinforcement of the defences in the Polar Area. On 15 October *Tirpitz* was moved to a berth near Tromsø and arrangements were made to protect her with anti-aircraft and smoke defences and land-based aircraft. This berth was supposed to conform to special requirements laid down at the Conference, one of which limited the maximum depth of water in the anchorage to a figure which would have prevented the ship from capsizing; the depth at the position in which *Tirpitz* was finally moored exceeding this limit and a hasty attempt was made to build up the sea-bed by depositing dredged material around and under the ship, which became known as "The Floating Battery".

On 29 October, 1944, Lancasters again attacked with 12,000 lb. bombs. Heavy cloud obscured the Tromsø anchorage and militated against accurate high level bombing but a near miss off the port quarter produced flooding aft.

Finally, on 12 November, 1944, the somewhat inactive operational career of *Tirpitz* was brought to a close when Lancaster aircraft bombed her with 12,000 lb. Tallboys for the third time, scoring hits which – aided by one near miss – caused the world's only "unsinkable" battleship to capsize in about ten minutes with the loss of some 1,000 lives.

Opposite, Fig. 1

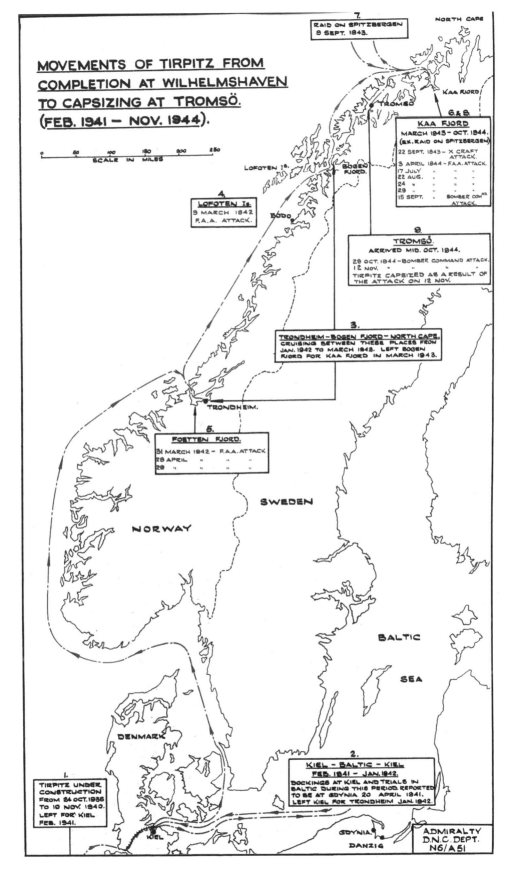

MOVEMENTS OF TIRPITZ FROM COMPLETION AT WILHELMSHAVEN TO CAPSIZING AT TROMSÖ. (FEB. 1941 – NOV. 1944).

SCALE IN MILES
0   50   100   150   200   250

NORTH CAPE

7.
RAID ON SPITZBERGEN
9 SEPT. 1943.

Kaa Fjord

TROMSÖ

6. & 8.
KAA FJORD
MARCH 1943 – OCT. 1944.
(EX. RAID ON SPITZBERGEN)
22 SEPT. 1943 – X CRAFT ATTACK.
3 APRIL 1944 – F.A.A. ATTACK.
17 JULY   "   "
22 AUG.   "   "
24   "   "   "
29   "   "   "
15 SEPT.   "   BOMBER COMMR. ATTACK.

Lofoten Is.

BOGEN FJORD.

4.
LOFOTEN Is.
9 MARCH 1942
F.A.A. ATTACK.

BODÖ

9.
TROMSÖ.
ARRIVED MID. OCT. 1944.
29 OCT. 1944 – BOMBER COMMAND ATTACK.
12 NOV.   "   "   "
TIRPITZ CAPSIZED AS A RESULT OF THE ATTACK ON 12 NOV.

3.
TRONDHEIM – BOGEN FJORD – NORTH CAPE.
CRUISING BETWEEN THESE PLACES FROM JAN. 1942 TO MARCH 1943. LEFT BOGEN FJORD FOR KAA FJORD IN MARCH 1943.

TRONDHEIM.

5.
FOETTEN FJORD.
31 MARCH 1942 – F.A.A. ATTACK
28 APRIL   "   "   "
29   "   "   "   "

SWEDEN

NORWAY

BALTIC

SEA

DENMARK

1.
TIRPITZ UNDER CONSTRUCTION FROM 24 OCT. 1936 TO 10 NOV. 1940. LEFT FOR KIEL FEB. 1941.

KIEL

2.
KIEL – BALTIC – KIEL
FEB. 1941 – JAN. 1942.
DOCKINGS AT KIEL AND TRIALS IN BALTIC DURING THIS PERIOD. REPORTED TO BE AT GDYNIA 20 APRIL 1941. LEFT KIEL FOR TRONDHEIM JAN. 1942.

GDYNIA

DANZIG

ADMIRALTY
D.N.C. DEPT.
N6/A51

The Ship

There was nothing sensational about the design of *Tirpitz*; she was merely a very large battleship, designed on conventional lines, propelled by three screws driven by steam turbines and mounting eight 38 cm. (approx. 15-in.) guns in twin turrets, arranged in the conventional way, two forward and two aft. This German mastodon was designed to a standard displacement of 42,600 tons, although the displacement reported for Treaty conditions was 35,000, the same as that of the *King George V* and *Washington* classes of battleship, which were genuinely designed to this size. In the deep condition she displaced 50,000 tons and had a draught of nearly 34 ft. Other things being equal this greater displacement would have been accompanied by greater ability to withstand damage. Although she measured 822 ft. overall, her most impressive dimension was her beam of 118 ft. which would have prevented her from passing through the Panama Canal. It was always thought that this implied a very deep "bulge" for protection against underwater attack, but it is now known that there was nothing remarkable about her underwater protection which was, in fact, inferior to that fitted in both British and American contemporary Capital Ships. The very large beam was adopted to provide an abnormally high initial stability. Such measures, however, may often reduce the resistance of the ship to the more severe states of damage. It is doubtful whether *Tirpitz* was at all better than her allied counterparts in this respect.

Information gained from a survey of the wreck and numerous drawings brought from Germany confirm that *Tirpitz*'s reputed fine watertight subdivision, and consequent "invincibility", were a complete myth; her subdivision was very similar to that of our own Capital Ships, and indeed those of all major sea Powers. Her watertight integrity was in several ways subordinated to requirements of convenience; for example, every transverse watertight bulkhead in the ship was pierced by watertight doors on the lower and middle platform decks, a menace which has been eliminated from H.M. ships for many years, and the engine rooms seemed to contain far more space than was needed.

Some of the available weight was used to secure a very high speed. *Tirpitz* was designed to develop 150,000 shaft horse-power which enabled her to make over 30 knots in the average action condition, and she was capable of developing 165,000 shaft horse-power for sudden bursts of over 31 knots. Her range based on an oil fuel capacity of 5,000 tons was over 10,000 sea miles. More fuel could be carried in an emergency.

More of the extra displacement in *Tirpitz* was accounted for by the fact that her 38 cm. guns were mounted in twin turrets rather than the weight saving triple and quadruple arrangements used in modern American and British Capital ships. Also the Germans fitted separate low angle and high angle secondary batteries rather than the dual purpose mountings used in Allied ships. She thus had twelve 15 cm. (5.9-in.) low angle guns in twin turrets, three on either side of the amidships superstructure, and sixteen high angle 10.5 cm. (4.1-in.) guns in twin mountings – four on each side. A further battery of sixteen 3.7 cm. (1.46-in.) mountings for close range anti-aircraft work was also provided.

This powerful armament was controlled by range-finders and director sights on the forward and after conning towers, and on the fore top. There were smaller range-finders for the secondary armament, one on each side of the bridge. The 10.5 cm. H.A. armament was controlled by four special gyro stabilized directors, one to port and one to starboard of the bridge, and two on the centre line abaft the main mast.

Tirpitz's general layout is illustrated by the small-scale drawing (Figure 2) which has been prepared for this report from larger scale drawings found in the Naval Arsenal at Kiel. It will be seen from the drawing that the machinery spaces, consisting of six boiler rooms, three engine rooms and miscellaneous compartments housing auxiliary machinery, the magazines and shell rooms, and other vital compartments such as fire control rooms, were well protected by a long armoured citadel. The sides were of 320 mm. (12.6-in.) thick cemented armour plates from 8 ft. below the waterline up to the battery deck and thinner plating of 145 mm. (5.7-in.) thickness to the upper deck. In addition, the third deck down was armoured with 80 mm. (3.15-in.) non-cemented plating over the machinery spaces and 100 mm. (3.94-in.) over the magazines between the torpedo bulkheads, while the sloping deck armour between the centre portion and the base of the side armour was 110 mm. (4.33-in.) in way of machinery spaces and 120 mm. (4.72)-in.) in way of magazines. There were extensions of the citadel by thinner armour, the lower belt being 60 mm. (2.36-in.) plating forward and 80 mm. (3.15-in.) aft and the upper belt being 35 mm. (1.38-in.) forward and aft. While there was no deck armour before the forward magazines, deck protection aft over the steering gear compartments was 110 mm. (4.33-in.) in thickness. This armoured citadel, re-inforced by a strength deck (the upper deck) which was 50 mm. (1.97-in.) thick generally, afforded efficient protection against splinters and all but the largest bombs dropped from a considerable height. Barbettes, and turret sides and roofs, and conning towers were protected by armour on the same generous lines.

Four sea-planes which were carried for spotting and reconnaissance were accommodated in special hangars abreast the funnel and under the main mast. They were launched by a fixed athwartships catapult between the funnel and the main mast.

It will be seen from this description that the *Tirpitz* and her sister ship, the *Bismarck*, were formidable – if conventional – fighting units which required our best ships and weapons to counter them, and which were capable of defeating attacks by heavy shell and all but the heaviest bombs. While *Tirpitz* remained in the Norwegian Fjords, powerful British units had to be kept in Home waters to protect our shipping.

Opposite, Fig. 2

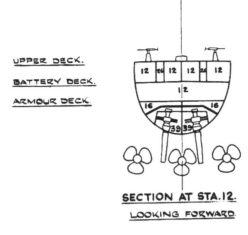

UPPER DECK.

BATTERY DECK.

ARMOUR DECK.

SECTION AT STA.12.

LOOKING FORWARD.

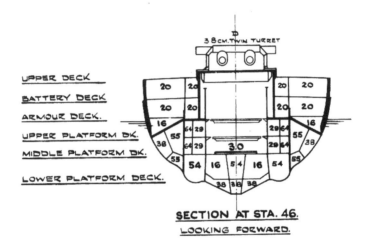

3·8CM.TWIN TURRET

UPPER DECK

BATTERY DECK

ARMOUR DECK.

UPPER PLATFORM DK.

MIDDLE PLATFORM DK.

LOWER PLATFORM DECK.

SECTION AT STA. 46.

LOOKING FORWARD.

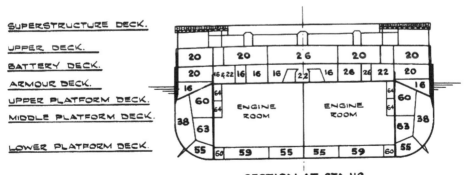

SUPERSTRUCTURE DECK.

UPPER DECK.

BATTERY DECK.

ARMOUR DECK.

UPPER PLATFORM DECK.

MIDDLE PLATFORM DECK.

LOWER PLATFORM DECK.

ENGINE ROOM   ENGINE ROOM

SECTION AT STA.112.

LOOKING FORWARD.

Tirpitz
General Arrangement

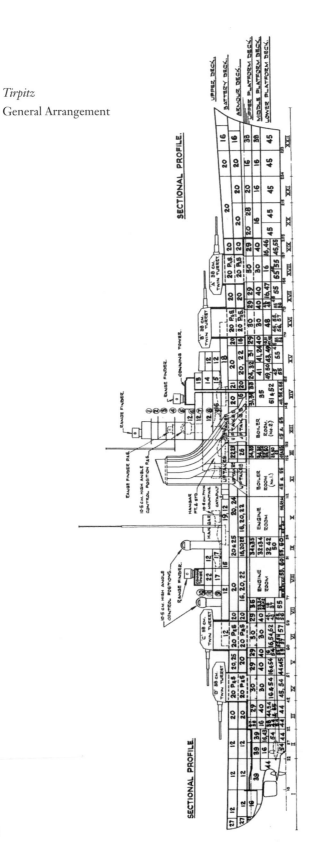

Fig. 2

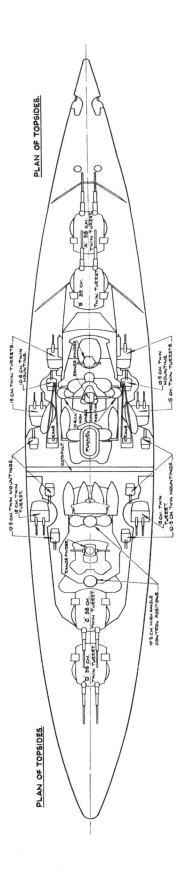

PLAN OF TOPSIDES.

PLAN OF TOPSIDES.

LOWER PLATFORM DECK.

1. FORE TOP.
2. UPPER SEARCHLIGHT PLATFORM.
3. LOWER   "   "
4. ADMIRAL'S BRIDGE.
5. UPPER MAST DECK.
6. LOWER   "   "
7. UPPER BRIDGE.
8. LOWER   "
9. SUPERSTRUCTURE DECK.

10. DECK HOUSE, AFT (UPPER)
11.   "   "   "   (LOWER).
12. CABINS.
13. ACTION INFORMATION CENTRE.
14. A/S OFFICE.
15. OFFICE.
16. STORE.
17. ADMIRAL'S APARTMENTS.
18. SICK BAY.

19. WARD ROOM.
20. CREW SPACE.
21. BAKERY.
22. WORKSHOP.
23. DRYING ROOM.
24. W/T OFFICE.
25. GALLEY.
26. LOBBY OR DECK SPACE.
27. SMOKE APPARATUS ROOM.

28. CAPSTAN MACHINERY COMPARTMENT.
29. 38 C.M. MAGAZINE.
30. 38 C.M. HANDING ROOM.
31. 3·7 C.M. MAGAZINE.
32. ANTI-AIRCRAFT TRANSMITTING STATION.
33. CONTROL CENTRE.
34. 15 C.M. MAGAZINE AND SHELL ROOM.
35. 10·5 C.M. MAGAZINE.
36. GUN CALCULATING POSITION.

37. FAN ROOM.
38. W.T.C.
39. STEERING GEAR COMPARTMENT.
40. 38 C.M. SHELL ROOM.
41. MAIN TRANSMITTING STATION.
42. THRUST-BLOCK COMPARTMENT.
43. PUMP ROOM.
44. BALLAST TANK.
45. RES. OIL FUEL TANK.

46. E/S GEAR.
47. REFRIGERATING MACHINERY.
48. COLD STORAGE.
49. GYRO ROOM.
50. SWITCH-BOARD ROOM.
51. AUXILIARY MACHINERY COMPARTMENT.
52. DYNAMO ROOM.
53. BOILER ACTION STATION.
54. SHAFT TUNNEL.

55. OIL FUEL TANK.
56. WASH WATER TANK.
57. FRESH   "   "
58. FEED   "   "
59. OVERFLOW TANK.
60. LUBRICATING OIL TANK.
61. ANTI-AIRCRAFT MAGAZINE.
62. MAGAZINE COOLING MACHINERY.
63. AVIATION SPIRIT TANK.
64. CABLE PASSAGE.

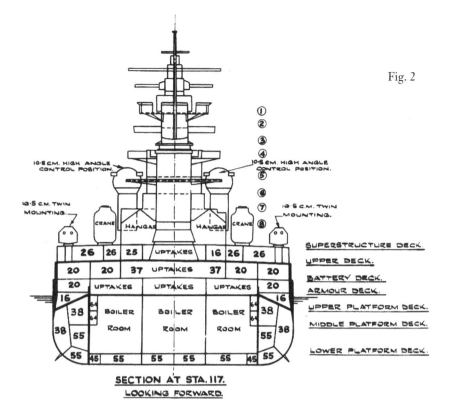

Fig. 2

10.5 C.M. HIGH ANGLE CONTROL POSITION.

10.5 C.M. HIGH ANGLE CONTROL POSITION.

10.5 C.M. TWIN MOUNTING.

10.5 C.M. TWIN MOUNTING.

① ② ③ ④ ⑤ ⑥ ⑦ ⑧

CRANE HANGAR HANGAR CRANE

26	26	25	UPTAKES	16	26	26	SUPERSTRUCTURE DECK.
20	20	37	UPTAKES	37	20	20	UPPER DECK.
20	UPTAKES	UPTAKES	UPTAKES	20			BATTERY DECK. / ARMOUR DECK.

16 / 38 / 38 / 55 / 55 / BOILER ROOM / BOILER ROOM / BOILER ROOM / 64 64 64 / 16 / 38 / 55 / 38 / 45 / 55 / 55 / 55 / 55 / 55 / 45 / 55

UPPER PLATFORM DECK.
MIDDLE PLATFORM DECK.
LOWER PLATFORM DECK.

SECTION AT STA. 117.
LOOKING FORWARD.

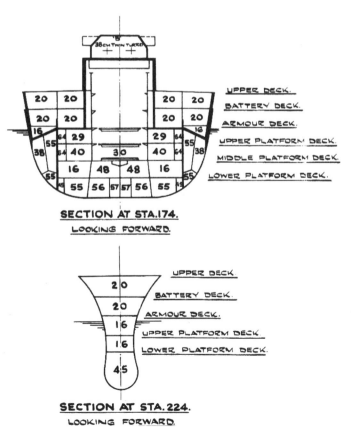

38 C.M. TWIN TURRET

20	20		20	20	UPPER DECK.
20	20		20	20	BATTERY DECK.
16				16	ARMOUR DECK.

55 / 64 / 29 / 29 / 64 / 55 / UPPER PLATFORM DECK.
38 / 64 / 40 / 30 / 40 / 64 / 38 / MIDDLE PLATFORM DECK.
16 / 48 / 48 / 16 / LOWER PLATFORM DECK.
55 / 55 / 56 / 57 57 / 56 / 55 / 55

SECTION AT STA. 174.
LOOKING FORWARD.

UPPER DECK
2 0
BATTERY DECK.
20
ARMOUR DECK.
16
UPPER PLATFORM DECK.
16
LOWER PLATFORM DECK.
45

SECTION AT STA. 224.
LOOKING FORWARD.

The Attacks

Attack by Fleet Air Arm Torpedo Bombers

On 6 March, 1942, H.M. Submarine *Sealion*, on patrol off the northern entrance to Trondheim, reported an enemy heavy ship proceeding on a north-easterly course. As a convoy on passage from Iceland to North Russia had been shadowed by a Focke-Wulf aircraft on the previous day, it was thought possible that the battleship *Tirpitz* might have left Trondheim to attack it. The C.-in-C., Home Fleet, in the *King George V*, with the *Duke of York*, *Renown* and *Victorious*, were at sea covering the convoy. On the following day C.–in-C., Home Fleet, intercepted a distress message from the Russian *Ijora* in position 72° 35' N, 10° 50' E. Early on 9 March six Albacores were flown off *Victorious* to search the area in which *Tirpitz* was believed to be operating. She was sighted at 0800 and a striking force of 12 Albacores armed with torpedoes, which had been flown off *Victorious* at 0735, was guided to the target by the shadowing aircraft. At 0842 *Tirpitz* was sighted by the torpedo planes which attacked in two waves, one on each side of the ship. The torpedoes appear to have been dropped at an excessively long range which enabled *Tirpitz* to "comb the tracks", turning sharply first to port and then to starboard. No hits were scored, but the German command seemed to have been somewhat scared because *Tirpitz* retired at high speed to her safe anchorage in the Foetten Fjord near Trondheim.

Early Bomber Command Attacks

In the Foetten Fjord she was immune from most forms of attack; she lay surrounded by mountains and was moored close in to the cliffs on one side and surrounded by torpedo nets on all others. On the occasional fine day which made air attack just possible she had only to put up a smoke screen to rectify the climatic defect. Despite these difficulties she was attacked by Bomber Command aircraft during the early hours of 31 March, and 28 and 29 April, 1942. The weather conditions during the first of these attacks were so bad that only one aircraft succeeded in finding *Tirpitz* at all, the usual smoke screen was in use and the attack was abortive. During the second and third attacks, most of the aircraft despatched, 32 and 30 respectively, managed to find the ship but again the smoke screen prevented useful results from being achieved. The Germans who were interrogated after the surrender reported that in one of these attacks the bombs (probably hydrostatically fused mines) rolled down the cliff into the sea – a mode of attack which they regarded as worthy of more success than it achieved.

Although the difficulties of carrying out an attack against a Capital Ship under these conditions are fully appreciated, the 4,000 lb. blast bombs with instantaneous fuses which seem to have constituted the major part of the bomb loads carried in these early attacks, were rather unsuitable. A hit would have caused only superficial damage to superstructures, while near misses would have detonated on the surface with little fragmentation and practically no effect on such a heavy ship. 2,000 lb. A.P. bombs dropped in level flight would have been a better choice, since twice as many of these bombs could have been carried and any hits would have had a direct effect on the vessel's fighting efficiency. The small Mk.XIX mines containing 100 lbs. of explosive and fitted with hydrostatic fuses to operate at 30 ft. depth had an almost negligible target, and the 500 lb. and 250 lb. G.P. bombs had little chance of producing serious damage against a ship of this size.

Operation Source

Tirpitz had a very quiet time from April, 1942, until March, 1943, during which period nothing useful was accomplished. At the end of this period *Scharnhorst* and *Lutzow* joined forces with her in the Altenfjord; these three ships with their attendant destroyers constituted a serious menace to the Russian convoys, which were suspended during the long daylight of the summer months for this reason. In early September, 1943, the squadron made a raid on Spitzbergen, showing that it was beginning to feel somewhat more aggressive, then returned to the anchorages in various branches of the Altenfjord. *Tirpitz* lay moored in Kaa Fjord – an arm of the Altenfjord some fifty miles from the sea – completely protected by torpedo nets. Though he disposed a superior Naval Force, it was extremely difficult for the C.-in-C., Home Fleet, to tempt the three ships to action from over 1,000 miles away, or to lay on a successful air or submarine attack against such secluded foxholes. It was finally decided to attack them with the new midget submarines officially known as X-Craft, which each carried two special ground mines, and which had been evolved after a careful study of the specific problem of attacking enemy units in such anchorages.

Six of these novel craft (X5 to X10) which had recently joined the Fleet, set out on the night of 11/12 September, 1943, on the hazardous journey to a position off the Norwegian coast, towed by 'S' and 'T' Class submarines. Two of them, X8 and X9, failed to complete this passage but the remaining four reached their rendezvous on 20 September, slipped their tows and proceeded independently to the attack.

X10's periscope and compasses immediately began giving much trouble and eventually failed completely; as a result, she had to retire from the attack. (The plan had been for X5, X6 and X7 to attack *Tirpitz*, X8 to attack *Lutzow* and X9 and X10 to attack *Scharnhorst*). During 20, 21 and 22 September, X5, X6 and X7 successfully negotiated the Altenfjord as far as the anchorage of *Tirpitz* in Kaa Fjord, passing en route mine fields, enemy surface vessels and the anti-submarine boom defence at the entrance to the Kaa Fjord.

X6 entered the torpedo net enclosure around *Tirpitz* at about 0705 G.M.T. using the official entrance which was open at the time for the passage of store ships (see Figure 3). After a series of instrumental defects had caused her to surface three times (she was mistaken for a porpoise on the first occasion, correctly identified on the second (at 0710) and attacked with machine-gun fire and hand grenades on the third), X6 succeeded in releasing her two charges under the ship abreast 'B' turret. As escape was then impossible, she was scuttled and her crew surrendered. Meanwhile, X7 endeavoured to penetrate the net defence by passing under it. She experienced a number of setbacks but eventually succeeded in entering the anchorage. Passing down it under the keel of *Tirpitz*, from forward to aft, she released one charge abreast 'B' turret and the other further aft, under the after Engine Room. This X-Craft left the enclosure at 0740, this time sliding over the nets, and then dived. During the manoeuvre she was sighted by the Germans and hit several times with machine-gun bullets. At 0812, while still submerged, the crew heard a tremendous explosion which they thought to be due to the explosion of the X-Craft charges. X7 subsequently became uncontrolled; it was decided to scuttle her and at 0835 she was brought to the surface, but sank again with her hatch open after only one member of the crew had managed to escape. The full movements of X5 are not known but she was seen at 0835 on the surface some 500 yards outside the nets, when she was fired upon by *Tirpitz* and appeared to sink.

There were thus four charges laid under or near *Tirpitz*, namely, one placed by X7 under the after engine room and three from X6 and X7 abreast 'B' turret.

From the German point of view, the first intimation that an attack was in progress came at about 0713 when a small craft (X6) – correctly identified as a submarine – was observed to break surface momentarily inside the torpedo nets about 200 to 250 ft. off the port beam. The submarine alarm was sounded, watertight doors were brought to the action state and the anti-aircraft guns were manned. The submarine was sighted again at 0720 and was attacked with 20 mm. and 37 mm. fire from *Tirpitz* and hand grenades thrown from a motor boat which had been despatched to attack her. The X-Craft was eventually brought to the surface and abandoned in a sinking condition by her crew. The motor boat tried to tow the submarine, which the Germans suspected might contain explosives, away from the battleship but it sank at 0732, some 50 to 60 yards off the port bow.

The Germans were aware of the existence of British midget submarines but had no information as to their armament. They were, therefore, undecided as to whether an attack by torpedoes, mines, or limpet charges had been made. To clear any limpets which might have been attached to the bottom, they pulled from stem to stern a wire strop slung around the ship under the keel. At the same time, preparations were made to get underway but, in view of the unknown menaces awaiting the ship in the fjord, it was ultimately decided to remain inside the nets. However, *Tirpitz*'s bow was moved away from the submarine known to have sunk off the port bow by tightening and slackening the port and starboard forward mooring cables. Unbeknown to the Germans this had the effect of clearing the forward part of the ship from the three charges placed abreast 'B' turret. The single charge aft remained effective.

Shortly after this evolution was complete at least two heavy explosions occurred in quick succession; spray was thrown up over the ship which shuddered violently. The other two X-Craft were destroyed in turn soon after this. An intensive depth charging of the fjord followed.

Although only one of the six charges originally intended for *Tirpitz* was effective, the results were undoubtedly worthwhile. Only a relatively small quantity of water entered the ship but damage to main machinery was enough to immobilize her for six months. It is doubtful whether the repairs carried out in Kaa Fjord restored the ship to her original standard of mechanical efficiency.

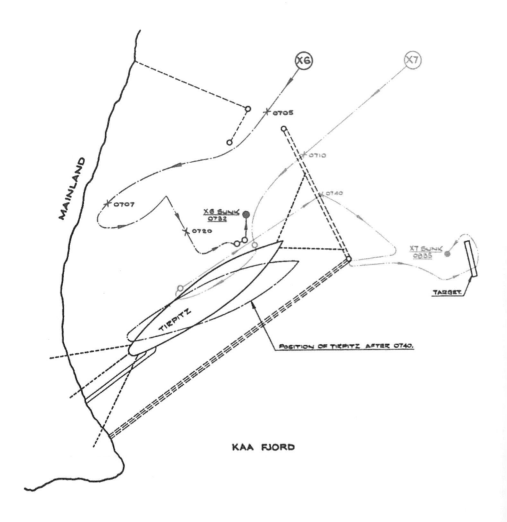

TIRPITZ.
OPERATION SOURCE.
TRACK CHART OF X-CRAFT.
SCALE: 1 IN. TO 220 FT.

Fig. 3

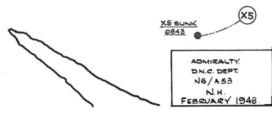

Operation Tungsten

The repair of damage caused by the X-Craft attack was complete by the beginning of March, 1944; *Tirpitz* then began a series of trials to test the efficacy of these repairs. These were to have culminated in prolonged sea trials in early April.

The first movements in Altenfjord were observed by our reconnaissance aircraft and C.-in-C. Home Fleet was therefore asked to lay on a bombing attack using Fleet Air Arm Aircraft. This attack took place on 3 April. Forty Barracudas were escorted by 81 Corsair, Hellcat and Wildcat fighters. Enemy reconnaissance was avoided by sending the Carrier force about a day behind a large Russia bound convoy. Complete surprise was achieved, the striking force reached the ship just as she was about to get underway for the open sea trials. Weather conditions were good.

The first strike began its attack at 0530 just as the second anchor was being weighed. Before a smoke-screen could be developed and before the flak batteries had been fully manned, the accompanying fighters were strafing the upperworks with machine-gun fire. Diving attacks by Barracudas carrying 1,600 lb. armour-piercing, 500 lb. semi-armour-piercing, and medium capacity bombs followed. A few 600 lb. anti-submarine bombs were also used. In all, nine hits (with one profitable near miss) were scored by this strike on the German ship. The second strike attacked at 0630 but found *Tirpitz* obscured by smoke, this time five hits and three near misses were obtained.

Unfortunately, owing to the low height from which the bombs were released (the Germans gave figures between 300 and 1300 ft.) none succeeded in penetrating the armour deck – in fact only two reached it. Two other bombs ricochetted off the 2-in. thick upper deck, and one lodged half-way through this deck. As all the vital parts of a large capital ship lie below armour, only superficial damage to living spaces and other unessential compartments was caused by the direct hits. This damage, however, was fairly extensive and several large fires resulted. Heavy casualties were caused both by the bombs and by the fighters. The greatest nuisance value was achieved by a bomb, probably 1600 lb. A.P., which struck the water a few ft. from the ship's side, penetrated the side plating beneath the armour belt and detonated near the main longitudinal protective bulkhead. This bomb flooded bulge compartments nearby and extensive work by divers was required to effect a repair.

In about a month *Tirpitz* was again operationally fit, no significant damage to armament or main machinery having been sustained in the attack. About two more months were required to complete the less important repairs.

Fleet Air Arm Attacks

Although *Tirpitz* showed no signs of leaving the Kaa Fjord it was suspected that the attack on 3 April had not inflicted any vital damage as it was realised that the bombs might not have been dropped from a height sufficient to enable them to penetrate the thick deck armour. Intelligence reports and reconnaissance photographs also indicated that the battleship was ready for further action. Attacks on the above dates were therefore made by bomber forces flown from Carriers of the Home Fleet in an attempt to prolong *Tirpitz*'s stay in the Kaa Fjord.

The first of these attacks developed during the early hours of 17 July, the Arctic summer being then at its height. Warning of the attack had been received about half-an-hour before the planes arrived and all necessary preparations, including the smoke-screen, had been made in *Tirpitz*. The aircraft dropped 1600 lb. armour piercing and 500 lb. bombs; no hits were scored.

Two attacks made at noon and in the evening of 22 August were also anticipated; again *Tirpitz* was enveloped in a smoke-screen, and no hits were registered. 500 lb. semi-armour-piercing bombs were used in these strikes.

The attack on 24 August was made during the afternoon, 80 aircraft being employed. The defences were once more in fully effective operation when the planes reached the *Tirpitz*, but this time, despite the difficulty of aiming through smoke, two of the 23 large armour-piercing bombs and 10 smaller semi-armour-piercing bombs which were dropped, scored hits. One of these detonated on the armour roof of 'B' turret which was only slightly damaged but the other – a 1600 lb. armour-piercing bomb – hit the port side of the upper deck abreast the forward conning tower, and penetrated through the armour deck to the lower platform (inner bottom) where it came to rest but – because of a fuse failure – did not detonate. Had this bomb been effective the main fire control rooms, switchboard rooms, etc., would have been put out of action. The resultant flooding would probably have extended to the forward auxiliary boiler room. In their official report on this attack the Germans stated:

"The attack on 24 August, 1944, was undoubtedly the heaviest and most determined so far experienced. The English showed great skill and dexterity in flying. For the first time they dived with heavy bombs. During the dive-bombing, fighter planes attacked the land batteries which, in comparison with earlier attacks, suffered heavy losses. The fact that the armour-piercing bomb of more than 1,540 lbs. did not explode must be considered an exceptional stroke of luck, as the effects of that explosion would have been immeasurable. Even incomplete smoke screening upsets the correctness of the enemy's aim, and it has been decided from now on to use smoke in wind strengths up to 9 m. per second irrespective of possible gaps."

The last of this series of attacks made on 29 August by 26 Barracudas, seven Hellcats, 10 Fireflies and 17 Corsairs from *Indefatigable* and *Formidable*, was carried out in exactly similar conditions. No hits were obtained.

Attack by Bomber Command Lancasters

A great improvement in technique was made on 15 September, 1944, when *Tirpitz* was attacked with the newly-developed Tallboy bombs. These massive bombs contained 5 100 lbs. of desensitized torpex in a comparatively thin streamlined case and were fitted with fuses having a slight time delay of 0.07 sec. Although it was anticipated that they might be damaged in passing through the heavy deck armour, it was hoped that the very large charge would compensate for any loss of efficiency and that even near misses would have considerable destructive value.

The operation was carried out by about 30 Lancasters which had previously flown from Scotland to North Russia, where they were based for the attack. The aircraft approached the target at high altitude from the South-East, descending to about 12,000 ft. for their attacks which they made in groups of about six, in close formation. The battleship was found moored at her berth; she had been given warning by shore radar installations so that shortly after the attack commenced an extensive and effective smoke-screen covered the greater part of the fjord, leaving only the boom surrounding *Tirpitz* and small portions of the ship visible. The main armament, directed by the shore radar installations, was used for putting up a barrage in way of the attacking aircraft.

Out of the 21 heavy bombs dropped, only one fell sufficiently close to *Tirpitz* to damage her. This bomb hit the upper deck on the extreme starboard side some 50 ft. abaft the bow, passed out through the flare of the forecastle into the water and detonated below keel level close to the ship. The explosion wrecked a large portion of the fore end, particularly that part below the waterline, and as a result of this damage the first 120 ft. of the ship became flooded to the waterline. Although this single hit did not seriously affect either machinery or armament, the damage to the fore end of *Tirpitz* could not be repaired without docking her, and she was henceforth unfit to undertake a voyage in the open sea and in consequence ceased to be an effective fighting unit.

The following resume, extracted from the translation of a captured German document shows the German reaction to this attack:–

"It was estimated that repairs, if they could be carried out without interruption, would take at least nine months.

"It was eventually decided at a conference on 23 September, 1944, at which the C.-in-C. and Naval War Staff were present, that it was no longer possible to make the *Tirpitz* ready for sea and action again. It was therefore considered that, in order to preserve the remaining fighting efficiency of the ship, she should be used as a reinforcement to the defences in the Polar Area. For this purpose *Tirpitz* was to be moved as soon as possible to the area west of Lyngenfjord, moored in shallow water and brought into the operation as a floating battery. A suitable berth had to be selected which would be reasonably secure and would offer favourable operational possibilities for the ship's armament. Adequate anti-aircraft, smoke-cover and net protection were to be provided. Makeshift repairs were to be made and the *Tirpitz* moved with the assistance of powerful tugs.

"The operation of moving the *Tirpitz* was carried out on 15 October, 1944. A berth was selected near Tromsø, Haakoy net enclosure, by F.O.I.C., Polar Coast in co-operation with Flag Officer, First Battle Group. The ship was protected against underwater attacks and aerial torpedoes by means of a double net barrage. Shore anti-aircraft guns and smoke-screen units were moved from Kaa Fjord to Tromsø. As the ship was only partially seaworthy, the crew, particularly the engine room complement, was decreased. It was found that there were varying depths of water at the selected berth; in particular there was a hollow below the midship section. Too many difficulties would have arisen if the ship were to be moved again, so it was decided to fill in the hollow till the water was 2 m. deep below the keel. Work was commenced by dredgers on 1 November, and by 12 November about 14,000 cm. had been filled in at both sides below the midship section."

Second Bomber Command Tallboy Attack

On 29 October, 1944, the lame *Tirpitz* now moored at Tromsø off Haakoy Island was again attacked by Bomber Command. A force of 32 Lancasters flying this time from British bases and carrying one Tallboy each, began bombing her at 0850. The target was seen obliquely as the aircraft approached, but low clouds obscured her from view during the bombing runs and made accurate bomb-aiming impossible. Once again, prior warning of the approaching raid was received and the ship was in a high state of readiness when the attack commenced. No direct hits were scored but the end was brought one stage nearer by a near miss off the port quarter, which damaged the port shaft and rudder and flooded about 100 ft. of the aft end of the ship on the port side.

Final Bomber Command Attack

The struggle between the British armed forces and *Tirpitz* came to an end on 12 November, 1944, when Bomber Command aircraft executed what was undoubtedly one of the most effective British air operations of the late war. 29 Lancasters, again carrying one 12,000 lb. M.C. bomb each, attacked the ship as she lay in her anchorage at Tromsø. Bombing commenced at 0941 and finished eight minutes later in clear weather and excellent visibility. *Tirpitz* had received ample warning by radio of the approach of the bombers and was again prepared when the attack developed. Intense anti-aircraft fire was augmented from nearby flak ships and shore batteries, but there was no effective smoke-screen. The bombing runs were made at heights varying between 12,500 ft. and 16,500 ft. *Tirpitz* received severe structural damage from, at least, two direct hits and one near miss, and as a result of this damage she capsized to port about ten minutes after the first bomb was dropped. Part of the starboard side of her hull is still to be seen above the surface – a reminder of the inability of a capital ship without adequate fighter cover to resist a determined and concentrated attack with modern airborne weapons.

Conclusions

The Second World War (1939–1945) has provided many striking lessons for those who would attack and for those who must defend a modern capital ship. None is more fundamental than those that can be learned from *Tirpitz*'s long struggle for survival among the Norwegian fjords. The history of *Tirpitz* is a classic example of the best way an inferior naval power can use one or more good battleships to pin down a superior enemy Naval Force over a long period, that is, by using them as a strategic threat in an almost unassailable anchorage. In contrast, the story of *Bismarck* illustrates the futility of operating an unsupported heavy unit in waters commanded by a superior enemy.

The example of *Tirpitz* also demonstrates that no anchorage is completely safe – not even the distant and narrow Norwegian fjords which lie in a rugged, mountainous country – unless adequate fighter cover can be provided, because no capital ship can be designed with a thick enough armour deck or sufficient underwater protection to defeat the most modern bombs.

As is indicated in pages 186-193, the German designers had done everything in their power to make *Tirpitz* invincible; half-way through her life they had firmly convinced themselves that this was so. But no capital ship yet designed is perfect. A very large armament and vast quantities of armour plate were built into *Tirpitz*, and to ensure a large margin of stability she was given a disproportionately large beam, but her free-board was small, and her stability at large angles of heel poor compared with contemporary Allied battleships. Because of the large beam, however, *Tirpitz*'s stability at small angles of heel was better than that of most ships, and, until heavy attacks were developed against them, both *Bismarck* and *Tirpitz* appeared to be able to withstand damage with the greatest of ease.

It may be profitable at this juncture to consider how best to attack a ship, or more particularly a capital ship such as *Tirpitz*.

The most fruitful attack is one which has as its result the sinking of the target. This can be accomplished by making it sink bodily, plunge or capsize.

Each method involves letting water into the ship; capsizing or plunging are more economical, and in that order, because less water is required.

If sufficient water to produce sinking cannot be let in, the aim should be to flood as many compartments as possible, underwater damage being particularly difficult to repair, and seawater an excellent auxiliary damaging agent.

Again, if flooding cannot be caused, the aim should be to damage the vitals, observing that the vitals of a capital ship are carefully arranged under armour.

The weapons which let water into ships and, therefore, have a chance of sinking them, are well known, being those which rupture the sides or bottom. Damage to vitals is produced by weapons of the same types and by the explosion of large charges at a distance, which often causes "shock damage". It is clear that high or medium capacity or general purpose bombs with instantaneous fuses and semi-armour piercing bombs with short delay fuses have little chance of producing vital damage.

The earlier attacks against *Tirpitz* failed, either because tactics were incorrect or the wrong weapons were used or insufficient of them to give a good probability of obtaining the requisite hits to sink. For example, the 4,000 lb. bombs used in the three Bomber Command attacks on *Tirpitz* during March and April, 1942, had no chance of producing damage except to upperworks. The charges laid by X-Craft went a large part of the way towards success because they let water into the ship and did extensive shock damage to the main machinery, but the water in which they were laid was too deep for them to produce sufficient flooding to sink the ship. The 1600 lb. armour-piercing bombs dropped during the Fleet Air Arm attacks were quite capable of penetrating *Tirpitz*'s deck armour and of causing vital damage and flooding if they had been released from a sufficient height. In the attack on 3 April, 1944, in particular, several hits were registered but the bombs were dropped from too small a height, and armour-piercing bombs were used in insufficient numbers to give a good probability of sinking.

The Tallboy bombs made up for their other deficiencies by their very large charge. As might have been expected they either broke up or detonated prematurely, or both, when they hit *Tirpitz*'s deck armour, but the radius of destruction was so large that damage to vitals and extensive flooding were inevitable. It is certain that, except when these bombs detonated in the water, the fuse delay of 0.07 sec. had no chance to function. The near miss effect of the bombs was disappointing; only detonation very close to the ship caused serious damage, and it is certainly not correct to attribute the sinking of *Tirpitz* primarily to the effects of near miss bombs. This poor performance as a near miss weapon is most probably due to the fact that the cavity of air, opened up by the swift passage of the bomb through the water, had insufficient time to close before the fuse functioned so that much of the energy of detonation was directed up this air cavity to the surface. Certainly, more spectacular results would be expected from such a large charge detonated statically in similar positions.

In the last attack, the two direct hits which, with one near miss, wrecked the port side of the amidships portion of the ship, detonated in the optimum positions for capsize. As is brought out in Appendix B.6 the effect of these three bombs would have capsized *Tirpitz* even had she sustained no damage previously. Had these three bombs been more widely distributed or had any one of them been in its corresponding position on the starboard side, three alone might not have proved fatal. This conclusion is, in fact, a perfectly general one; the best place to damage any ship is amidships and on one side only.

It is natural to ask – "What of the future?". Should attempts be made to strengthen the case of bombs as big as these to enable them to penetrate intact the deck armour of ships like *Tirpitz* (*Yamato* had an armour deck 7-in. thick)? – or should the decrease in charge/weight ratio which such strengthening implies be avoided at all costs to retain a very large charge as in Tallboy? The history of *Tirpitz* provides no answer to this question.

Appendix A

Detailed Accounts of Damage

A.1. X Craft Attack at Kaa Fjord on 22 September, 1943 (Operation 'Source')

A.2. F.A.A. Attack at Kaa Fjord on 3 April, 1944 (Operation 'Tungsten')

A.3. F.A.A. Attack at Kaa Fjord on 24 August, 1944

A.4. Bomber Command Attack at Kaa Fjord on 15 September, 1944

A.5. Bomber Command Attack at Tromsø on 29 October, 1944

A.6. Bomber Command Attack at Tromsø on 12 November, 1944

Illustrations

A.1 – Damage Sustained as a Result of X–Craft Attack in Kaa Fjord, 22 September, 1943 (Operation 'Source')

Narrative and Evidence
See pages 194-203.

Weapons Used
Each midget submarine (X craft) used in the attack carried two detachable side charges, resembling in shape the main tanks of a normal submarine, each of which contained two tons of Amatex. The charges were fitted with clock time fuses which could be set before release. Four such charges from two X-craft were released under *Tirpitz*, one under the port side of the Section VIII (centre engine room), one abreast the port side of 'B' turret and rather further from the ship. These charges were off the port side of the ship after the fore end had been moved to starboard as a precautionary measure. Two of these four charges, namely the one under the engine room and one off the port bow, are known to have detonated within a fraction of a second of each other.

The Depth of Water
The depth of water in the anchorage varied between 35 and 40 m. (i.e. approximately between 115 and 130 ft.) and the ship's draught at the time was about 10 m. (about 33 ft.).

Subsequent Events
The two heavy explosions occurred at about 0812 G.M.T. and caused heavy spray but no appreciable water columns. The whole ship was shaken violently. All lights and most of the electrical equipment failed immediately. The mooring cables remained intact and the ship listed gradually 2 degrees to port.

Structural Damage (See Figure A.1)
The bottom plating in way of the engine rooms was split and dished, the longest split being about 8 m. (approximately 26 ft.). The inner bottom and longitudinals in the damaged area were forced upwards and buckled and all the pipes, including condenser inlets and outlets, were subjected to shock.

At the fore end the explosion of the second charge caused a small split about 1 metre (3.3 ft.) long in the port side plating of Section XXII between the upper and middle platform decks. Plating in the vicinity was dished.

Whipping of the whole ship was most probably responsible for a sudden discontinuity in the straight line of keel and buckled panels of bottom plating in Section XI of the ship.

Flooding

Double bottom compartments in Sections VII to X (mainly on the port side) and No. 2 diesel generator room were flooded, and leakage into the port and centre engine rooms, No. 1 diesel-generator room, No. 2 dynamo control room, the after anti-aircraft control position and No. 2 steering gear compartment, was controlled by pumping. This flooding caused *Tirpitz* to heel to port 2 degrees. It was estimated that 800 tons of water entered the ship.

All pumps were put out of action by lack of electric power but one hour after the explosion the centre and port engine rooms were pumped out and, by 1800, No. 2 diesel-generator room had been pumped out using the hull and fire pumps.

Damage to Machinery

All turbine ft., plummer-blocks, thrust blocks and much of the auxiliary machinery were distorted or cracked and as a result of the propeller shafts could not be turned. The main defects were in Sections VII to IX. Damage to the port unit was more intense, for example, the port condenser and turbine casings were fractured. None of the boilers could be flashed up for some time because the auxiliary burners were damaged, particularly in the after boiler room; failure of electric current also prevented the fitted pumps being started. The damage took six months to repair.

Damage to Armament

All turrets jumped off their roller paths and turret clips were stretched. 'A' and 'C' turrets were put out of action temporarily and P.III 15cm. twin turret was jammed. The after anti-aircraft control position was put out of action by shock and flooding and a considerable amount of range-finding and other optical equipment were severely damaged and needed replacement, including the equipment in the 38 cm. director control towers and the 15 cm. secondary armament control towers on either side of the bridge.

Damage to Electrical Equipment

Most of the ship's lighting and nearly all her electrical equipment, including her W/T equipment, were put out of action by the explosions. There was some delay before a diesel generator and a small auxiliary plant could be started to supply the ship with power. Turbo-generators were brought into operation about 2½ hours after the explosions. Seven of the eight diesel-generators were put out of action by shock damage to casings and cracked holding-down bolts.

Damage to Communications Equipment

In addition to the temporary failure of communications and W/T equipment generally, due to loss of power, much of the W/T equipment and aerials were permanently damaged. Similar breakdowns occurred in the radar and echo ranging equipment.

Miscellaneous Damage

The port rudder installation was put out of action by shock which caused the stuffing gland to leak and the steering gear compartment to flood. Fire and bilge pumps were put out of action by electrical failures and mechanical damage. Two aircraft were badly damaged.

Tirpitz
X-Craft attack
22 September 1943

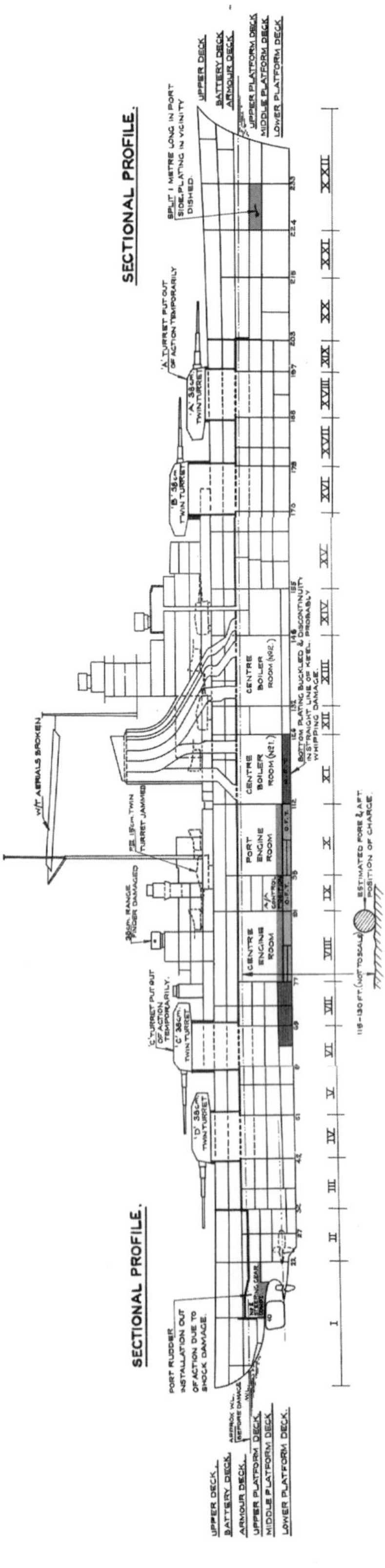

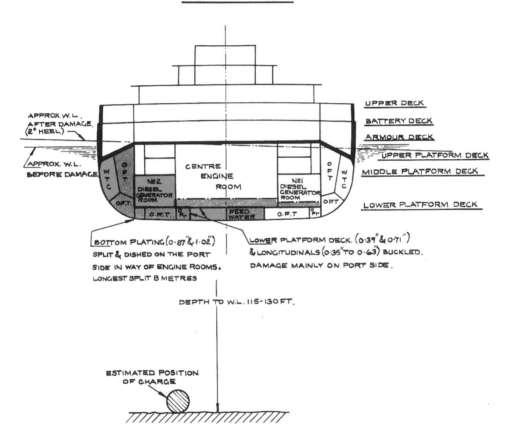

SECTION AT STA. 88.

(LOOKING FORWARD)

SCALE:- 1 IN. TO 32 FT.

Bottom compartments

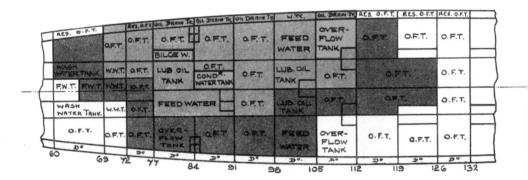

FLOODING KEY.

UNCONTROLLED RAPID FLOODING.

CONTROLLED FLOODING.

LIQUID PRESENT BEFORE DAMAGE

FLOODING INTO LIQUID PRESENT BEFORE
DAMAGE.

Lower platform deck

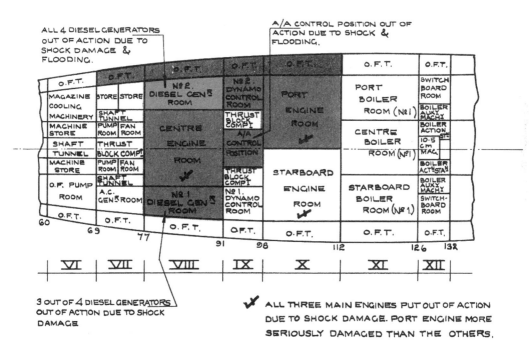

ALL 4 DIESEL GENERATORS
OUT OF ACTION DUE TO
SHOCK DAMAGE &
FLOODING.

A/A CONTROL POSITION OUT OF
ACTION DUE TO SHOCK &
FLOODING.

3 OUT OF 4 DIESEL GENERATORS
OUT OF ACTION DUE TO SHOCK
DAMAGE

ALL THREE MAIN ENGINES PUT OUT OF ACTION
DUE TO SHOCK DAMAGE. PORT ENGINE MORE
SERIOUSLY DAMAGED THAN THE OTHERS.

A.2. – Damage Sustained as a Result of F.A.A. Attack at Kaa Fjord on 3 April, 1944. (Operation 'Tungsten')

Narrative and Evidence
See pages 194-203.

Weapons Used
The following bombs were dropped during the attack:–

1600 lb. A.P. bombs fused .08 secs. delay	......	7+2
500 lb. S.A.P. bombs fused .14 secs. delay	......	27+39
500 lb. M.C. bombs fused Nose instant	....	9+9
600 lb. A/S bombs fused Hydrostatic 35 ft	....	4+1

where the two numbers indicate the number of bombs dropped during the first and second strikes respectively.

Structural Damage (See Figure A.2.)
The damage sustained by *Tirpitz* was mainly of a superficial nature. No bomb passed through the armour deck and only two penetrated to it. In the detailed summary of the damage given below, the bomb hits are numbered from forward; hits 3, 6, 8 and 9 and 10 to 14, occurred during the first strike and the remainder during the second strike; the near miss abreast the funnel occurred during the first strike.

Hit No. 1 (1600 lb. A.P. ?) penetrated the starboard side of the upper deck (1.97-in.) at station 218 over the junction of a deck beam and girder. The bomb failed to detonate and remained lodged in the deck plating.

Hit No. 2 (500 lb. M.C. ?) detonated on impact with the upper deck (1.97-in.) near station 172 on the port side. The deck was dished slightly and the surrounding structure was damaged by blast and splinters.

Hit No. 3 (500 lb. S.A.P. ?) detonated on impact with the lower mast deck at its forward starboard corner causing severe blast and splinter damage to surrounding structure; splinters were embedded in the conning tower armour (13.8-in.).

Hit No. 4 (500 lb. S.A.P. ?) detonated while passing through the port side of the upper deck (1.97-in.) near station 144 and blew a hole in this deck about 2 m. (6.5 ft.) in diameter, the edges being petalled downwards.

The surrounding structure above the upper deck and compartments below it in Section XIII were damaged by blast, splinters and a large fire.

Hit No. 5 (500 lb. M.C. ?) detonated on impact with the port upper deck edge at about station 125 causing splinter damage to superstructure and to the degaussing cable.

Hit No. 6 (1600 lb. A.P. ?) struck a boat on the starboard side near station 130, passed through the boat, and the roof (1.38-in.) and gun platform (0.8-in.) of S2, 15 cm. twin turret. It then struck the upper deck (3.15-in.) and was deflected along it into the gun room where it detonated just above the deck at about station 126 and caused severe blast and splinter damage to the surrounding structure. A large fire started in this area which caused extensive damage.

Hit No. 7 (500 lb. S.A.P. ?) perforated the after end of the roof of the starboard hangar and the superstructure deck. It rebounded from the upper deck (3.15-in.) and detonated just above that deck at about station 123 on the starboard side of the gun room. This detonation was in close proximity to that of Hit No. 6 and added to the damage caused by that bomb.

Hit No. 8 (500 lb. M.C. ?) struck the funnel a glancing blow on the port side, detonated a short distance from it and caused considerable blast and splinter damage. The port side of the funnel and six of the twelve uptakes in it were crushed, the roof of the port hangar collapsed and the port searchlight on the funnel was blown from its seating. A fire caused slight damage.

Hit No. 9 (1600 lb. A.P. ?) perforated the superstructure deck (0.4-in.), upper deck (1.97-in.), battery deck (0.24-in.), and detonated about station 110, port in contact with the top edge of the sloping deck armour (4.3-in.) just outboard of the main protective bulkhead. The armour deck was bulged downwards but not holed, and the continuation of the main protective bulkhead (1.8-in.) above the armour deck was torn away from the bulkhead proper at the horizontal riveted lap between the battery and armour decks, and was blown inboard. The battery deck outside this bulkhead was torn at its connection with the bulkhead and forced up against the upper deck. The inboard portion of the battery deck was arched upwards. Severe blast and splinter damage occurred in compartments on the battery and armour decks in Sections X and XI of the ship.

Note. The Germans considered it improbable that the damage done to the main protective bulkhead could have been caused by the explosive in an armour-piercing bomb. They suspected that petrol vapour from the damaged pipe line for fuelling the aircraft exploded and enhanced the effect of the bomb.

This opinion is not necessarily true since 1600 lb. bombs contain slightly more explosive than the 500 lb. G.P. bombs.

Hit No. 10 (500 lb. M.C. ?) detonated on impact with the top edge of the starboard side armour (5.7-in.) at about station 102. Slight damage was caused.

Hit No. 11 (500 lb. S.A.P. ?) struck and perforated a boat at about station 100, on the port side, the roof of the after hangar, the superstructure deck (.4-in.) and detonated in the wardroom in contact with the upper deck (1.97-in.) just to starboard of the middle line. The detonation dished but did not rupture the thick upper deck; surrounding light structure was damaged by blast, splinters and a subsequent fire; the wardroom and adjacent cabins were wrecked.

Hit No. 12 (1,600 lb. A.P.?) perforated the starboard side plating (0.55-in.) just below the lower edge of the side armour at about station 97 and penetrated the bulge and detonated in the vicinity of the main protective bulkhead (1.77-in.). The main protective bulkhead was dished inboard to a maximum depth of 6-in. for a length of about 16 ft., some riveted connections in the lower portion of the bulkhead were strained and permitted leakage. Bulkheads in Sections IX and X of the bulge were damaged and there was a hole in the side plating about 3 ft. by 1.5 ft.

Hit No. 13 (500 lb. S.A.P. ?) perforated the superstructure deck (0.4-in.), struck the upper deck (1.97-in.) and rebounded into the air where it detonated some 3 ft. above the starboard side of the upper deck at about station 72. Splinters from the bomb penetrated the upper deck and several cabins were wrecked by blast and splinters; there was a small hole in the upper deck due to the ricochet of the bomb.

Hit No. 14 (500 lb. S.A.P. ?) perforated the upper deck (1.97-in.) and the battery deck (0.24-in.) and broke up on impact with the sloping armour deck (4.72-in.), about station 40, starboard. There was probably a low order detonation of a portion of the bomb filling and the remainder burned causing a fire.

Near Misses – There were probably four near misses, all off the starboard side. One, probably 500 lb. M.C. or 600 lb. A/S, detonated close to the ship's side abreast the funnel and caused a hole in the side plating (0.5 and

0.8-in.) about 7 ft. long by 3 ft. deep, and another abreast the outer shaft bracket caused splits and dishing in the adjacent bottom plating.

Flooding

Starboard bulge compartments in Sections VIII, IX and X flooded to the waterline from Hit No. 12 and in Section XI through the near miss abreast the funnel. (See Near Misses above). A slight list to starboard resulted. Sea water also entered compartments aft as the result of the near miss abreast the starboard shaft bracket.

Damage to Machinery

There was no damage to main or auxiliary machinery.

Damage to Armament

The pedestal mounting of P1, 10.5 cm. twin anti-aircraft gun was damaged by blast and splinters, the gun platform was bent upwards and the gun was put out of action, from Hit No. 4. Two machine guns on the starboard side of the lower mast deck were damaged by Hit No. 3 and the port quadruple gun on the funnel was damaged by Hit No. 8. An armour-piercing bomb (Hit No. 6) perforated the roof and gun platform of S.II 15 cm. twin turret without affecting its efficiency.

The 10.5 cm. flak batteries were put out of action soon after the commencement of the attack by machine gunning of the guns' crews.

Damage to Communications Equipment

All W/T aerials were damaged.

Casualties

There were 122 killed and 316 wounded. Many of the casualties were the result of machine gunning by the fighters, which accompanied the bombing force and strafed the upperworks before the bombers went in.

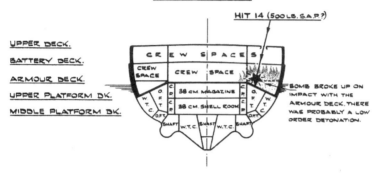

SECTION AT STA.40.
LOOKING FORWARD.

HIT 14 (500 LB. S.A.P.?)

UPPER DECK.

BATTERY DECK.

ARMOUR DECK.

UPPER PLATFORM DK.

MIDDLE PLATFORM DK.

CREW SPACES

CREW SPACE | CREW SPACE

38 CM. MAGAZINE

38 CM. SHELL ROOM

W.T.C. | SHAFT | W.T.C. | SHAFT | W.T.C. | SHAFT

BOMB BROKE UP ON IMPACT WITH THE ARMOUR DECK. THERE WAS PROBABLY A LOW ORDER DETONATION.

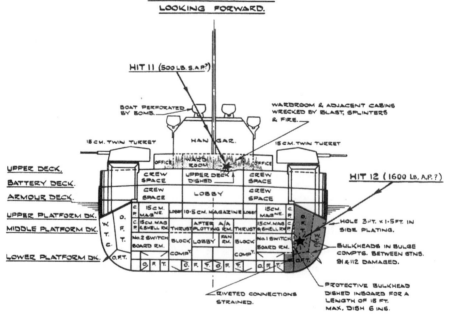

SECTION AT STA.97.
LOOKING FORWARD.

HIT 11 (500 LB. S.A.P.?)

BOAT PERFORATED BY BOMB.

WARDROOM & ADJACENT CABINS WRECKED BY BLAST, SPLINTERS & FIRE.

15 CM. TWIN TURRET

HANGAR.

15 CM. TWIN TURRET

UPPER DECK.

BATTERY DECK.

ARMOUR DECK.

UPPER PLATFORM DK.

MIDDLE PLATFORM DK.

LOWER PLATFORM DK.

OFFICE | WARD ROOM | OFFICE

CREW SPACE | UPPER DECK DISHED | CREW SPACE

CREW SPACE | LOBBY | CREW SPACE

15 CM. MAGNE. | 10·5 CM. MAGAZINE | 15 CM. MAGNE.

15 CM. MAG & SHELL RM | THRUST | PLOTTING RM. | THRUST | 15 CM. MAG & SHELL RM

No.2 SWITCH BOARD RM. | BLOCK | LOBBY | FAN RM. | BLOCK | No.1 SWITCH BOARD RM.

COMPT | AFTER A/A | COMPT

HIT 12 (1600 LB. A.P.?)

HOLE 3 FT. × 1·5 FT. IN SIDE PLATING.

BULKHEADS IN BULGE COMPTS. BETWEEN STNS. 91 & 112 DAMAGED.

PROTECTIVE BULKHEAD DISHED INBOARD FOR A LENGTH OF 18 FT. MAX. DISH 6 INS.

RIVETED CONNECTIONS STRAINED.

Fig. A.2

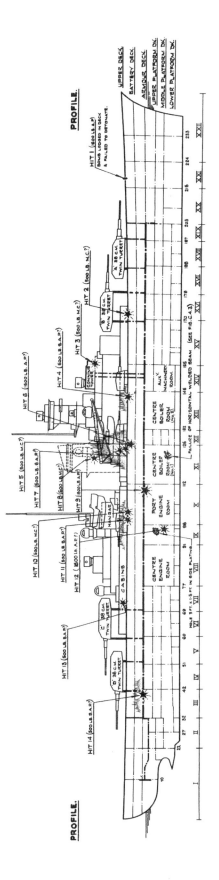

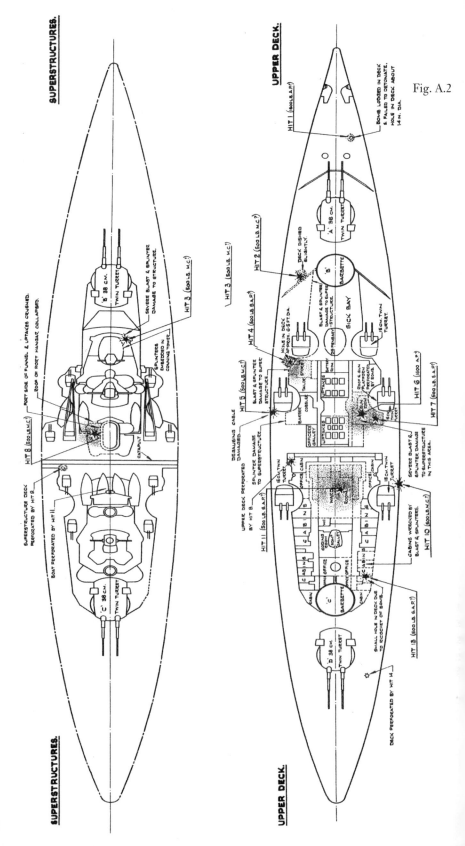

Fig. A.2

SUPERSTRUCTURES.

SUPERSTRUCTURE DECK PERFORATED BY HIT 8.

BOAT PERFORATED BY HIT 11.

'C' 38 CM. TWIN TURRET

PORT SIDE OF FUNNEL, & UPTAKES CRUSHED.
ROOF OF BOAT HANGAR COLLAPSED.

SEVERE BLAST & SPLINTER DAMAGE TO STRUCTURE.

SPLINTERS EMBEDDED IN CONNING TOWER.

'B' 38 CM. TWIN TURRET

HIT 3 (500 L.B. M.C.?)

CATAPULT

HIT 8 (500 L.B. M.C.?)

UPPER DECK.

HIT 1 (500 L.B. A.P.?)

BOMB LODGED IN DECK & FAILED TO DETONATE. HOLE IN DECK ABOUT 14 IN. DIA.

'A' 38 CM. TWIN TURRET

HIT 2 (500 L.B. M.C.?)

DECK DISHED SLIGHTLY.

'B'

BARBETTE

HOLE IN DECK APPROX. 6.5 FT DIA.

HIT 4 (500 L.B. S.A.P.?)

BLAST & SPLINTER DAMAGE TO SUPER-STRUCTURE.

15 CM. TWIN TURRET

SICK BAY

HIT 5 (500 L.B. M.C.?)

BLAST & SPLINTER DAMAGE TO SUPER-STRUCTURE.

BARBER'S TAILOR

DEGAUSSING CABLE DAMAGED.

CABLE

OFFICERS GALLEY

UPTAKES

SECONDARY BATTERY GUN

BLAST & GUN PLATFORM PERFORATED BY BOMB.

HIT 6 (500 L.B. A.P.?)

15 CM. TWIN TURRET

HIT 7 (500 L.B. S.A.P.?)

SPLINTER DAMAGE TO SUPERSTRUCTURE.

UPPER DECK PERFORATED BY HIT 8.

15 CM. TWIN TURRET

OFFICE CABIN

COOLING ROOM

ROOM GALLEY

WARD ROOM

15 CM. TWIN TURRET

OFFICES

SEVERE BLAST & SPLINTER DAMAGE TO SUPERSTRUCTURE IN THIS AREA.

HIT 11 (500 L.B. S.A.P.?)

C A B I N S

CABIN OFFICE

BAKERY

C A B I N S

OFFICE

C A B I N S

CABINS WRECKED BY BLAST & SPLINTERS.

HIT 10 (500 L.B. M.C.?)

'C'

CABIN OFFICE

BARBETTE

FIRE OFFICE

CABIN

C A B I N S

SMALL HOLE IN DECK DUE TO RICOCHET OF BOMB.

'D' 38 CM. TWIN TURRET

HIT 13 (500 L.B. S.A.P.?)

DECK PERFORATED BY HIT 14.

Fig. A.2

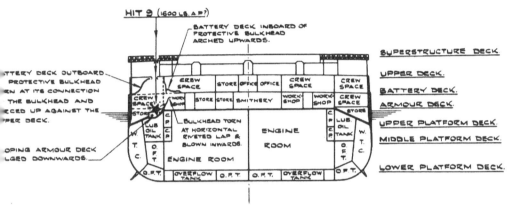

SECTION AT STA.110.
LOOKING FORWARD.

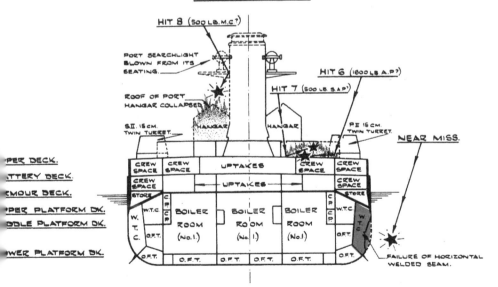

SECTION AT STA.122.
LOOKING FORWARD.

A.3. – Damage Sustained as a Result of F.A.A. Attack at Kaa Fjord on 24 August, 1944

Narrative and Evidence
See pages 194-203.

Weapons Used
The following bombs were dropped during the attack:–

1600 lb. A.P. bombs fused   .08 secs. delay – 18 in No.
1000 lb. A.P. bombs fused   .08 secs. delay – 5 in No.
500 lb. S.A.P.A.P. bombs fused.14 secs. delay – 10 in No.

Damage Sustained (See Figure A.3.)
Tirpitz sustained the following damage as the result of two hits:–

Hit No. 1 (1600 lb. A.P.) which failed to detonate, perforated the upper deck (1.97-in.), battery deck (.24-in.), armour deck (3.15-in.) and upper and middle platform decks (.24-in. and.28-in. respectively) and came to rest on the lower platform deck (.35-in.), about station 161, port.

Hit No. 2 (500 lb. S.A.P. ?) detonated on top of 'B' turret, the roof (5.1-in.) of which was dished. A four-barrelled gun on top of 'B' turret was destroyed.

TIRPITZ.
F.A.A. ATTACK – 24ᵀᴴ AUGUST 1944.

Fig. A.3

SCALES AS SHOWN.

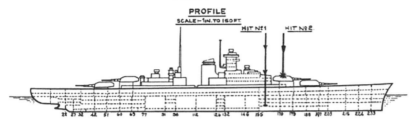

PROFILE
SCALE – 1IN. TO 150 FT.

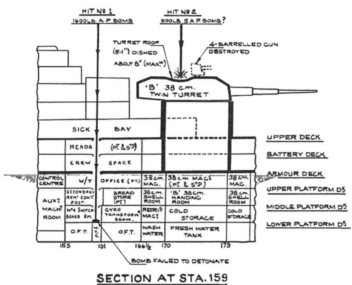

PART SECTIONAL PROFILE
SCALE – 1 IN. TO 32 FT.

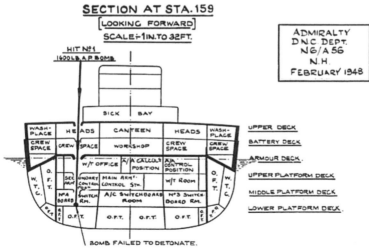

SECTION AT STA. 159
[LOOKING FORWARD]
SCALE – 1 IN. TO 32 FT.

A.4 – Damage Sustained as a Result of Bomber Command Attack at Kaa Fjord on 15 September, 1944

Narrative and Evidence
See pages 194-203.

Weapons Used
The following weapons were dropped during the attack:–

12,000 lb. M.C. (Tallboy) bombs fused.07 secs. delay – 16 in No. J.W. Mk. II Mines (Special Type) – 72 in No.

Their details are as follows:–

12,000 lb. M.C. bomb
  Type of filling – Torpex II
  Weight of filling – 5,100 lbs.
  Charge/weight ratio – 44%

J.W. Mark II
  Type of filling – Torpex
  Weight of filling – 100 lbs.
  Charge/weight ratio – 25%

Structural Damage (See Figure A.4)
Severe structural damage was caused to the fore end of the ship by a 12,000 lb. M.C. bomb which passed through the ship via the upper deck (1.97-in.) and out through the flare of the starboard side plating (1.38-in.) and detonated in the water below keel level and very close to the ship.

The structure below the armour deck from the stern up to the transverse armour bulkhead at station 203 was blown away or wrecked. The starboard side was more severely damaged than the port side. The upper, battery and armour decks were bulged upwards, the latter a maximum of about one metre.

Flooding
The portion of the ship forward of station 203 was flooded to the waterline and the draught forward increased about 2.5 m. (8.2 ft.) in consequence.

Counter-flooding and Transference of Oil Fuel

Counter-flooding of port and starboard wing compartments aft was carried out; it was estimated that about 1,500 tons of water were admitted to the ship.

Damage to Machinery

The main engines were damaged by vibration and required overhauling. Eight days were taken to make them serviceable. Auxiliary machinery, which was seated on special resilient mountings was unaffected.

Damage to Communications Equipment

The aerials were broken.

Casualties

There were 5 casualties.

Fig. A.4

TIRPITZ.
BOMBER COMMAND ATTACK – 15TH SEPT. 1944.
SCALES AS SHOWN

PROFILE.
SCALE:-1IN TO 150 FT.

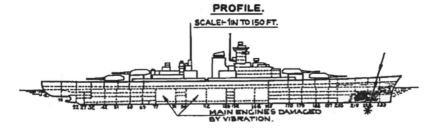

MAIN ENGINES DAMAGED
BY VIBRATION.

PART PROFILE
SCALE:- 1IN TO 32 FT.

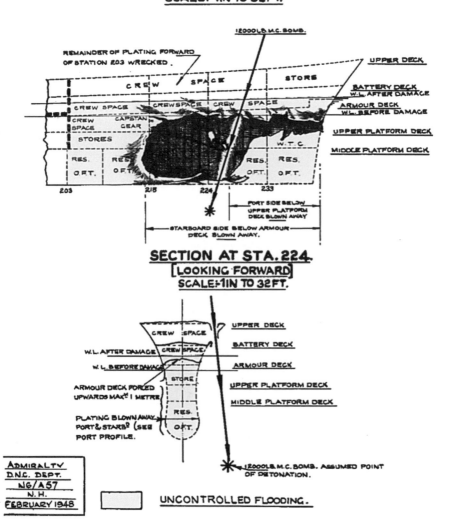

12000 LB. M.C. BOMB.

REMAINDER OF PLATING FORWARD
OF STATION 203 WRECKED.

UPPER DECK

CREW SPACE · STORE

BATTERY DECK
W.L. AFTER DAMAGE

CREW SPACE · CREW SPACE · CREW · SPACE

ARMOUR DECK
W.L. BEFORE DAMAGE

CREW
SPACE · CAPSTAN
GEAR

UPPER PLATFORM DECK

STORES

W.T.C.

MIDDLE PLATFORM DECK

RES.
O.F.T. · RES.
O.F.T. · RES.
O.F.T. · RES.
O.F.T.

203 · 218 · 224 · 233

PORT SIDE BELOW
UPPER PLATFORM
DECK BLOWN AWAY

STARBOARD SIDE BELOW ARMOUR
DECK BLOWN AWAY.

SECTION AT STA. 224.
[LOOKING FORWARD]
SCALE:- 1IN TO 32 FT.

UPPER DECK

CREW SPACE

BATTERY DECK

W.L. AFTER DAMAGE · CREW SPACE

W.L. BEFORE DAMAGE

ARMOUR DECK

STORE

ARMOUR DECK FORCED
UPWARDS MAXE 1 METRE

UPPER PLATFORM DECK

MIDDLE PLATFORM DECK

RES.

PLATING BLOWN AWAY
PORT & STARBD (SEE
PORT PROFILE.

O.F.T.

12000LB. M.C. BOMB. ASSUMED POINT
OF DETONATION.

ADMIRALTY
D.N.C. DEPT.
NS/A57
N.H.
FEBRUARY 1948

UNCONTROLLED FLOODING.

A.5 – Damage Sustained as a Result of Bomber Command Attack at Tromsø on 29 October, 1944

Narrative and Evidence
See pages 194-203.

Weapons Used
Thirty-two 12,000 lb. M.C. bombs were dropped during the attack.

Structural Damage (See Figure A.5)
The port side plating at the after end of the ship was strained and split by a near miss which is reported to have hit the water off the port quarter between 10 and 25 m. (about 30 to 80 ft.) from the shipside.

Flooding
Water entered compartments on the port side aft over a length of approximately 35 m. (about 115 ft.); those affected included the steering gear compartment and shaft passages. No serious leaking of decks and bulkheads occurred far inboard. It was estimated that about 800 cm. of water entered the ship. Some of the flooded compartments were subsequently pumped out.

Damage to Shaft and Rudder
The port shaft was bent and the port rudder was damaged by the explosion.

Casualties
There were 3 casualties.

Fig. A.5

TIRPITZ
BOMBER COMMAND ATTACK —29TH OCT. 1944.
SCALES AS SHOWN.

PROFILE
SCALE :-1IN TO 150FT.

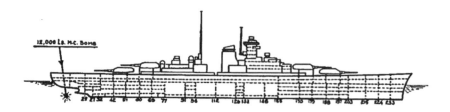

PART PLAN OF UPPER PLATFORM DECK
SCALE :-1IN. TO 32FT.

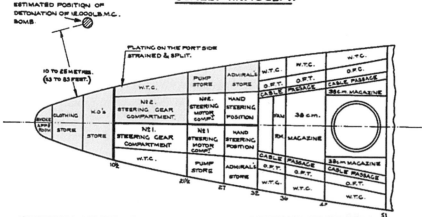

SECTION AT STA. 13.
LOOKING FORWARD
SCALE :-1IN. TO 32FT.

SECTION AT STA. 39.
LOOKING FORWARD.
SCALE :-1IN. TO 32FT.

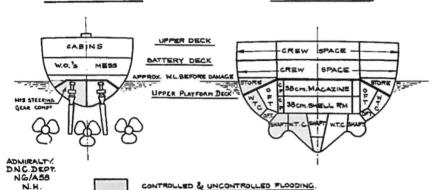

ADMIRALTY.
D.N.C. DEPT.
NG/A58
N.H.
FEBRUARY 1948

CONTROLLED & UNCONTROLLED FLOODING.

A.6 – Damage Caused by the Final Bomber Command Attack at Tromsø on 12 November, 1944

Narrative and Evidence
See pages 194-203 and Appendix B.

Weapons Used
Twenty-nine 12,000 lb. M.C. bombs each containing 5,100 lbs. desensitised Torpex and fused 0.07 secs. delay were dropped by the attacking aircraft.

Structural Damage
Deduced from survey of wreck at Tromsø – see Figure A.6 and pages 263-273 of Appendix B.

Hit No. 1 – The bomb struck the port side of the ship on the upper deck near the end of the athwartships catapult at about station 113 and penetrated to about the armour deck (3.2-in.). It is considered that it detonated while passing through the armour deck, a short distance inboard of the protective bulkhead. The bomb blew a large hole about 45 ft. long in the side plating (0.55 to 0.8-in.), extending from below the bilge keel probably to the upper deck, between stations 107 and 118. The plating at the edges of this hole was petalled outwards.

The protective bulkhead (1.8-in.) was blown outwards and the hole in it took the form of a large 'V', apex downwards, giving the impression that it had failed down the line of welding connecting it to the transverse bulkhead at station 111.

The main side armour in this area was probably blown off the ship's side. The position of parts of the 110 mm. (about 4.3-in.) sloping deck armour indicated that some of the side armour had hinged outwards about the upper deck connection.

The 110 mm. (4.3-in.) sloping armour deck in the damaged area had been fractured in at least two places and was displaced outboard. A considerable portion of the 80 mm. (3.2-in.) armour deck was missing.

Hit No. 2 – This bomb struck the port side of the ship about station 99. It is impossible to deduce an exact point of detonation from the evidence obtained during the survey of the wreck, the only certainty is that the bomb detonated prematurely somewhere between the upper deck and about mid-draught.

The bomb blew a hole about 45 ft. long in the side plating (0.55 to 0.8-in.) between stations 95 and 106. This hole extended from just above the bilge keel probably to upper deck level. There was also a smaller hole about 13 ft. deep x 6 ft. wide between stations 92 and 94, the top edge coinciding with the lower edge of the 320 mm. (12.6-in.) side armour. The edges of each of these holes were petalled outwards.

There was a very large hole in the protective bulkhead in the same area.

Side armour plates in this area had either been ripped completely away or hinged outboard about their upper edge.

The 110 mm. (about 4.3-in.) sloping deck armour in the same area was bent downwards, but not ruptured, into the form of a trough 7 to 8 ft. deep.

The hit abreast the after range-finder (Hit No. 2) was followed by an explosion, and some time after this *Tirpitz* moved bodily to starboard, a line of white froth was seen along the port side of the hull and the near miss which followed developed into a high column of black smoke. No other bomb which fell in the water produced a similar disturbance. This suggests that ammunition exploded subsequent to this bomb hit but it is improbable that this explosion was responsible for the majority of the damage which followed this bomb hit.

Note:– The two large holes caused by hits 1 and 2 were joined just below the waterline into one large uninterrupted hole about 100 ft. long.

Near miss:– This occurred close to the port side abreast station 128, probably when the ship was heeled about 20 degrees. It blew a hole 40 ft. long x 17 ft. deep in the side plating between stations 122 and 134, the top edge of the hole being from 3 to 10 ft. below the lower edge of the thick side armour. The plating around the hole was petalled inwards. Side plating over a more extensive area was dished inwards and split.

The protective bulkhead was dished inwards over a large area and there was at least one split about 9-in. wide caused by the fracture of the welding connecting this bulkhead to transverse bulkhead 132.

There was probably a direct hit on turret 'B' which caused damage to superstructures of unknown extent. There is also a possibility that a further near miss off the starboard side of the fore end accentuated the damage caused by the near miss during the 15 September attack.

Flooding

It was impossible to ascertain the extent of uncontrolled flooding but it is certain that the following sections of the ship at least flooded very rapidly:–

All bulge compartments between stations 77 and 146
All port machinery spaces over the same length of the ship

– that is, at least 5,000 tons entered the ship. The Germans estimated that about 12,000 tons of water entered the ship in all.

Subsequent Events

The ship heeled rapidly to port immediately after the first hit, attained an angle of about 20 degrees and steadied momentarily, probably owing to the port bilge keel coming into contact with the mud of the sea bed. During this period the second direct hit and the near miss occurred extending the damage and increasing the rate of heeling. The ship continued to list and at some angle between 25 degrees and 70 degrees there was an explosion in the after main armament magazines as a result of which turret 'C' was blown out of the ship. The order to abandon ship was then given and she subsequently heeled 145 degrees, the angle at which she still lies.

Casualties

About 1,000 officers and men were drowned.

Tirpitz
Bomber Command attack
12 November 1944

PROFILE.

UPPER DECK
BATTERY DECK
ARMOUR DECK
UPPER PLATFORM DECK
MIDDLE PLATFORM DECK
LOWER PLATFORM DECK

PROFILE.

UPPER DECK
BATTERY DECK
ARMOUR DECK
UPPER PLATFORM DECK
MIDDLE PLATFORM DECK
LOWER PLATFORM DECK

D 38 c.m. TWIN TURRET

C 38 c.m. TWIN TURRET

HIT 2 (1,000 LB M.C.)

NEAR MISS (1,000 LB M.C.)

HIT 1 (1,000 LB M.C.)

PORT SIDE PLATING RUPTURED FROM TURN OF BILGE TO AT LEAST THE W.L. FOR 220FT. APPROX.

HIT 3 (2,000 LB M.C.) TO PORT OF TURRET.

B 38 c.m. TWIN TURRET

A 38 c.m. TWIN TURRET

NEAR MISS (12,000 LB M.C.) UPPER STARBOARD SIDE.

THIS BOMB DETONATION MAY HAVE EXTENDED THE DAMAGE CAUSED TO THE BOW IN THE ATTACK ON THE 15TH SEPTEMBER, 1944.

PROFILE.

FLOODING KEY.

UNCONTROLLED RAPID FLOODING
DUE TO 12TH NOVEMBER ATTACK
(NOTE:- EXTENT SHOWN IS THE
MINIMUM THAT OCCURRED - SEE
8.6.3. OF ENCLOSURE 6.)

UNCONTROLLED FLOODING PRESENT
IN SHIP IMMEDIATELY PRIOR TO ATTACK
ON 12TH NOVEMBER. - DUE TO ATTACKS
ON 15TH SEPTEMBER. (FLOODING FORWARD)
& 29TH OCTOBER. (FLOODING AFT.)

Fig. A.6

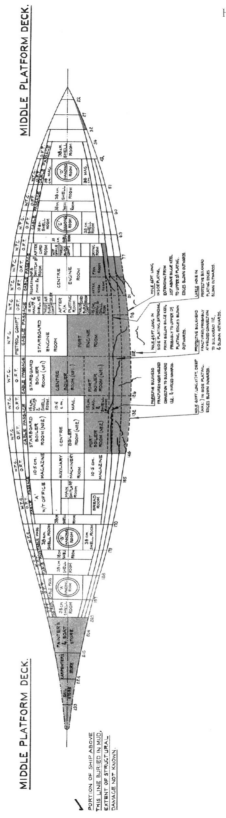

MIDDLE PLATFORM DECK.

MIDDLE PLATFORM DECK.

PORTION OF SHIP ABOVE
THIS LINE BURIED IN MUD.
EXTENT OF STRUCTURAL
DAMAGE NOT KNOWN.

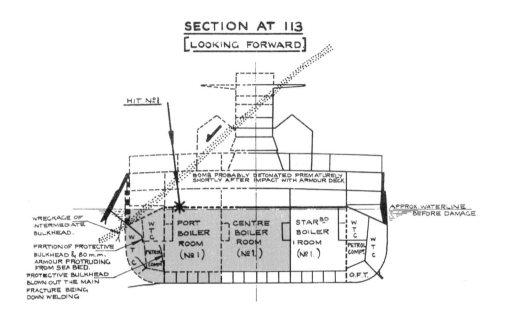

SECTION AT 113
[LOOKING FORWARD]

HIT Nº1

BOMB PROBABLY DETONATED PREMATURELY
SHORTLY AFTER IMPACT WITH ARMOUR DECK.

APPROX. WATERLINE
BEFORE DAMAGE.

WRECKAGE OF
INTERMEDIATE
BULKHEAD.

PORTION OF PROTECTIVE
BULKHEAD & 80 m.m.
ARMOUR PROTRUDING
FROM SEA BED.

PROTECTIVE BULKHEAD
BLOWN OUT THE MAIN
FRACTURE BEING
DOWN WELDING

W T C | PORT BOILER ROOM (Nº1) | CENTRE BOILER ROOM (Nº1.) | STARᴮᴰ BOILER ROOM (Nº1.) | W T C | PETROL COMPᵗ | W T C

W T C | PETROL COMPᵗ

O.F.T.

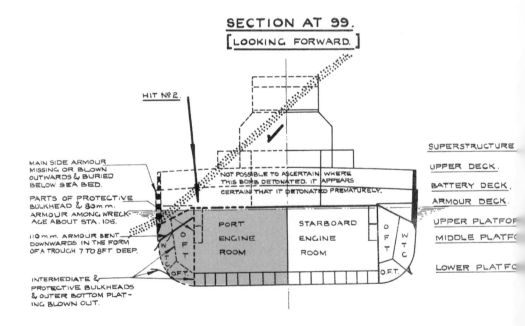

SECTION AT 99.
[LOOKING FORWARD.]

HIT Nº2.

MAIN SIDE ARMOUR
MISSING OR BLOWN
OUTWARDS & BURIED
BELOW SEA BED.

NOT POSSIBLE TO ASCERTAIN WHERE
THIS BOMB DETONATED. IT APPEARS
CERTAIN THAT IT DETONATED PREMATURELY.

PARTS OF PROTECTIVE
BULKHEAD & 80 m m.
ARMOUR AMONG WRECK-
AGE ABOUT STA. 105.

110 m.m. ARMOUR BENT
DOWNWARDS IN THE FORM
OF A TROUGH 7 TO 8FT DEEP.

INTERMEDIATE &
PROTECTIVE BULKHEADS
& OUTER BOTTOM PLAT-
ING BLOWN OUT.

W T C | O F T | PORT ENGINE ROOM | STARBOARD ENGINE ROOM | O F T | W T C

O.F.T. | O.F.T.

SUPERSTRUCTURE

UPPER DECK.

BATTERY DECK.

ARMOUR DECK.

UPPER PLATFOR

MIDDLE PLATFO

LOWER PLATFO

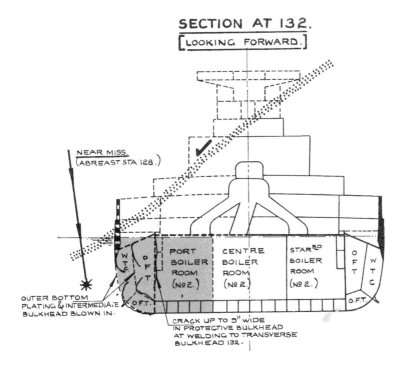

Appendix B

B.6 Conclusions

Illustrations

Appendix B – Survey of Wreck at Tromsø, 4 September to 15 October, 1945

B.1 – Introduction

Tirpitz was the second capital ship to be despatched by bombs alone, the first being the Italian battleship *Roman* which was sunk in deep water off Sardinia by German rocket bombs shortly after the Italian surrender. *Tirpitz* however was sunk in very shallow water by the new massive Tallboy bombs. She therefore provided a unique opportunity for:–

(a) Obtaining direct evidence of the effectiveness of direct hits and near misses with the 12,000 lb. M.C. (Tallboy) bombs, which was then urgently required because this weapon was being recommended as a Category 1 bomb for the attack of Japanese capital ships, aircraft carriers and cruisers;

(b) Examining the effectiveness of her structure against this form of attack;

(c) Ascertaining the extent of flooding caused by the bombs and the reason for her capsizing;

(d) Providing information as to the fuse delay achieved by the bomb in practice, with particular reference to the susceptibility of its Torpex filling to premature detonation when used against heavy deck armour.

A further consideration was that no facilities existed for carrying out controlled tests with the bomb, because its large diameter (38-in.) was more than twice that of our largest gun and its weight of 12,000 lbs. prevented it being fired even from projected rocket runways. The possibility of obtaining useful information from tests against an actual battleship was remote owing to the great difficulty of obtaining a suitable modern battleship for such trials and the very small probability of scoring the right sort of hits from the operational bombing level of about 12,000 ft.

The Director of Naval Construction therefore considered it imperative that the opportunity of carrying out a careful survey of the wreck should not be missed and in March, 1945, when the end of the war with Germany was in sight, the collection of information as to the enemy's intentions regarding possible demolition of the wreck was commenced and it was also stated officially that D.N.C was anxious to carry out such a survey if at all possible.

Information obtained by D.N.C's representatives in Northern Germany confirmed that it was essential to inspect the wreck to assess the damage caused by the Tallboy bombs during the last attack, and in June, 1945, D.N.C. sought approval to carry out the survey which would include inspection by divers of the underwater portions of the damage. Board approval for this operation was given in mid-July but there were certain difficulties which had to be overcome before the survey could proceed. The only British diving tender, HMS *Tedworth*, could not be used owing to her lack of endurance for the lengthy sea voyage to Tromsø and urgent requirements for her use elsewhere. Consideration was then given to obtaining an American salvage vessel, but this was found to be impossible. It was then suggested that the German salvage vessel SS *Richard* which had been standing by *Tirpitz* and which was being used to bring armour plate ex-*Tirpitz* to England, might be used for the purpose. There was some delay in getting *Richard* sailed to England but she was inspected at Rosyth on 17 August when it was found that, contrary to previous reports, she was a ship designed for harbour use only and that her speed, endurance and accommodation were unsuitable for the operation. Action was therefore taken to obtain an L.C.Q. for use as the accommodation ship and D.N.C's representatives visited Tromsø by air (through the courtesy of the Air Ministry) to make preliminary arrangements for the survey. It was found that a pontoon suitable for use as a diving platform was available at Tromsø. Arrangements were also made for the supply by D.T.M. of an Officer and twelve divers with all the necessary diving and underwater cutting equipment required for the inspection and the supply by D.A/S.M. of an echo sounding set and a competent officer to carry out a survey of the sea-bed in the vicinity of the wreck.

L.C.Q.492 was allocated for the operation by C.-in-C. Roysth and she was sailed on 31 August for Tromsø, arriving there on 4 September. The Officers then assembled in L.C.Q.492 for the survey were:–

Constructor Captain J. L. Bessant, directing the operation;
Constructor Lieutenant North, who supervised the operation at the site during the whole period;
Lieutenant Hughes, R.N.V.R., commanding H.M. L.C.Q.492;
El. Sub Lieutenant Tennent, R.N.V.R., in charge of echo sounding operations;
Mr. Chadwick, Commissioned Gunner, R.N., with twelve divers from HMS *Vernon*.

The first few days at Tromsø were spent in arranging for the use of auxiliary craft and equipment, including an ex-German motor minesweeper to act as general diving tender and a motor cutter for operating the echo sounding set, and in rigging a 65 ft. x 20 ft. concrete pontoon as a diving stage. The survey proper began on 8 September and falls conveniently into four main sections:–

(a) Interrogation of witnesses;
(b) Survey of the area surrounding the wreck for bomb craters;
(c) Survey of the above water portions of the wreck; and
(d) Survey of underwater portions of the wreck.

These are described in the following sections B.2, B.3, B.4 and B.5 of this enclosure.

B.2 – Interrogation of Witnesses

A number of people who had either seen the sinking of *Tirpitz* or who could give any useful evidence about the ship were interrogated. The most useful information about the actual final attack was given by two Norwegian civilians, Anton and Edmund Rikkardson, who live on Kvaloy and witnessed the action from beginning to end, and by the master of the German salvage ship *Scheibenhof*, who supervised the German diving operations which followed the capsizing.

Anton and Edmund Rikkardson

The point from which they witnessed the sinking is indicated on the plan of the anchorage given in Figure B.2 and was about two miles on the starboard quarter of *Tirpitz*.

During their interrogation a one-hundredth scale model of *Tirpitz* (prepared in D.N.C. Department) was used to obtain a clear reconstruction of what the witnesses saw, including the position of hits and the subsequent angles of heel. They agreed that the large quantity of smoke produced during the attack might have obscured later bomb hits, but stated that the sequence of bombs affecting the ship was as follows:–

(i) Hit on the upper works just forward of the bridge and slightly to starboard which blew away all the superstructures in the vicinity but did not damage the ship below the upper deck;

(ii) Hit on the port side in way of the catapult and about 20 ft. inboard from the ship's side which produced a great deal of smoke but no flame, the ship began to heel immediately. This hit has been confirmed by other sources;

(iii) Near miss just off the port side abaft hit number (ii). (A direct hit in this vicinity was confirmed by the diving survey; it is thought that this was mistaken for a near miss);

(iv) Near miss, starboard side forward, some distance from the ship's side. The survey of the seabed confirms this near miss. No damage additional to that caused by the September attack was found by diving;

(v) Direct hit on the starboard side of the quarter-deck after the ship had heeled to about 25 degrees which produced red flame and a considerable amount of smoke.

There is evidence that there was a magazine explosion and an explosion in turret 'C'. With the ship at 25 degrees, turret 'C' would be in line with the estimated position of the direct hit and the magazine explosion may have been mistaken for a bomb hit.

Master of *Scheibenhof*

Three German vessels, *Richard*, *Scheibenhof* and *Mellum*, were used after the capsizing to remove the propellers and main side armour. The Master of *Scheibenhof* obtained, from one of the survivors, sketches of the after end of *Tirpitz* which showed the position of the wine stores aft. He had considerable spare time and made several attempts to gain access to the stores by diving. Using a system of small charges detonated simultaneously, he blew off an area of plating 36 ft. x 16 ft. from the ship's side aft and found that the accommodation spaces aft on the battery deck and armour deck had been wrecked by a major explosion which had occurred forward of this. On reaching the wine stores he discovered only 36 bottles intact, the remainder were either smashed or had their corks blown in by the explosion. His evidence was useful in that it gave the extent of the damage aft due to the internal explosion. This is indicated in Figure B.5.

Kristian Pettersen

His house and farm were very close to where *Tirpitz* was moored and one of his buildings had been damaged during the first attack; he was much impressed by the accuracy of the bombing.

Petterson was able to give accurately the position of the local anti-aircraft sites; these are shown on Figure B.2. The guns had been sited before *Tirpitz* arrived but a number of her crew were put ashore on arrival to assist in manning them.

Every day between the last two attacks, two or three 120 foot barges brought what he described as a mixture of gravel and clay and dumped it around *Tirpitz*.

There was a persistent local rumour that a large party was held onboard *Tirpitz* the night before the final attack and that the crew was far from efficient as a result. Petterson had heard this rumour but could give no evidence. He said that the survivors had behaved very oddly and were either frightened or drunk.

Oberleutnant Mohrmfelt

This officer was on shore on the mainland (See Figure B.2) and did not see the attack but visited the ship between 3 and 4 o'clock in the afternoon when rescue operations were in progress. He said that about 50 men were rescued after the ship capsized.

A number of liberty men were ashore at the time of the attack and the majority of the "technical" personnel (he presumably meant engine room personnel) had not been onboard for some time. (Kapitan Sommer, an engineer officer and probably the damage control officer, was ashore during the attack). He did not think that *Tirpitz* had settled very much after capsizing, possibly a metre or so. After the attack he spoke with Ober Lieutenant (Ing.) Schultz who was below in the engine room when the ship was attacked but who managed to reach the upper deck and jump overboard before she capsized. Schultz stated that there was a direct hit on the port side which caused the ship to heel to about 45 degrees, at which angle she stopped for some time. "C" Magazine then blew up, the order to abandon ship was given and *Tirpitz* continued to heel into the position she now holds. He felt certain that all watertight doors would have been closed before the attack commenced but considered that many would have been opened again on the order to abandon ship.

Mohrmfelt said that it had been decided to make up the sea bed around *Tirpitz* and silt was dredged from the northwest end of Tromsø and dumped around the ship continuously for three weeks before the final attack.

Oberleutnant Hamann
This officer was in command of Repair Ship F171 which had been detailed to carry out rescue work on *Tirpitz*. Work was commenced about noon on 12 November and continued for approximately 24 hours. Attempt was made to burn through the sea inlet of the starboard engine room but the equipment available was inadequate. Eventually access was gained into the electrical machining room (Section XIV of the ship) and from there an effort was made to enter the starboard boiler room but this compartment was so hot inside that the attempt was abandoned.

Obermaschinemann Sneuer
Sneuer was also attached to F171. He stated that about 50 men were rescued; small holes were burned into the electrical machinery room and food and drink passed in to survivors trapped inside, later larger holes were burned to allow the men to escape.

Baurat Voss
Voss was in no way connected with *Tirpitz* and had not seen the attack but being a technical officer he had given some thought to the capsizing of the ship and his views were borne out to a great extent by the diving survey.

He considered that to capsize the ship the damage must have been along one side only. He had heard that there had been at least one direct hit on the port side. He thought that the bomb would defeat the armoured deck and that, if it detonated just inside the protective bulkhead sufficient damage would be caused to produce uncontrollable flooding.

He said that turret 'C' had been blown a distance of 20 m. (66 ft.) and that it had been seen in this position in the sea bed from a boat. (Note: It was not possible to see the turret from the surface during the survey, but by diving it was found that it was 30 to 40 ft. further outboard than it would have been had it merely dropped out as the ship capsized.) He thought that the explosion of 'C' Magazine was the main cause of the capsizing. (Other evidence does not confirm this).

He realized the menace to watertight integrity of watertight doors in main bulkheads low down in the ship. On the order to abandon ship many of these doors would be left open, the explosions would blow off a number of them and many would be jarred open by shock.

The sequence of events as he saw it was:–

(i) Hit(s) on the port side produced a heel to about 45 degrees;

(ii) Turret 'C' then blew up, the order to abandon ship was given, and the ship gradually capsized to her present position.

A number of other witnesses were interrogated, including a member of the Gestapo, but no useful information additional to the above was obtained.

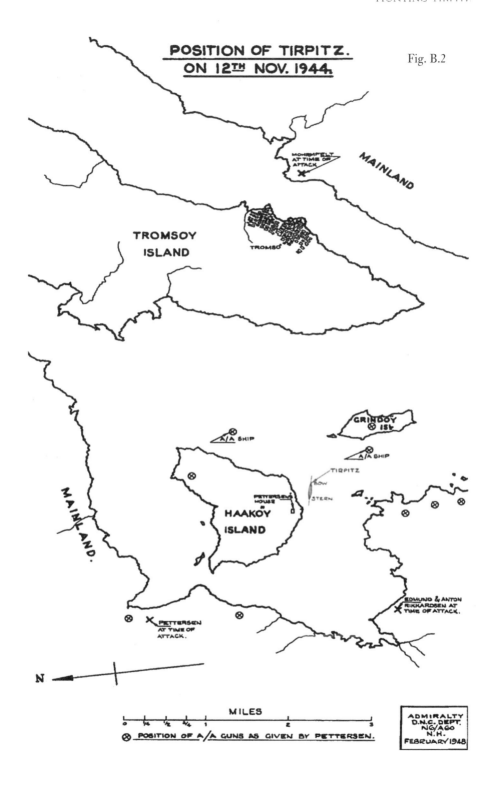

POSITION OF TIRPITZ.
ON 12TH NOV. 1944.

Fig. B.2

MAINLAND

MOHRENFELT
AT TIME OF
ATTACK.

TROMSOY
ISLAND

TROMSO

MAINLAND.

GRINDOY
ISt

A/A SHIP

A/A SHIP

TIRPITZ

PETTERSEN'S
HOUSE
BOW
STERN

HAAKOY
ISLAND

EDMUND & ANTON
RIKKARDSEN AT
TIME OF ATTACK.

PETTERSEN
AT TIME OF
ATTACK.

N

MILES

0   ¼   ½   ¾   1   2   3

⊗ POSITION OF A/A GUNS AS GIVEN BY PETTERSEN.

ADMIRALTY
D.N.C. DEPT.
NG/A60
N.H.
FEBRUARY 1948

B.3 – Survey of Area Around Ship

A systematic survey of the sea-bed around the wreck was made using a Type 766 echo sounding set to obtain the positions of the bomb craters. The set gave good records from which the craters were easily identifiable (Figure B.3.1. shows two typical records). Figure B.3.2 is a chart of the area around *Tirpitz* showing depth corrected to mean low water springs and areas in which the sea-bed close to the wreck had been made up by dumping silt. As a result of the latter the area around the wreck was of a very uneven nature.

Sixteen craters were found within the area shown in the figure and one just outside it in a roughly easterly direction. The craters within the area have been lettered 'A' to 'P' and include those caused by bombs dropped in the 29 October attack. It is known that some of these bombs were dropped during the last attack, namely C, D, E, G, H, J and L, the positions of which are shown in Figure B.3.2. In addition bomb 'K' can be identified with a burst 300 yards East North-East of the ship and bomb 'I' with the near miss off the port quarter which caused extensive flooding, both dropped in the 29 October attack. This leaves bombs F, M, N, O and P of those dropped near the ship, as unidentified and they may have been dropped in either the second or third Tallboy attacks. Of these latter bombs it is unlikely and there is no evidence that bombs F, M, N and P did material damage owing to their distance from the ship, while bomb O in the vicinity of the fore end would account for the very shattered state in which the latter was found during the survey. As there is no evidence of this bomb having been dropped on 29 October, it may be concluded that it was dropped during the last attack and escaped notice in the general confusion which followed the first bomb hit. It is unlikely that it caused much extension of the damage to the fore end produced by the bomb on 15 September attack in Kaa Fjord.

It can therefore be stated definitely that *Tirpitz* received at least one effective near miss off the port quarter during the attack on 29 October and one effective near miss on the port side abreast the bridge on 12 November and that in addition there was one near miss very close to the fore end which may have occurred on the former date but more probably on the latter date and which did not materially alter the damage produced by the bomb on 15 September or appreciably affect the loss of the ship.

TIRPITZ

Fig. B.3.1

TYPICAL ECHO SOUNDING RECORDS.

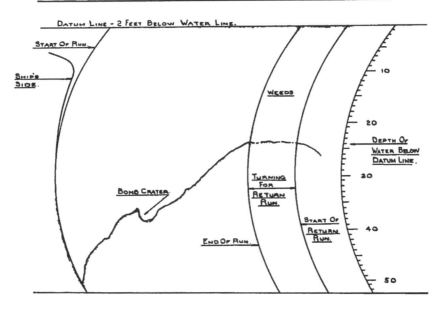

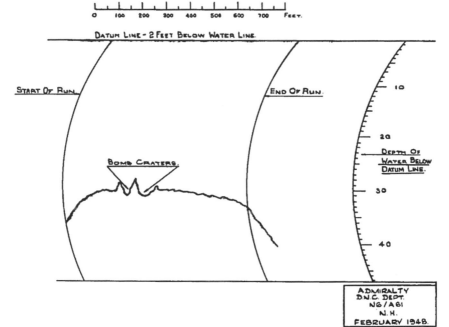

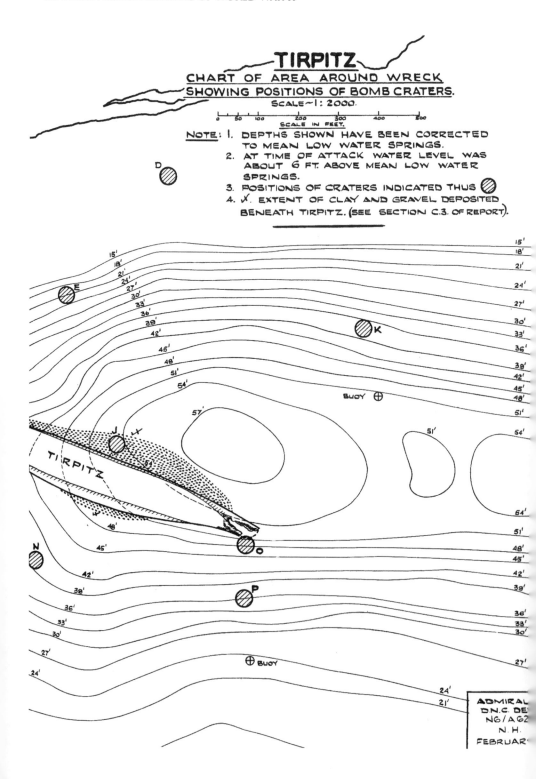

TIRPITZ
CHART OF AREA AROUND WRECK
SHOWING POSITIONS OF BOMB CRATERS.
SCALE ~ 1: 2000.

SCALE IN FEET.

NOTE: 1. DEPTHS SHOWN HAVE BEEN CORRECTED
   TO MEAN LOW WATER SPRINGS.
2. AT TIME OF ATTACK WATER LEVEL WAS
   ABOUT 6 FT. ABOVE MEAN LOW WATER
   SPRINGS.
3. POSITIONS OF CRATERS INDICATED THUS ⊘
4. ⨯. EXTENT OF CLAY AND GRAVEL DEPOSITED
   BENEATH TIRPITZ. (SEE SECTION C.3. OF REPORT).

ADMIRAL
D.N.C. DE
N6/A62
N.H.
FEBRUAR

B.4 – Survey of Above Water Portion of Wreck

Object of Survey
The above water portion of the wreck was examined for evidence of damage and anything noteworthy in the construction of the ship.

Damage Due to Internal Explosion Aft
It was found that considerable damage had been caused by an internal explosion in the vicinity of 'C' and 'D' magazines. The majority of this damage was underwater at the time of the survey, but it was possible at very low water to get access to the area through holes burnt for escape purposes and along the cable passages.

The seat of the explosion was in the magazine between turrets 'C' and 'D'. On the starboard side of the ship the explosion damaged the inboard bulkhead of the cable passage and vented down the cable passage damaging decks and bulkheads as far aft as bulkhead 36 and as far forward as bulkhead 68.5. In both cable passages there were watertight doors at each transverse bulkhead. The hinges of all these doors in the area were broken and one of the doors was blown aft about 27 ft. The longitudinal bulkhead forming the starboard boundary of the shell room just forward of turret 'C' had a number of holes blown in it and gave the impression that a number of explosions had occurred in the shell room rather than one large explosion such as had occurred in the magazine. The products of the explosion had had sufficient force however to blow the watertight door in the main transverse bulkhead 68.8 on the lower platform deck a distance of 20 ft. aft. Everything in this shell room had been blackened by products of the explosion.

'C' gun-house when examined by divers was also found in a badly wrecked state. The starboard longitudinal protective bulkhead on the outboard side of the cable passages did not appear to be damaged.

Damage Caused by Underwater Hit with 1600 lb. A.P. Bomb in Fleet Air Arm Attack of 3 April, 1944
Most of the damage caused by this bomb had been repaired. A large bulge in the protective bulkhead had been left but all other damaged structure had been made good by cutting away the damaged portions and welding in new. The hole in the ship's side caused by the entry of the bomb had been stopped by welding a square patch over it under water. A crack in

the outer bottom plating caused by the detonation of the bomb had been made watertight by driving in steel liners and underwater welding. The compartment had subsequently been pumped dry and the repair continued from inboard.

Damage Caused by 500 lb. M.C. or 600 lb. A.P. Bomb in Fleet Air Arm attack of 3 April, 1944

Figure B.4.4 shows damage caused by a near miss which detonated off the starboard side abreast the funnel. The dishing in the outer bottom plating extended over an area of 50 ft. x 16 ft., the maximum inboard deflection at the centre being about 33-in.. Some authorities have wrongly supposed that this damage had been caused by a near miss with a Tallboy. The bomb had caused splits in way of welding over a considerable area and these splits had been made watertight by driving in steel liners and welding on patches under water. The repair had been continued from inboard after pumping out the compartment.

Damage to plating and frames was extensive and the repairs must have taken many weeks. No attempt had been made to alter the shape of the bulge in the bottom plating and fabricated transverse frames had been built around it. The pressure pulse from this near miss had caused considerable damage at the inboard end of the sea inlet which was close to the above-mentioned damage. As this was quite inaccessible no repair work had been carried out.

Damage to Flat Bottom Probably Due to X Craft Attack

Buckled panels of plating near the flat keel Section XI were caused by excessive whipping of the whole ship. A number of chalk lines were drawn on the plating to show up the buckling more clearly. This damage suggested that the ship had received a permanent set and observations made to ascertain the breakage discovered a hog of 5-in. between the forefoot and the after cut up, the discontinuity being local in the region of the buckling. Panels of bottom plating in Sections VIII, IX and X of the ship were dished over a large area in the manner typical of the detonation of a large charge at some distance. Seams of plating split along welds had been made watertight by driving in wooden wedges from inboard, no attempt at further repairs had been made. The whole of this damage is consistent with that expected from the X craft attack (see A.1 of Appendix A).

Damage Caused by Explosion Subsequent to the Sinking

Although this damage had no bearing on the loss of the ship, it throws some light on the quality of her construction. The transverse bulkhead failed along a line of welding to the longitudinal bulkhead and was torn away from the stiffeners which had been designed with tapered ends. The intermittent welding which had been used to connect the stiffeners to the bulkhead was of such poor quality that when the explosion occurred the welding failed and the stiffeners took only a small proportion of the load for which they had been designed. It was observed that all similar stiffeners throughout the ship were likewise connected by intermittent welding. Detailed examination carried out at H.M. Dockyard, Portsmouth, of a number of specimens of welding cut from *Tirpitz* indicated that the German welding technique was of a poor standard.

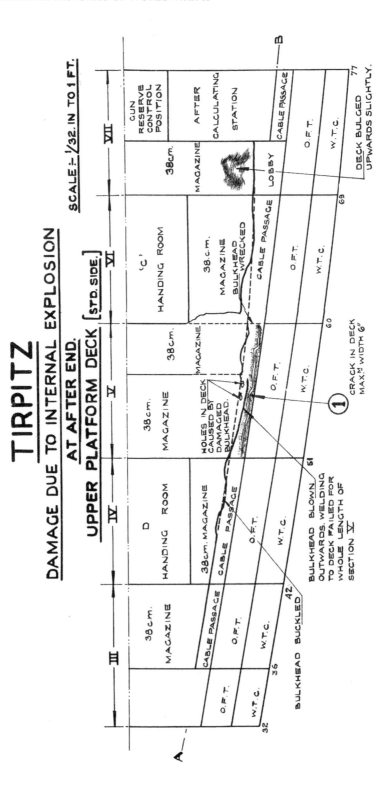

TIRPITZ

DAMAGE DUE TO INTERNAL EXPLOSION
AT AFTER END.
UPPER PLATFORM DECK [STD. SIDE.]

SCALE :- 1/32. IN TO 1 FT.

Fig. B.4.2

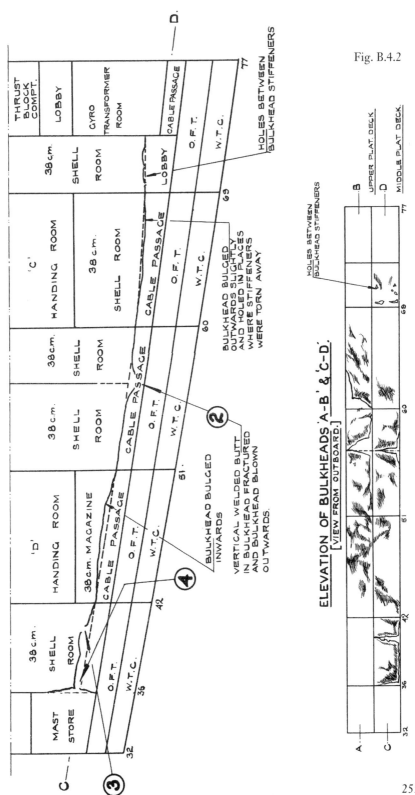

MIDDLE PLATFORM DECK.

MAST STORE

38 c.m. SHELL ROOM

'D' HANDING ROOM

38 c.m. SHELL ROOM

38 c.m. SHELL ROOM

'C' HANDING ROOM

38 c.m. SHELL ROOM

THRUST BLOCK COMPT.

LOBBY

GYRO TRANSFORMER ROOM

38c.m. MAGAZINE

38 c.m. SHELL ROOM

38 c.m. SHELL ROOM

LOBBY

CABLE PASSAGE

CABLE PASSAGE

CABLE PASSAGE

CABLE PASSAGE

O.F.T.

O.F.T.

O.F.T.

O.F.T.

O.F.T.

O.F.T.

W.T.C.

W.T.C.

W.T.C.

W.T.C.

W.T.C.

W.T.C.

BULKHEAD BULGED INWARDS

VERTICAL WELDED BUTT IN BULKHEAD FRACTURED AND BULKHEAD BLOWN OUTWARDS.

BULKHEAD BULGED OUTWARDS SLIGHTLY AND HOLED IN PLACES WHERE STIFFENERS WERE TORN AWAY

HOLES BETWEEN BULKHEAD STIFFENERS

32 36 42 51 60 69 77

C

D

③ ④ ②

ELEVATION OF BULKHEADS 'A-B' & 'C-D'.
[VIEW FROM OUTBOARD.]

HOLES BETWEEN BULKHEAD STIFFENERS

A

C

B UPPER PLAT. DECK.

D MIDDLE PLAT. DECK.

32 36 42 51 60 69 77

TIRPITZ.
DAMAGE CAUSED BY NEAR MISS BOMB.
[POSSIBLY 500LB. M.C. OR 600LB.A/S.]
DURING F.A.A. ATTACK ON 3RD APRIL.'44.

SCALE:-1IN TO 32FT.

PART PROFILE
STARBOARD.

Fig. B.4.4

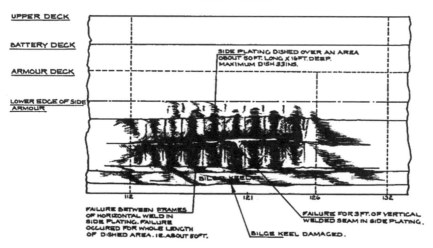

UPPER DECK

BATTERY DECK

ARMOUR DECK

LOWER EDGE OF SIDE ARMOUR

SIDE PLATING DISHED OVER AN AREA OBOUT 50FT. LONG X 16FT. DEEP. MAXIMUM DISH 33INS.

112   121   126   132

FAILURE BETWEEN FRAMES OF HORIZONTAL WELD IN SIDE PLATING. FAILURE OCCURED FOR WHOLE LENGTH OF DISHED AREA. IE. ABOUT 50FT.

FAILURE FOR 3FT. OF VERTICAL WELDED SEAM IN SIDE PLATING.

BILGE KEEL DAMAGED.

PART SECTION AT STA.121.
LOOKING FORWARD.

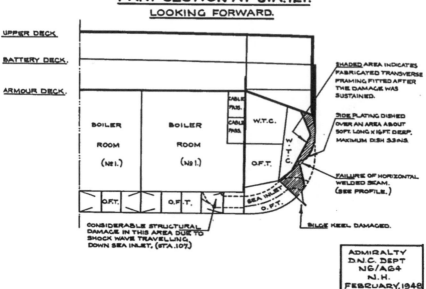

UPPER DECK.

BATTERY DECK.

ARMOUR DECK.

BOILER ROOM (N°1.)

BOILER ROOM (N°1.)

CABLE PASS.

CABLE PASS.

W.T.C.

W.T.C.

O.F.T.

O.F.T.   O.F.T.   SEA INLET   O.F.T.

SHADED AREA INDICATES FABRICATED TRANSVERSE FRAMING FITTED AFTER THE DAMAGE WAS SUSTAINED.

SIDE PLATING DISHED OVER AN AREA ABOUT 50FT. LONG X 16FT. DEEP. MAXIMUM DISH 33INS.

FAILURE OF HORIZONTAL WELDED SEAM. (SEE PROFILE.)

BILGE KEEL DAMAGED.

CONSIDERABLE STRUCTURAL DAMAGE IN THIS AREA DUE TO SHOCK WAVE TRAVELLING DOWN SEA INLET. (STA.107.)

ADMIRALTY
D.N.C. DEPT
N6/A64
N.H.
FEBRUARY, 1948

B.5 – Survey of Underwater Portion of the Wreck

Note: In the following sections "above" and "below" refer to the ship as she was at the commencement of the last attack, that is, upright and on even keel.

General Considerations Affecting the Survey

The programme of diving had to be arranged so that at any given time a maximum of useful information was being obtained, because it was clear that lack of daylight and bad weather would eventually put an end to diving. Any tendency to concentrate on one specific part of the damage had to be resisted. Diving was made difficult by the fact that the slightest movement stirred up the soft mud of the sea-bed and reduced visibility in the water to two or three feet. The water never really cleared during the time for which the diver was down. Entry into damaged areas released large quantities of oil fuel which also hampered diving.

At the commencement a quick survey of the whole of the submerged portion of the wreck was made to determine the position and nature of the major areas of damage. This preliminary survey, which took about eleven days, made it clear that the most important damage had occurred along the port side of the ship in Sections VIII to XIII, and it was decided to carry out a more detailed survey of this region. The damage to the bow, which occurred during the attack in Kaa Fjord on 15 September, 1944, may have been increased by a near miss during the final attack but, in view of the limited time available, was not considered to justify a detailed examination. The remainder of the damage to bottom plating was mainly in the nature of splits along welded butts and seams.

Damage Resulting From Direct Hit by 12,000 l.b. M.C. Bomb at Approximately Station 113

Damage to side plating is shown in Figure B.5. It will be seen that there was a large hole about 45 ft. long in this plating extending from below the bilge keel up to the level of the bottom of the side armour. Plating at the edges of the hole was petalled outwards. The centre of damage was approximately at station 113. The level of the sea bed in this area was just above the lower edge of the side armour and it was not possible to find out whether the side armour had been displaced by the explosion, but parts of the 110 mm. (4.33-in.) sloping deck armour were sticking out of the mud almost vertically. The general disposition of this armour and wrecked structure indicated that the main side armour had been blown out into some such position as indicated in the appropriate section of Figure B.5 and it is highly probably that the ship's side in this area was damaged right up to the upper deck.

It was possible, but only with some difficulty to get through the wreckage, consisting of portions of 110 mm. (4.33-in.) and 80 mm. (3.12-in.) deck armour and parts of the intermediate bulge bulkhead, as far as the longitudinal protective bulkhead. It was found that the latter had been blown outwards and that the hole in it was in the form of a large 'V', apex downwards, giving the impression that failure had occurred down the line of welding connecting it to the transverse bulkhead at station 112. The cables in the cable passage just inside the bulkhead were visible but it was impossible to get further inboard.

Having in mind the 0.07 secs. fuse delay which for bombs dropped from 12,000 ft. or over, implies detonation 50 ft. or more after impact, the sensitivity of even desensitized Torpex and the weakness of other Tallboy bombs, (for example, those which broke up on the concrete roofs of U-boat pens and the broken nose of a bomb found on Haakoy Island) it appears probable that this bomb detonated prematurely after hitting the deck armour.

Damage Resulting From Direct Hit by 12,000 lb. M.C. Bomb at Approximately Station 99

There was another large hole in the side plating, with edges petalled outwards, centred about station 99 as indicated in Figure B.5. This hole was about the same length as that described in the previous section, that is about 45 ft., but the damage to side plating was confined to an area above the bilge keel. A smaller hole centred about station 92 was also petalled outwards and was tightly packed with 15 cm. ammunition, which prevented access into it.

The level of the sea bed fell rapidly towards the fore end of Section VIII of the wreck and, at station 88, it could be seen that the main side armour had been ripped off the ship's side. Forward of this at about station 90, one of the side armour plates was either missing or had been blown out so far that it was completely buried in the mud. It was possible to gain access into the ship above the sloping armour deck at this point but only for a short distance because of the way being barred by debris and wrecked structure. In the vicinity of station 98 the main side armour was also missing or completely buried in the mud and the 110 mm. (4.33-in.) sloping deck armour was well clear of the sea bed, being bent downwards into the form of a trough 7 to 8 ft. deep. It is probable that in this area also the ship's side was damaged up to the upper deck.

Debris made it impossible to gain access through the larger hole up to the protective bulkhead, but the type of wreckage found in this area made it quite clear that there was a very large hole in that bulkhead and the general impression of the divers was that it had been blown outwards.

It is impossible to reach any definite conclusion as to where this bomb detonated as it is somewhat difficult to reconcile the sloping deck armour being arched downwards, but not ruptured, with a hole in the side plating extending to just above the bulge keel. The first feature suggests that this bomb detonated directly above and some distance from the sloping deck armour, but this thick deck plating should have screened the side plating below it. The evidence does, in fact, indicate that there may have been two explosions, one above and the other just below the level of the deck armour. For the same reasons as given on page 263 it is most improbable that this bomb detonated correctly.

There was a combined magazine and shell room, supplying P.III 15 cm. mounting just inboard of the protective bulkhead between stations 91 and 98. It is possible that the ammunition in it exploded and in fact, the evidence does suggest a small explosion in this area, but it is most improbable that such an explosion would have produced a hole of the same shape and position as that found in the side plating. Had the protective bulkhead abreast this magazine not been damaged previously, such an explosion would have vented through the thinner transverse bulkheads at the ends of the magazine. It is therefore concluded that the damage in this area was caused by a bomb which detonated prematurely.

Damage Resulting From the Near Miss with 12,000 lb. M.C. Bomb at Approximately Station 128

The extent of damage to the outer bottom is shown in Figure B.5. It will be seen that there was a hole about 40 ft. long x 17 ft. deep, the plating around this hole being dished over a larger area. As the hole in the wreck was above the sea bed a ladder had to be rigged to gain access and it was found that the intermediate longitudinal bulkhead was blown in. The longitudinal protective bulkhead could not be examined in detail in the time available but one diver gained access through the wreckage up to the protective bulkhead at the point where it joins transverse bulkhead 131.8. He found that the protective bulkhead was dished inwards and had fractured near the welding, the resulting gap varied up to 9-in. in width.

Damage to Bow

Damage to the bow was consistent with various reports of the damage caused at Kaa Fjord on 15 September, 1944 except that a large portion of the wreckage was so loose and insecure that it was difficult to imagine that *Tirpitz* could have steamed from Altenfjord to Tromsø without it having been torn away. It was deduced that a further near miss had aggravated the damage in this area, but as this was of little importance as regards the capsizing the matter was not pursued further.

Damage in Vicinity of Port Shaft Swell

Interrogation of survivors had reported a near miss off the port quarter and, as pointed out in Section B.3, there was a crater caused by a near miss off the port side towards the after end abreast Sections III and IV of the ship. Diving confirmed considerable damage to the outer bottom plating in this region consistent with a near miss. Panels of plating were dished inwards and there were a number of cracks in welded seams. For example, there were two cracks 25 ft. long and 12 ft. long, both about 3-in. wide, along welded seams in the outer bottom, and several cracks in the port shaft swell, one being about 3 ft. long x 4-in. wide.

Miscellaneous Damage

There were a number of instances of dishing, cracks and splits of a minor nature in the outer bottom plating chiefly at the after end of the ship, which could not be directly attributed to any particular attack. The majority of the cracks and splits had been made watertight by underwater welding or by welding patches over them.

One area of plating had been blown away from the ship's starboard side, just above the upper deck in Section I of the ship and had been hauled up on to the wreck. The mess decks inside this hole showed evidence of damage having been caused by an explosion forward of this position. Although it was not at first clear what had caused this damage, later interrogations elicited that it had been cut away by a salvage party. (See Section B.2.)

There was a hole in the outer bottom plating between the arms of the port "A" bracket about 10 ft. square. Inside the hole the structure had been wrecked by an internal explosion which had occurred somewhere forward of this position. It could not be ascertained whether the hole had been made by this internal explosion or whether it had been made deliberately by salvage parties.

Damage in Turret 'C'

As had been expected, all turrets had fallen out of the ship as she turned over and all were on the sea-bed and partly buried in the mud. It was found, however, that turret 'C' was some 30 to 40 ft. further outboard than had been expected and wreckage inside the up-turned gun house indicated that a large explosion had occurred inside the turret and had thrown it overboard. It was not possible to find the source of the explosion and suggestions that a bomb had hit turret 'C' or the deck in the vicinity led to a second survey being made. The whole of the quarterdeck, with the exception of small regions to port of the turrets, was examined and was found to be intact. Had a bomb penetrated the regions which could not be examined, damage to the outer bottom plating on the port side would have occurred but no such damage could be found. Neither had turret 'C' roof been penetrated by a bomb and it was therefore concluded that no bomb had hit the ship in this area and that the explosion must have resulted from internal causes.

B.6 – Conclusions

Hits and Near Misses which Caused Damage to the Ship

Consideration of the evidence obtained from this survey, in conjunction with all the other evidence given, strongly suggests that in the final attack *Tirpitz* received the following direct hits and near misses:–

(a) Direct hit on the port side at about station 113 which detonated prematurely very shortly after impact on the armour deck just inside its junction with the longitudinal protective bulkhead.

(b) Direct hit on the port side at about station 99 which detonated prematurely.

(c) Direct hit to port of turret 'B' detonated prematurely shortly after impact.

(d) Near miss off port side abreast station 128.

(e) Near miss very close to starboard bow.

Structural Damage

It is not known whether near miss (E) added materially to the damage caused by the previous near miss in a similar position in September, but there is no evidence to suggest that this bomb appreciably affected the loss of the ship; nor is there any evidence as to the damage caused to the upper works by hit (C) but the survey confirmed that there was no damage to side or bottom plating in this area.

It was impossible completely to dissociate the damage caused by direct hits (A) and (B) and near miss (D), but between them they ruptured port side plating from the turn of bilge to at least the waterline over a length of approximately 200 ft. amidships in Sections VIII to XIII. The longitudinal protective bulkhead, the bulge bulkheads outboard of it and the sloping armour deck were ruptured over a similar length. While it is probable that damage inside the ship extended inboard and above this, it was impossible to confirm these points in the survey as these parts of the ship were either obscured by a mass of debris or by the wreck being buried in the mud.

Flooding

The following sections of the ship at least would have been open to the sea and would have flooded very rapidly as a result of the damage indicated in the proceeding paragraph:–

> All bulge compartments between stations 77 and 146.
> All port machinery spaces over the same length of the ship.

The Germans stated that immediate flooding extended forward of this to station 155, which is quite probable.

Note:– Calculations, using authentic stability data for *Tirpitz* brought back from Germany by D.N.C's. officers, show that the immediate flooding indicated above, together with the known flooding at the fore end and after end caused by the two previous attacks, was more than sufficient to capsize the ship. Flooding was probably much more extensive than this and may have been spread by the water-tightness of doors in main bulkheads being vitiated, or doors may have been left open by the escaping crew. In addition the internal explosion aft undoubtedly increased the extent of the flooding. Nevertheless, further calculations show that the above-mentioned immediate flooding with the ship otherwise intact and in the best condition to resist capsize, would have produced the same ultimate result but, as pointed out elsewhere, the two hits and one near miss which caused this flooding could not have been in more effective places.

Capsizing

As a result of the flooding the ship heeled rapidly to port, attaining an angle of 20 degrees and then steadied momentarily. (At this angle of heel the port bilge keel would come into contact with the mud of the sea-bed which would check the rate of heeling). Some time after this, at an angle variously stated to be between 25 degrees and 70 degrees, an internal explosion occurred in the vicinity of the after main armament magazines, the order to abandon ship was given and the ship subsequently heeled to 145 degrees. She still lies in this position with the port side and the superstructures resting on the sea-bed.

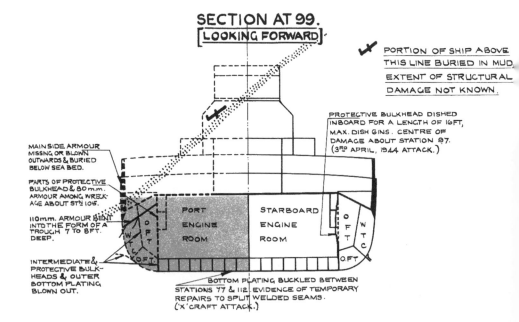

SECTION AT 99.
[LOOKING FORWARD]

PORTION OF SHIP ABOVE
THIS LINE BURIED IN MUD,
EXTENT OF STRUCTURAL
DAMAGE NOT KNOWN.

PROTECTIVE BULKHEAD DISHED
INBOARD FOR A LENGTH OF 16FT,
MAX. DISH 6INS. CENTRE OF
DAMAGE ABOUT STATION 97.
(3RD APRIL, 1944 ATTACK.)

MAIN SIDE ARMOUR
MISSING OR BLOWN
OUTWARDS & BURIED
BELOW SEA BED.

PARTS OF PROTECTIVE
BULKHEAD & 80 m.m.
ARMOUR AMONG WRECK-
AGE ABOUT STN 105.

110mm. ARMOUR BENT
INTO THE FORM OF A
TROUGH 7 TO 8FT.
DEEP.

INTERMEDIATE &
PROTECTIVE BULK-
HEADS & OUTER
BOTTOM PLATING
BLOWN OUT.

PORT
ENGINE
ROOM

STARBOARD
ENGINE
ROOM

O
F
T

W
T
C

O.F.T

O
F
T

W
T
C

O.F.T

BOTTOM PLATING BUCKLED BETWEEN
STATIONS 77 & 112. EVIDENCE OF TEMPORARY
REPAIRS TO SPLIT WELDED SEAMS.
('X' CRAFT ATTACK.)

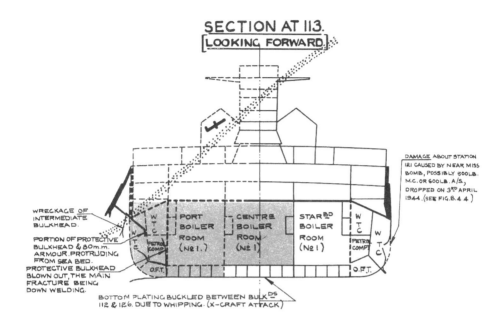

SECTION AT 113.
[LOOKING FORWARD.]

DAMAGE ABOUT STATION
121 CAUSED BY NEAR MISS
BOMB, POSSIBLY 500LB.
M.C. OR 600LB. A/S,
DROPPED ON 3RD APRIL
1944. (SEE FIG.B.4.4)

WRECKAGE OF
INTERMEDIATE
BULKHEAD.

PORTION OF PROTECTIVE
BULKHEAD & 80 m.m.
ARMOUR. PROTRUDING
FROM SEA BED.
PROTECTIVE BULKHEAD
BLOWN OUT, THE MAIN
FRACTURE BEING
DOWN WELDING.

BOTTOM PLATING BUCKLED BETWEEN BULKDS
112 & 126. DUE TO WHIPPING. (X-CRAFT ATTACK)

W T C · PETROL KOMP · O.F.T.

PORT BOILER ROOM (No1.)

CENTRE BOILER ROOM (No1)

STARBD BOILER ROOM (No1)

W T C · PETROL COMPT · O.F.T.

W T C

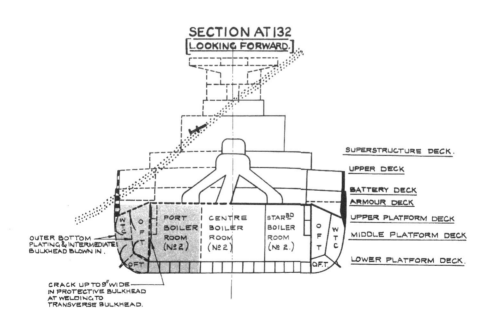

SECTION AT 132
[LOOKING FORWARD.]

SUPERSTRUCTURE DECK.

UPPER DECK

BATTERY DECK

ARMOUR DECK

UPPER PLATFORM DECK

MIDDLE PLATFORM DECK

LOWER PLATFORM DECK.

OUTER BOTTOM
PLATING & INTERMEDIATE
BULKHEAD BLOWN IN.

CRACK UP TO 9" WIDE
IN PROTECTIVE BULKHEAD
AT WELDING TO
TRANSVERSE BULKHEAD.

W T C · O F T · O.F.T.

PORT BOILER ROOM (No2)

CENTRE BOILER ROOM (No2)

STARBD BOILER ROOM (No2.)

O F T · O.F.T. · W T C

265

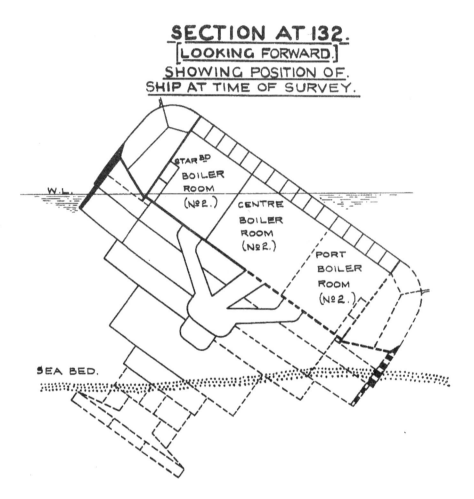

SECTION AT 132.
[LOOKING FORWARD.]
SHOWING POSITION OF.
SHIP AT TIME OF SURVEY.

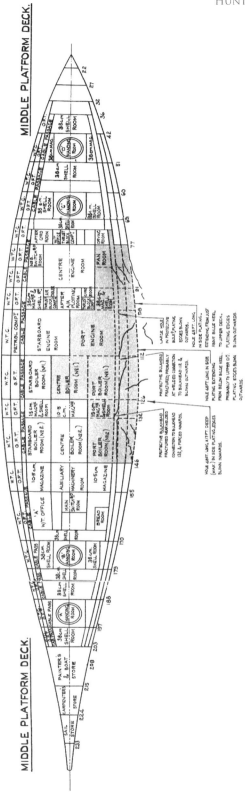

Tirpitz
Damaged deduced from
survey of wreck

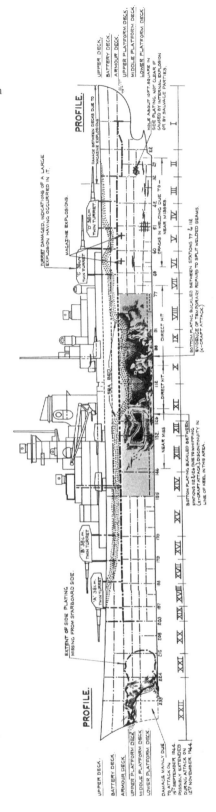

Part V

Personal Accounts

The *Tirpitz* Sank on 12. 11. 1944

I wrote this report for my family and friends in order to illustrate to them the pointlessness of wars so that they may get an idea of what great suffering men cause one another by going to war (to this day). This report cannot be a comprehensive description, especially since – as a survivor of the attack of 12 November 1944 – I can only provide evidence of events during that year. From my battle station, I could only observe the events in my immediate vicinity, as I had to concentrate on my job as an anti-aircraft gunner. I have therefore also included statements from my comrades, whom I only conferred with after the attack.

On 12 November, 1944, around 0900, the alarm bells of the aeroplane alarm signal shrilled across the ship. The crew, as practiced repeatedly, rushed to their battle stations and reported those to be ready.

The music corps, which had been playing just a moment before, immediately cleared the stern in order to man their battle stations. All occurred with lightning speed. The crew waited intently for announcements from the ship's command. They fearfully awaited the expected attack of the Royal Air Force. Everyone was aware what this could mean for them. The previous attack, on 29 October, of 39 Lancaster bombers, had shown what could happen to the ship if the attackers scored even a single close hit. This had not helped improve the crew's confidence. However, they appeared to put negative thoughts aside.

The *Tirpitz* was the newest, heaviest and most modern ship of the German Navy. Built especially for sea battle, the ship's length was 251 m with a width of 36 m at a draught of 10.5 m. The displacement weight in action was 52,600 tons. The sea target arms comprised 8 x 38 cm guns in four double towers with 12 x 15 cm guns in double carriages and strong air raid defences, which I will come back to later. However, the ship could never live up to everyone's expectations. Her sister ship, the *Bismarck*, had, on her first Atlantic deployment, sunk the pride of the British Home Fleet, the battleship *Hood*, but was afterwards destroyed by the superior surface forces of the enemy.

After a hit on the bow, the *Tirpitz* was at her old anchorage in the Kaa fjord near Alta. Through emergency repairs, the combat readiness of the ship had been maintained, but she was no longer seaworthy. She was therefore dragged to her last anchorage at Tromsø, near the island of Haaköy. The small island of Grindoy is located east of Haaköy. The *Tirpitz* moored here, so as to be used as a swimming battery. At 16 m sea depth, this seemed to be a relatively safe anchorage, even if damage to the ship could cause considerable water to enter her. The ship could only have been fully repaired at a German shipyard; this however was already impossible in wartime. The German armies were retreating everywhere and the enemy had already reached the then Reich territory. Manufacturing plants and many cities had been destroyed by non-stop British and American air attacks, with great loss of life.

Here in Northern Europe, after the fall of the Finnish front, the German troops retreated to Norway, clearing Norwegian civilians from the Finnmarks and recklessly destroying villages and homes. Thus, the marine bases in these areas also had to be abandoned. Against all expectations, however, the Russian troops stopped their advance in Kirkenes, after they had set fire to the city. At that time the *Tirpitz*, together with other naval forces, had orders to secure the northern flank and to fight the allied convoys in the North Sea. This proved to be effective and lead to a temporary stop of convoys into the Soviet Union, though the Soviet Union was desperately dependent on these deliveries of aid.

During the deployment against convoy PQ17, the *Tirpitz* missed the actual convoy, but the British commander, admiral Sir D. Pound, ordered his backing forces to retreat and the convoy to disperse, as he regarded the presence of the German units as a considerable threat. This was a fiasco for the cargo vessels and their crews. They were now helpless against the attacks of German submarines and air forces. Only 12 out of 30 ships reached Russian harbours.

This resulted in the British Prime Minister, Winston Churchill, demanding the destruction of the *Tirpitz*, declaring, "the entire naval situation throughout the world would be altered". All heavy units, who were kept in the North of England through the presence of the *Tirpitz*, were missed by the Allies elsewhere. This resulted in many different attacks by the British, in this aim to destroy the then largest, and apparently feared, battleship of the German Navy.

During the arming of the *Tirpitz* in the naval shipyard Wilhelmshaven, the Royal Air Force made two unsuccessful bomb attacks against the ship. After the transfer into Norwegian waters, these attacks were continued, but again they were unsuccessful. The *Tirpitz*'s anti-aircraft guns were already outmoded by this time, and thus not sufficient, although they were updated at a later stage. This became particularly pertinent when comparing them to the anti-aircraft guns used by the American battleships like *Iowa*. Such arms would later on prove to be ineffective against high-flying heavy bombers.

On 3 April 1944, aeroplanes from the aircraft carriers *Furious* and *Victorious* attacked the *Tirptiz* in the Kaa fjord. There were great losses among the operators of the anti-aircraft guns, with 122 men dead and another 316 injured. Parts of the superstructure were severely damaged. However, the British had losses to report as well. *The Times* newspaper declared, "Attack at dawn. *Tirpitz* paralysed…" and "… must be regarded as worthless" in their leading article.

We were all waiting for the firing command, when the attacking aircrafts strafed from the stern. Their strikes sputtered across the deck around us, but had no impact. When the firing command finally came, I had to quickly load the grenades. This was a heavy task and poor visibility made breathing difficult. I did not even notice the bomb attack on and next to the ship, due the unbelievable noise around us. Suddenly I felt a stream of hot air that pushed me aside. At first I could not see anything around me, due to the smoke of the explosion. Yet we continued firing until we ran out of ammunition. Behind us, the aircraft hangar was burning. Simultaneously, the siren on the chimney wailed non-stop. During a lull in combat, the fire-fighter group came into action. A hit on the officer cadet's lavatory beneath us had ripped open the deck behind us, but none of our gun-operation crew was seriously injured. This seemed to be a miracle. Our standby ammunition, including its container, had fallen into the hole created by the bomb, where it had caught fire. The ship's plane, which had previously been standing on the catapult, ready for take off, was now lying on the deck below us, severely damaged. Moments later, a second attack took place, but this time we were much better prepared. Again, I did not notice much going on around me, since I was busy loading the gun and had to concentrate very hard. Only when we had a chance to draw breath did my comrades tell me that half my face was burnt. Strangely, I had not felt this until that point. They sent me off to the sickbay. The sick bay had been hit and the situation inside was indescribable. Only the emergency lighting was on and a few medics were looking after the injured who had managed to reach the sick bay, though transporting the injured had not yet begun. I returned to my gun as soon as my burn had been treated. It was only later that evening when I noticed that I also had a slight injury on my right shin.

On 13 April 1944, the ship's commander reported to High Command for Naval Warfare – among other things – the following:

"506 shot   10.5 cm high explosive fragmentation shell cartridge
400   shot   3.7 cm high explosive fragmentation shell cartridge
8,260 shot   2 cm   high explosive fragmentation shell cartridge

Loss of personnel
122 dead, amongst them 8 officers and civil servants, 22 corporals, 90 men, 2 shipyard employees;
316 injured, amongst them 18 officers, 31 corporals, 266 men, 1 shipyard employee.

Conduct of the crew
The crew's conduct was exemplary, especially when one considers the constant change of men and how little experience most crew members had in battle. The L anti-aircraft team deserves special mention as they got through both attacks well despite the complete lack of coverage and great losses. The machine team also deserves special mention, as they fought hard against any strikes and their impact on the ship. This attack was the first big practical test for the crew. Their conduct and efforts enabled us to move the damaged ship safely to its anchorage."

Junge

Another four such attacks by the British followed during July and August, after the shipyard employees had repaired all damage from the attack of 3 April. According to British sources, a total of 180 machines were used during these operations, with only six of them being lost. These attacks were of little success as the Kaa fjord was being secured with fog batteries and so the *Tirpitz* was beyond the pilots' sight. The pilots therefore had to drop their bombs almost blindly into the fog.

The Royal Air Force received orders to attack and destroy the *Tirpitz* with long-range bombers and a specially designed 5,400 kg bomb. This bomb possessed a hitherto unimaginable destructiveness and had so far been used against German submarine bunkers in France and barrages in Germany. The target was outside the range of Lancaster bombers, so on 15 September 1944, 27 aircraft, which had stopped at Russian airports, began an attack on the ship. During this, they managed to make a crucial strike against the ship's forecastle. As a consequence of this, the *Tirpitz* was now no longer seaworthy and could not be repaired on site. The British ended the attack without losing a single aircraft. Only six bombers had crashed on Soviet airfields during the transfer flight from Scotland to Russia.

The Soviet Union also joined in the fight against the *Tirpitz*. A message from a Soviet submarine commander about the bombing and damaging of the *Tirpitz* later turned out to be false and an air attack by the Soviet North sea air fleet was unsuccessful because the pilots were unable to find their target.

The last act of this 'drama' began with the *Tirpitz*'s transfer to Tromsø. An attack on 29 October 1944, by 27 long-range bombers, which could now reach their target directly from England, proved unsuccessful. Again the bombers missed their target. Two had to make a forced landing in Sweden due to severe damage. It turned out that due to the small number of kills, the anti-aircraft guns were virtually ineffective, making the shooting of the British formation from the 38 cm and 15 cm towers a merely desperate defence.

In November 1944, the ship received its death blow. The enemy formation, which had been noticed very early, approached the anchored ship from the east, so that only the starboard artillery could engage. The 38 cm towers' first volley went below the formation. The 15 cm towers and heavy anti-aircraft guns were only able to open fire once the formation had moved within their reach. The anti-aircraft carriers *Nymph* and *Thetis* joined the defence, as did several anti-aircraft batteries stationed ashore. The noise, due to the gunfire in the fjord, which was surrounded by mountains, was indescribable. The light anti-aircraft guns also aimed at the enemy, even though the machines were attacking at such an altitude that they were completely out of range of those guns. The first bomb fell into the sea and threw an enormous wall of water into the sky. Shortly afterwards a huge explosion on port side shook the ship and showered the anti-aircraft teams with sea water. Thereupon the ship tilted towards the port side as a second strike, also on port side, shook her body. Later, the 38 cm firing tower Cäsar exploded and was found at a distance of approximately 50 m from the wreck. A great deal of the ship's side had been destroyed by the bomb strikes, causing sudden flooding. Counter-flooding proved ineffective. The upper deck inclined so quickly that operation of the guns became impossible. The ship then keeled over completely and lay at an angle of 135°. The anti-aircraft guns ashore stopped firing. The Lancaster bombers veered south, with individual planes flying over the capsized wreck before they did so.

An oil film spread inside the net cage surrounding the ship. Debris floated alongside the surviving crew who were fighting for their lives. They tried to swim towards the net cage's buoys. Few had been able to put on their life jackets. A few swimmers even attempted to reach the beach of the small island of Haaköy, which was covered in a thin layer of snow.

The dead were floating in the water, being held up for a while by their inflated clothing. Escape from inside the ship was as good as impossible. Individual groups inside the ship were able to reach levels which the sea had not yet filled only because the ship's hull was out of the water. Some men clambered onto the hull. Help came quickly from Tromsø and from two anti-aircraft carriers and a factory ship, so 82 of the men trapped inside the ship were rescued. Most of those trapped inside the ship met their death. Many drowned in the icy water, while others died from lack of oxygen. Their bodies were found several days later where the water had not yet penetrated, looking as if they were asleep on pipes or huddled in corners. The death of those comrades locked inside the processing centre was particularly traumatic, as these men had still had voice communication with the rescue units. Unfortunately it was impossible to save them in time.

"I experienced this last bomb attack from the very beginning and I want to describe it. The aeroplanes flew in close formation from starboard. We were able to follow events clearly as we had already been at our guns at the early anti-aircraft alarm. We expected the arctic sea fighters from Bardufoss to take action against the Lancaster bombers, but nothing happened, even though their take-off had been announced through the ship's loudspeakers. There was fear in everyone's eyes as we sensed that this might be our last day. After the heavy artillery had opened fire and the first volley had detonated beneath the enemy formation, the formation drifted apart, though keeping their attack course. We received permission to fire as the formation came closer and the anxiety I had experienced disappeared. I caught a glimpse of a large bomb being released from the lower body of an aircraft, following the path of the aircraft for a short while and then disappearing from view. It then reappeared as a shadow, quite a distance from the ship, dived into the sea with a splash and sent an enormous wall of water skywards. I could not see the effect of our defensive fire. The light anti-aircraft guns were now also firing at the enemy formation, although it was beyond their reach. The noise was indescribable and it was impossible to distinguish between individual shots from different calibres. The noise increased even more as a great shaking ran through the ship. This was the first strike on port side. Large amounts of water came down on us. The second strike I did not even notice as the ship immediately tilted to port side. The ammunition no longer reached our gun and so I picked up a few grenades from the standby ammunition. A tender that had fallen out of its fastener blocked the access to the ammunition lift. The ammunition men also could no longer reach the gun. In the meantime, the heeling had become so strong that I could not load the pipe anymore. The ammunition fell out of the standby locker and tumbled over the aeroplane deck into the water. Much debris followed. From our original operation team, only one comrade and myself were left. The others were probably still in their positions inside the armoured protection.

By this time, we were no longer able to stand upright on deck and had to hold on to the rail. The gunfire died away and, only occasional shots were still being fired. The occasional bomb was still dropped into the sea around the ship. We noticed nothing of the explosion of the tower Cäsar because the ship continually shook under the close strikes. At approximately 80° list, my comrade and I climbed over the upper deck's rail onto the starboard side armour. I pulled my steel helmet off my head and threw it away. It bounced over the side armour into the water, which looked grotesque somehow. There was no trace of fear: I only thought about how to get away from the ship as quickly as possible, because further explosions were expected inside the ship. We moved to the stern as the distance to the coast seemed shortest there. We briefly took cover behind the starboard propeller as a few aeroplanes approached the ship again. When no fire came from the aircraft, I took off my boots and my jacket and we jumped over the rudder blade and into the water. My comrade did not re-emerge as I swam for the coast. The water surface was covered in a film of oil emerging from the fuel reservoirs. Before I reached the buoys at the net cage, there was a tree trunk in my way, which I climbed on to. Another comrade from our gun joined me and together we saw a metal life-raft drifting past, so we moved to it. Too many men were already holding onto the buoys of the net cage that slowly sank deeper due to the added weight. Among the many dead floating around us there were also comrades who tried to save themselves by swimming. Very few of them had put on their life-jackets, I had not put mine on either. After some time, we were picked up and taken to the anti-aircraft cruiser *Thetis*. There we were taken care of and they took us ashore to Tromsø the next day. Cleaning off the oil with soap and a coarse scrubbing brush under a hot shower is an unpleasant, vivid memory.

By chance, a neighbour of my father's saw me ashore and told him that I had survived. I do not know how long I had been swimming; I had lost all sense of time. I did not feel how cold the water was either, though it cannot have been more than a few degrees above freezing."

The *Tirpitz* had a regular crew of 2,608 men. Many of the technical personnel had disembarked a few days earlier and were on their way home. We have to thank some of those men – as they remained in Tromsø for a while – for putting their knowledge to use during the rescue mission, which was of great help. Yet the losses of human life were considerable. Nearly 800 were saved: 900 people had remained on the ship. From these 800, several met their death during the last months of the war, or in captivity. We do not know exact numbers. The Reich's Federation for War Graves could only allocate graves on the military cemetery Botn-Rognan for very few of the dead. The remains of dead soldiers found during the breaking up of the ship were also entombed there.

Two Lancaster bombers from the Allied formation had to make a forced landing in Sweden and their crews were able to return to England. All other aeroplanes reached their stations in Scotland. None of their men were lost.

The great tragedy of this event is that the German Air Force with its fighter formation stationed in Bardufoss, did nothing to assist the *Tirpitz*, even though there had been a telephone connection between the airfield commander and the ship's command before, and during, the attack.

Commander Major Heinrich Ehrler of Fighter Squadron III/5, a highly decorated soldier, later had to answer for this at court martial.

For the Norwegian people, especially those in Tromsø, which was overflowing with evacuees and soldiers, the destruction of the *Tirpitz* came as a great relief. People had been afraid that the city would be damaged during the battle. The 'lonely queen', as they called the *Tirpitz*, was now no longer a threat to them.

British Air Vice Marshal R. A. Cochrane announced to his staff on the morning of 13 November 1944, that "the 'beast' had finally been slain after five years of tremendous efforts."

The report from the high command of the Wehrmacht stated " … the battleship *Tirpitz* has been disabled".

We, the former crew of the battleship *Tirpitz*, have formed a group, Bordgemeinschaft, and meet once a year to conduct a ceremony at the memorial in the honorary cemetery in Wilhelmshaven to remember our fallen comrades. The comrades of the Bordgemeinschaft have collected the names of the dead in a memorial book in order to preserve their memory.

While looking through the pages of the book with 1,067 names of the fallen, the wife of one of our comrades said: "For each of these names there stands a mother."

But the volunteers from other nations – e.g. Dutch, Belgian, French and Polish – shall not be forgotten either. It is not our place to judge, nor do we want to adjudicate on their reasons for serving in the German Navy. To us, they were our comrades. At the same time, on this 60th anniversary of the destruction of the *Tirpitz*, we shall remember the fallen enemies, the pilots, navy sailors, merchant ship sailors and the Norwegian freedom fighter that committed suicide during German captivity, so as not to betray his friends.

Fleet Admiral Karl Dönitz, Supreme Commander of the Navy, wrote:

"… Through the loss of the *Tirpitz* the German naval warfare with surface vessels came to a halt. Here it was already obvious that heavy ships would be endangered more and more by the air force; this development finally lead to the decommissioning of the British and American battleships in 1957 and 1958."

Klaus Rohwedder

Reports by Other Members of the *Tirpitz* Crew

"I arrived onboard towards the end of 1940, as tower commander for tower BruNo. At this time the ship was being run in and the crew became acquainted with her. When the *Bismarck* was to clear the port in May 1941, I was onboard for the last shooting against the target ship *Zähringen*. We were supposed to accompany the *Bismarck* and our commander, Captain Topp, tried to make this happen. The navy supreme command denied this however, stating that we were not yet trained well enough. Perhaps everything would have been different. The *Tirpitz* could have kept the *Bismarck* on course after the hit on the rudder and both ships could have reached a French harbour.

At the start of 1941, the *Tirpitz* was moved to Norway. At first we were located in the Faettenfjord near Drontheim, where the ship was attacked by British bombers. We were smoked out, but the forecastle could still be seen, so every time one bomber after the other appeared it was shot. At times we counted over 20 planes, but they always attempted to escape over the close Swedish border in order for the crews to return to England.

The bombers carried barrels filled with explosives, whose fuses were set to a 12 m depth. They dropped these explosives into the gloom. On one occasion, the jolting caused by the explosions damaged the helm and all the artillery equipment had to be readjusted. The fjord was full of dead fish at such times and many of the crew collected and ate them, though the seagulls ate most.

When we received notification that a convoy with weapons of the Allied Forces for Russia had been seen, we cleared the port and tried to attack. This however was always unsuccessful. We were once attacked by British torpedo planes from an aircraft carrier. First they came from starboard so that we managed to avoid the torpedoes, then they came from port side and again we avoided their torpedoes and shot down three planes.

Later, I spoke to a British officer from this aircraft carrier and he told me that in schools this attack was used as a bad example, as the attack should really come from both sides at the same time, so that it would be impossible to avoid the torpedoes. He also told me that the aircraft carrier had moved west at top speed in fear of an attack from us because they had no protection against battleships, while at the same time we had gone east between the Lofoten islands into the Vestfjord near Narvik at top speed, expecting an attack from several battleships and the aircraft carrier. As a consequence, none of the Albacore biplanes were able to return to the aircraft carrier.

From then on, we remained inside the Vestfjord and later waited in a fjord near the North Cape (Kaa fjord), in order to be as close as possible to the convoy route. Since the English knew the combat strength of the *Bismarck* and did not want to enter into battle with us, they stopped the convoy traffic during daylight, i.e. during summer, when we were approaching, or later when we were located inside the fjord near the North Cape.

We had become a 'Fleet in being' and had the same problems as the imperial fleet had had in their time. Therefore, the commander had already given me orders to entertain the crew, while we had been in the Faettenfjord near Drontheim. Everyone used spoon lures to catch their fish, which they could then fry and eat over homemade electric cookers. There was also a lot of singing and the best choir received a prize. During winter, we went skiing among many other things. The crew was thirsty for action. Spitsbergen was only attacked in 1943 and the coalmines were set on fire, supposedly they burned on for years (30 years). After this time, I was transferred to Supreme Command."

Friedrich Wilhelm Rasenack
(Captain-Lieutenant), La Falda, Argentina

"During the attack, 12 November 1944, I was on the astern bridge as a lieutenant and responsible for the firing of the light anti-aircraft guns. I was awaiting orders from Lieutenant Commander Fassbänder. Since the telephone was no longer working, I gave orders for all canons to shoot. In the meantime, a series of bomb hits caused the *Tirpitz* to start capsizing. When the rail, and part of the port side weapons, were underwater, I jumped into the cold sea without a life-jacket. Tower Cäsar exploded as I reached the water. The resulting suction pulled me a few meters under. This probably saved my life. As I re-emerged I saw many dead comrades. I then swam approximately 100 m to the net cage and held on to it. After about 20 minutes, a lifeboat picked me up. The machine oil in the water and on my body was also a lifesaver. It kept us warm. After my rescue

I stayed in the hospital in Tromsø for three to four days, then went on holiday."

Hans Mueller
(Lieutenant), New Bern, North Carolina, USA

"… But what we had been expecting happened on 15 September. Twenty five four-engined Lancasters, so called 'flying fortresses', were reported by our observation stations via radio. We had devised the zone shooting for the defence and opened fire on this day with 38 cm calibres at 25 km. Through this, we disrupted the attack; the enemy had not expected bombardment at this distance. They scored a near hit, which damaged the forecastle severely. From that point onwards, we could only operate at a speed of three knots, i.e. the *Tirpitz* could no longer be used as a battleship on the open sea.

During this attack, a 9 m long dud dropped on the spit in front of where we were trying to anchor. At the sight of this 6 ton bomb, we realised that a direct hit would mean the end for our ship.

… We found totally different geographical conditions in the Tromsø Fjord. There were no mountains around, instead visibility was clear at a radius of 30 km. The observation posts ashore thus lost their meaning. The first attack in Tromsø occurred on 29 October 1944. A sailor was on the lookout and caught sight of the enemy at 0810 at a distance of 70 km. …

We had plenty of time to prepare and to man all stations. On that day, I had command over the communications centre for the heavy artillery. Our volleys covered a large area and so the English had to drift apart. We received a near hit that caused 8,000 cm. of water to leak in. The list was levelled out through counter-flooding. We shot down a few Lancasters, others got lost on their way home.

…12 November, 1944 came, which brought the end of the *Tirpitz*. The air raid warning went off at 0800. The weapons reported "clear for action" 40 seconds later. The Commander spoke a few words of encouragement and motivation and announced the support of the Arctic Sea fighters. The commander at the time was Captain Weber. As we had so far survived without foreign support, everyone's confidence was much higher this time.

My predecessor, Lieutenant Mettegang, had the command over the communications centre again on this day. He was onboard because he had not yet managed to find a means of transport to Germany.

The measurements from the five processing centres were very different. I got the values from the five measuring devices on my screen in the communications centre electronically. Here they were averaged and sent to the weapons automatically. Radar engineering was in its infancy. At sea we could handle problems, but inside the Tromsø-Fjord with its mountains we had difficulties. The shaking, due to all the attacks, meant constant readjusting was required. The measurements were never further apart than on this day. A 25 km shooting zone for the heavy artillery was cleared. The volleys went too far. Fire had been opened too late. Approach altitude was 6,000 m. At a distance of 10 km the planes descended to 2,500 m so increasing their speed during approach. Hits could no longer be distinguished from our own shots.

Only a few minutes after the start of the battle the ship began to list. Within 45 seconds we had a list of 90° port side. The ship turned a further 135° and remained in this position.

At 90° list the crew had left the communications centre. The light had gone out and the emergency lighting dispersed a low light. I left last. The hatchway was blocked. Water was coming in everywhere. Wood and equipment was floating around chaotically. Air and water was gushing from all corners. It was as though we were in the pool beneath a waterfall, which could swallow us up at any moment. We were completely disorientated.

I finally reached the front radio room, where 50 to 60 men were lying on the ceiling. I felt uncomfortable around so many people. I looked for another exit and went with a sailor, into the front *mutterrichtraum*, where there were 14 men. We stayed there until our rescue. The sea hadn't penetrated these rooms yet. All around us there was the sound of gurgling water. Anything could happen.

The ship capsized at 0920. At around 1500 the emergency lighting went out too. Now we were in darkness and there was a morbid silence: everyone dwelled on their own thoughts.

I was the senior in the room and so gave a few orders after the light had gone out, such as urging everyone to keep quiet and move as little as possible so as not to waste any oxygen. We had four oxygen cylinders that we emptied gradually, so that none of us suffered from breathing difficulties or tinnitus. We had no idea of time. Eight or nine hours may have gone by when we heard noises that we could not yet identify, but that seemed to come from the outside. We knocked against the exterior walls. We heard knocks in reply.

There was no doubt that somewhere someone was taking care of us; they would try to rescue us. Our hopes rose when we could clearly here the sound of welding at the exterior wall. Our elation reunited us with our comrades and with life itself.

Finally, a welded section of the wall fell into our prison. Our comrades had worked their way through empty fuel cells and had found us at last. We were once again connected to the outside world and were pulled out one by one.

It was dead of night. The sight of the night sky full of stars was overwhelming and filled me with faith and thanks…

…Eighty-six men owed their rescue to the engineer officer, Lieutenant Commander Sommer, who knew the ship inside out and who had been ashore at the time of its destruction. He obtained some welding equipment and hired a Norwegian boat to come to our aid."

Willibald Vösling
(Lieutenant), Giesen-Hasede

"12 November, 1944 was a clear, cold day with no clouds in the sky. Shortly after 2000 there was suddenly an air raid warning. The whole crew ran across the ship like ants – each to their battle stations. I, too, ran as fast as I could. My battle station was inside the 15 cm tower on starboard I. Just like the 38 cm towers, these 15 cm towers had bottom sections in which the ammunition arrived via lifts. My destination was the ammunition room in the ship below.

After a short while, the 38 cm towers started to fire. Only a few minutes later the middle artillery, the 15 cm guns, opened fire too. It was like a hurricane. The ship shook at each shot from the 38 cm towers. A terrible shock followed. This had to be a hit. Shortly afterwards a second great shock. We must have received two serious hits. The ship slowly tilted to port. Then another great explosion. The whole ship trembled like a windswept tree. The list now reached 45°. Since the speaking tubes had been crushed, we tried to reach the gun platform via telephone. There was no connection at all, not even to other stations. "The ship is sinking," everyone shouted, "we need to get out," but where? Besides, we had not received orders to abandon ship.

I suggested that we should climb up to the gun platform and from there through a small hatch to the upper deck, from where we could jump into the sea and swim away from the ship as quickly as possible. So we climbed up, one after the other. I was second. I constantly shouted at the man in front of me to move faster. When we arrived at the hatch we could not open it. The man in front of me pushed with all his strength and shouted: "I can't open the hatch, it has jammed." In the meantime the ship was tilting port side more and more. Finally, the hatch opened! At that precise moment the ship turned over completely. A giant column of water pushed into the tower and the man in front of me fell right into this surge. He was carried away by the water, washed into the tower and did not make another sound. He died instantly. Horrified, I screamed to the others: "Quick, quick, back to the ammunition room." We climbed back as fast as we could – now upwards since the ship had turned by 180°. The capsizing had only taken eight to nine minutes. In the ammunition room we encountered a few other comrades. The emergency lighting was still on – that was quite a feeling …

I cannot remember exactly what happened afterwards. Other comrades joined us. We crouched in a room that was half filled with water. Then the light went out. Someone had a torch, so we were able to find our orientation in an emergency.

There was much more – which I cannot remember – until we reached the power station control room with 37 men. There a great fear came over us. We were afraid that the steam boilers in the nearby boiler room could explode. One comrade hugged me and said: "Ernst, now we all have to die – now I will never see my mum again…"

Above us there was an empty fuel cell. An oval manhole cover was located directly above us. We were now in an air bubble above the water level. Fortunately for us, the fuel cell was empty. With a lot of effort and an adjustable screw wrench, a so-called 'French', we managed to open the manhole cover. When all screws had finally been loosened, the cover fell with a terrible bang. Then a few comrades climbed into the cell and started knocking against the walls. After some time we heard knocking and steps from outside. When the knocking was directly above us we were just about able to communicate with our saviours. They told us to remain calm and not to talk, so as to save air.

Outside, our saviours were working feverishly. It took ages for the flame cutters to penetrate the steel wall. A circular hole was cut. Breathing was difficult for us. With a bang, the cut steel disc fell through the smoke into the room. Then we climbed, one by one, injured first, through the hole. Lieutenant Commander Sommer, who was leading the rescue mission, congratulated us. First of all, everyone was given *schnapps*. We gave our names and were brought ashore immediately. A gym, laid out with straw, served as an initial emergency shelter. The rescue operation onboard continued feverishly. Aside from our group, another 50 men were rescued from the wreck."

Ernst Renner
Petty Officer, Munich

Part VI

An Arado Ar196A-3 floatplane being catapulted from *Tirpitz*. After
missions, the plane would land near the ship to be hoisted by a crane.
The battleship was equipped with hangars for the storage of up to four
floatplanes.

Source: from the collection of M. S. Laarman. Many such photographs
were taken by Herr Wendt, a photographer onboard *Tirpitz*. He sold
prints, such as this one, to the crew.

Cleaning of one of the 38 cm gun barrels. Inside is Oberleutnant Ernst Bogs, Artillerie Technische Offizier, who did not survive *Tirpitz*'s final fate.

Source: Wolfgang Piwowarsky 1. Wachoffizier en Turmkommandant on *Tirpitz*, courtesy Rolf Piwowarsky.

Kapitän zur See Karl Topp, who was Commander of *Tirpitz* between
February 1941–1943, with two members of the crew.

Source: from the collection of M. S. Laarman.
Photographer: Herr Wendt.

A relaxed moment onboard *Tirpitz* in the mess. The sailors share
Kujambel, a sweet drink typically consumed in the German Navy during
World War II.

Source: Albert Buddensiek, crewmember of *Tirpitz*.

The battleship was protected by anti-torpedo netting. It can still be found
on shore at her former anchorage and lies, metres thick, in the garden of
Tromsø War Museum in Trømsdalen, Norway.

Source: Jac Baart.

SCHLA
1.4.
UNSEREN

The Wilhemshaven Ehrenfriedhof Cemetery was first used in 1912 as a naval garrison's cemetery. It contains numerous graves of World War I and II casualties. The *Tirpitz* memorial stone was placed there by the *Tirpitz* Veteran's Association and reads:

BATTLESHIP TIRPITZ
1.4.1939-12.11.1944
TO COMMEMORATE OUR DEAD

Source: Klaus Rohwedder

SCHIFF TIRPITZ

 – 12. 11.1944

EN ZUM GEDENKEN

The *Tirpitz* Veteran's Association

Soon after World War II, Heinz Assmann, who had served on *Tirpitz* until 1942 as Kapitän zur See, began to meet with former crew of the battleship, made possible due to his work in the GM/SA, the German Minesweeper Administration. This unit operated minesweeping in German vessels with German staff under Allied control, after German capitulation, which continued until 1947. Thanks to Assmann, the former crew began to reunite and became a large, family like group of people with a shared history. In 1947, the first gatherings were held in various locations, mostly around the date of 12 November, the day the ship sank. Today, these gatherings still take place, although the number of participants is increasingly fewer.

The ship's newspaper, *Der Scheinwerfer* (*Search Light*), which was printed onboard in wartime, was revived in 1958. It still exists and publishes information for and about the crew and the ship.

Besides the contact with each other, the Association tackled other matters. Much effort was put into preparing a complete list of crew, which unfortunately was not achieved. But a book with the personal data of all fallen comrades was published. This book contains the names of 1,100 crew who died on or before 12 November, 1944. Furthermore, the Association assisted with other books about *Tirpitz*, films and documentaries. Strong ties exist with British veterans' associations, Norway's *Tirpitz* Museum in Kaa fjord and the exhibition in Tromsø. In Wilhelmshaven in Germany and Kaa fjord and Tromsø, memorials testify to the ship's history and tragic end.

Nature dictates that there will be an inevitable end to the Association in the near future, but *Tirpitz* has an established place in naval history and the Association gave the ship a place in the life of many former crew, their relatives and friends.

With thanks to Artur Mary
Bordgemeinschaft Slachtschiff *Tirpitz*

Admiral Sir Mark Stanhope

As the First Sea Lord and Chief of Naval Staff, Mark Stanhope is the Royal Navy's professional head and Chairman of the Navy Board. He is responsible to the Secretary of State for the fighting effectiveness, efficiency and morale of the Naval Service, and as a member of the Defence Council supports the Secretary of State in the management and direction of the Armed Forces through prerogative and statutory powers. As a member of the Chiefs of Staff Committee and Armed Forces Committee, he advises CDS on maritime aspects of all operations and the underlying strategy and policy. He is also the Top Level Budget holder for the Naval Sector and advises the Permanent Under Secretary on resource allocation and budgetary planning in the light of defence policy and naval priorities.

Joining the Royal Navy in 1970, Mark Stanhope's career has included command of submarines and surface ships as well as broad experience in Whitehall and the NATO Alliance. During the Cold War he commanded the conventional submarine HMS *Orpheus* (1981–1983) and the nuclear powered submarine HMS *Splendid* (1986–1989). His final sea command was the aircraft carrier HMS *Illustrious*.

In between sea appointments he has worked in the Ministry of Defence for the Naval Staff and as a personal staff officer to the Chief of Defence staff (1994–1996), followed by a short secondment to the Cabinet Office. His initial NATO assignment was in the Regional Headquarters of Allied Forces North, in Holland. Following this he served as the Deputy Commander-in-Chief Fleet before returning to NATO, this time in Norfolk, Virginia, as the Deputy Supreme Allied Commander Transformation. His most recent appointment as Commander-in-Chief Fleet combined both his operational and alliance experience exercising full command over all deployable Fleet units, including the Royal Marines, while also holding the post of Allied Maritime Component Commander at Northwood.

Awarded the OBE in 1990, he was knighted in 2004 and further honoured in 2010 with a GCB and is a recipient of the US Legion of Merit (Officer).

Dr G. H. Bennett

Dr G. H. Bennett is the author of over a dozen books covering military, diplomatic and maritime history. His works include: *Destination Normandy: Three American Regiments on D-Day; Hitler's Admirals; Survivors; British Merchant Seamen in the Second World War;* and *The RAF's French Foreign Legion: De Gaulle, the British and the Rebirth of French Airpower 1940–1945*. He has worked at Plymouth University since 1992, where he is an Associate Professor of History. Dr Bennett is a Trustee of The Britannia Museum, Britannia Royal Naval College, Dartmouth.